A Prayer Strategy
For Jesus' Victory over Radical Islam
Book II

A Prayer Strategy for
The Victory of Jesus Christ

Defeating the Demonic Strongholds of
Radical Islam

Zeb Bradford Long

PRMI Exousia Press

A PRAYER STRATEGY FOR THE VICTORY OF JESUS CHRIST
DEFEATING THE DEMONIC STRONGHOLDS OF ISIS AND RADICAL ISLAM

Published by PRMI Exousia Press,
a ministry of the Presbyterian-Reformed Ministries
International Dunamis Institute
Black Mountain, North Carolina, USA
www.dunamisinstitute.org

Cover design and graphics by Joe Schlosser, Excellent Adventures Inc.

Scripture quoted by permission. All scripture quotations, unless otherwise indicated, are taken from the NET Bible® copyright ©1996-2016 by Biblical Studies Press, L.L.C. All rights reserved.

Because of the dynamic nature of the Internet, any web addresses or links contained in this book may have changed since publication and may no longer be valid.

ISBN-13: 978-0692596463
ISBN-10: 0692596461

Library of Congress Control Number: 2016945837
PRMI EXOUSIA PRESS, Black Mountain, NC USA

DEDICATION

This book is dedicated to the intercessors through all the ages through whom, God the Father, Son and Holy Spirit have defeated Satan's plans for evil and advanced the Kingdom of Jesus Christ on earth.

The War

[15]Moses built an altar, and he called it "The LORD is my Banner," for [16]he said, "For a hand was lifted up to the throne of the LORD— that the LORD will have war with Amalek from generation to generation." (Exodus 17:15-16)

[12]For our struggle is not against flesh and blood, but against the rulers, against the powers, against the world rulers of this darkness, against the spiritual forces of evil in the heavens. (Ephesians 6:12)

The Victory

[14]Jesus replied, "I am the way, and the truth, and the life. No one comes to the Father except through me. (John 14:6)

[8]He humbled himself, by becoming obedient to the point of death—even death on a cross! [9]As a result, God exalted him and gave him the name that is above every name, [10]so that at the name of Jesus every knee will bow—in heaven and on earth and under the earth— [11]and every tongue confess that Jesus Christ is Lord to the glory of God the Father. (Philippians 2:8-11)

ACKNOWLEDGMENTS

First, I acknowledge my three great teachers of intercession. The Rev. Archer Torrey, the great grandson of R.A. Torrey and founder of Jesus Abbey in South Korea. He mentored me in following Jesus Christ in the power of the Holy Spirit. The Rev. Tom White, the author of the book *Believers Guide to Spiritual Warfare* and Director of Frontlines Ministries, first introduced me to the dynamics of spiritual warfare while I was in Taiwan as a missionary. The Rev. Doug McMurry, my older brother in the Lord, connected me to the historical moves of the Holy Spirit. Together we have coauthored books on prayer and the work of the Holy Spirit. He provided me with the encouragement as well as the example of both doing the work of prayer and writing about it so that others could join in this work. He opened the door for me to the Messianic Jewish ligament of the Yeshua body. My thanks also to Dr. Dan Juster, Asher Intrater and the ministries *Tikkun International* and *Revive Israel.* Together they welcomed me to Israel where I experienced God fulfilling Romans 11. There I saw not only Satan's schemes to replace God's way of salvation by the deception of Islam, but also the culmination of the Westward blowing wind of the Holy Spirit fulfilling the Great Commission. Without this, I would not have grasped God's strategy for defeating the demonic strongholds based on Islam.

I cannot name them, but over three decades there are many intercessors who, along with me, were formed into prayer teams and deployed by Jesus Christ on the frontlines of his battles with demonic strongholds. As I have often functioned as visionary leader, I owe these fellow warriors my thanks and indeed my life and sanity. I owe these fellow warriors my thanks and indeed my life and sanity. Together in the battlespace, I learned the tactics and strategies presented in this book.

Thanks to the PRMI Board of Directors and ministry staff who have all taken part in the discernment of this work and provided the prayer covering as well as the administrative support for me to do the research and writing of this book.

In addition to intercessors and PRMI staff, I have worked closely with the following team who helped directly with the formation of the ideas, writing, and editing of this book, work made immensely more difficult by my own profound learning disability. So, my thanks to Judy Cook, Doug McMurry and Cindy and Steve Strickler. Danielle King mastered the details of the interior layout of the book. Thanks to Joe Schlosser who formed the graphics for the book.

I am especially thankful for my wife, Laura. She has been an anchor of love, peace and stability during this extended project. Many a Sunday I have listened to her preach and the Lord has sustained and spoken to me through the Word.

With your help this project moved from vision to reality. Thank you.

Finally, I acknowledge that all glory and praise belongs to the Father, Son, and Holy Spirit, whose Kingdom of life, truth and freedom will prevail over Satan's plans for death and tyranny in Radical Islam.

Table of Contents

Part I
Preparing for War

1. Facing the Dire Threat of Radical Islam 12

2. Who Serve in the Army of Intercessors? 23

3. Cohorts of Intercessors for Defeating Strongholds 35

4. Opposing War Aims of the Lord and of Satan 55

5. Into the Gap: Engagements with the Enemy 65

6. The Holy Spirit's Strategy and Tactics 72

7. Intelligence Preparation of the Battlespace 76

Part II
First Battlespace
Engaging the Demonic Powers

8. Tactics for Piercing the Demonic Cloaking.................................. 109

9. Are Intercessors Authorized to Engage the Archons? 127

10. The Intercessor Standing Between Heaven and Earth 137

11. Binding the Demons at Work in the Leaders 150

12. Breaking Satan's Curses 179

13. Dividing Satan's Kingdom 205

14. Unity in Biblical, Trinitarian Faith 212

15. The Authority of Born Again Jews and Gentiles in Unity 220

Part III

The Second Battlespace
Engaging the Demonized Leaders

16. God Removes the Leaders through Conversion to Christ 234

17. God Removes the Leaders of Radical Islam by Death 251

Part IV

The Third Battlespace
Defeating the Jihadist Armies of Radical Islam

18. Military Force Destroying Jihadist Armies 265

19. The Responsibility of Government to Wage War 277

20. The Role of Joshua the Warrior 285

21. Interceding for President Bush and Soldiers on the Frontlines . 297

Part V

Closing the Ring
Four Waves of the Holy Spirit Converging on Jerusalem
to Fulfill the Great Commission

22. The Father's Strategy to Fulfill the Great Commission 311

23. Jews Returning to the Land of Israel and to Yeshua 320

24. The "People Who Use Chopsticks" Taking the Gospel Back to
    Jerusalem 332

25. Closing the Ring on Fortress Islam 342

26. The Holy Spirit Mobilizing, Equipping and Deploying Jesus' Army of
    Intercessors 354

    Notes 366

Part I
Preparing for War

Facing the Dire Threat
of Radical Islam

Book I of this series, A Prayer Strategy for Jesus' Victory over Radical Islam, *Discerning the Times*, focused on gathering the intelligence needed for exposing Satan's plans in the world today. This process led to deeply disturbing conclusions that the Church of Jesus Christ and cultures of freedom and democracy based on our Judeo-Christian values are facing an imminent and deadly threat from Radical Islam.

Satan's Plans and Means Exposed

The conclusion of Book I is that at the beginning of the 21st century Satan is using the history, culture and sacred texts of Islam to construct a genre of demonic strongholds aptly called "Radical Islam." As demonstrated in the previous book, these demonic/human intermingled organizations have taken various distinct expressions reflecting either the Shia or Sunni branch of Islam from which they arise. The Sunni branch contains the Taliban in Afghanistan and its Tehrik-e-Taliban Pakistan (TTP) affiliate in neighboring Pakistan, al-Qaeda and its various affiliates, ISIS and its al-Qaeda in Iraq (AQI) precursor, and Boko Haram in Nigeria which has pledged allegiance to ISIS.[1] From the Shia stream, the main demonic stronghold is the Islamic Republic of Iran which as of 2016 is the chief state sponsor of Islamic terrorism. They are expressing their evil through their proxies such as Hezbollah and many others.[2]

While these various groups mutually hate each other and may well destroy one another, they all fit within the category of Radical Islam. They all spring from the same set of lies sown by Satan in the heart of Muhammad that are believed to be the infallible word of a deity named Allah. This spiritual being whose nature and character as revealed by Islam's prophet in the Quran and in the examples and sayings of the prophet in the Hadith, is completely contrary to the One True God who has revealed Himself in the Old and New Testaments.

These Radical Islamic strongholds provide Satan with the human means of implementing on earth four schemes. These were exposed by the Holy Spirit through our discernment process detailed in Book I to be:

1. Replace God's way of salvation revealed in the Old and New Testaments with the deception of Islam.

2. Exterminate Jews and Christians in order to replace Yahweh's Covenants of salvation for humanity.

3. Strangle the winds of the Holy Spirit blowing in the house of Islam that is bringing Muslims to saving faith in Jesus Christ.

4. Establish the Islamic Caliphate from which to wage offensive jihad to accomplish the genocide of Jews and Christian and impose Islamic hegemony through Sharia law. This includes destroying the State of Israel and subverting and/or destroying the "Nations of the Cross" which have the military, cultural and spiritual

power to block the vision of establishing the Caliphate.

From the daily news reports, it is clear that Satan has already started carrying out these four plans through the strongholds based on Islam. Already in this second decade of the 21st century there are "wars and rumors of war" and turbulence in the human and spiritual realms. The Islamic State has already declared itself the Caliphate. The genocide of Christians has already begun; the hatred and assaults on Jews are escalating. Credible threats to destroy Israel are publicly made by Muslim nations and terrorist groups with ever more deadly arsenals. There are forebodings of impending and catastrophic evil, just as there were in the 1930s when the demonic strongholds of Nazism, Communism and Japanese Imperialism were growing in power and strength. I documented these movements of evil in Book I. Now I move to the task of Book II, which is to provide the actual prayer strategies and tactics that the Holy Spirit is calling intercessors to deploy to defeat Satan's plans in Radical Islam and to advance the Gospel of Jesus Christ into the Muslim world.

Father's Strategic Plans Revealed

Storm clouds of impending evil are gathering, but so too are the countervailing winds of the Holy Spirit. We are at an extraordinary time in the history of advancing the Kingdom of Jesus Christ. The Father is sending four great waves of the Holy Spirit which are in succession with the two thousand year westward blowing winds of the Holy Spirit that started in Jerusalem and are now converging back on Jerusalem. These four waves are:

1. The Holy Spirit is bringing the Jewish people back to the Land of Israel and to faith in Jesus—Yeshua the Messiah. Over the

last 150 years there have been more Jews coming to faith in Jesus Christ as Lord and Savior while keeping their Jewish identity, than at any other time since the beginning of the Church.

2. A great outpouring of the Holy Spirit is occurring among Asian Christians, empowering them for witness to Muslim peoples worldwide—the "back-to-Jerusalem" movement.

3. The third great wave is the outpouring of the Holy Spirit within the Church globally, renewing Trinitarian faith and mobilizing the vanguards within the Body of Christ to contribute to the fulfillment of the Great Commission.

4. The fourth great wave of the Holy Spirit is within the fortress of Islam itself, bringing Muslims to freedom and life in Jesus Christ. There are more Muslims coming to saving faith in the true Isa today than at any other time in the last fourteen hundred years.

The Triune God is advancing the Kingdom by these waves of the Holy Spirit, each in succession of the outpouring of the Holy Spirit originating from Jerusalem at Pentecost in Acts 2, and then over the centuries continuing in a predominantly westward movement to return and converge in Jerusalem. The purpose is to fulfill the Great Commission of the Gospel going to all nations on earth.

Satan's frantic work of building the strongholds of Radical Islam is no doubt in response to these waves of the Holy Spirit relentlessly moving to fulfill God's redemptive purposes. Satan knows his time of final defeat is drawing near. In the quickening pace of what could be the prelude to the End Times, he is driven to the desperate measures contained in his four schemes, which would lead to the extermination of all who do not submit to Islam's deception—which could mean the murder of billions of human beings. Even more terrible than the threat of genocide is the quenching of the light of salvation through Jesus Christ, condemning humanity to eternal death.

Satan is terrified that these present waves of the Holy Spirit are intended to negate and abolish his fourteen-hundred-year project of constructing the religion, culture and political system of Islam as a replacement for Yahweh's way of salvation established through his covenants with Israel and fulfilled in Yeshua, Jesus Christ, the Jewish Messiah for all nations and peoples. (Isaiah 49:6 and John 4:22)

These moves of the Holy Spirit are, in turn, part of the Father's master plan for defeating the strongholds of Radical Islam, and then pushing toward the culmination of Jesus' victory by overturning Satan's master deception of Islam itself with the truth that, [12]*there is salvation in no one else, for there is no other name under heaven given among people by which we must be saved.* (Acts 4:12)

Our Role as Intercessors is Praying for and Participating in these Waves of the Holy Spirit

These waves or pulses of the Holy Spirit come at the Father's initiative; however, we do contribute to his sending these waves. He has decreed that we will cooperate with him by means of prayer. All through the history of the advancement of the Kingdom of God, the Father has determined that the prayers of his children would precede and initiate these waves. The strategic role of prayer in God's plans is revealed in the book of Acts. Each wave of the Holy Spirit is preceded by the work of earnest prayer. The first move of the Holy Spirit in the New Covenant era is the prayer meeting preparing for the outpouring at Pentecost that took place after Jesus ascended into heaven from the Mount of Olives.

> [13]When they had entered Jerusalem, they went to the upstairs room where they were staying. Peter and John, and James, and Andrew, Philip and Thomas, Bartholomew and Matthew, James son of Alphaeus and Simon the Zealot,

and Judas son of James were there. [14]All these continued together in prayer with one mind, together with the women, along with Mary the mother of Jesus, and his brothers. (Acts 1:13-14)

This gathering of the fellowship —not just the apostles, but other men and women who were followers of Jesus—praying in one accord, is the model for all future outpourings of the Holy Spirit. The second wave comes shortly after Pentecost when the nascent Church came under persecution. In prayer, they cried out to God:

[27]For indeed both Herod and Pontius Pilate, with the Gentiles and the people of Israel, assembled together in this city against your holy servant Jesus, whom you anointed, [28]to do as much as your power and your plan had decided beforehand would happen. [29]And now, Lord, pay attention to their threats, and grant to your servants to speak your message with great courage, [30]while you extend your hand to heal, and to bring about miraculous signs and wonders through the name of your holy servant Jesus. (Acts 4:27-30)

In response, the Father answers as recorded in Acts 4:31, [31]*When they had prayed, the place where they were assembled together was shaken, and they were all filled with the Holy Spirit and began to speak the word of God courageously.* Thus, the Church grew among the Jewish believers.

The next wave enabled the Gospel of Jesus Christ to bridge the chasm separating Jews and Gentiles. This move of the Spirit is prepared for by prayer, but not by the Jewish believers. Their Jewish worldview, despite the promises of their own prophets about the messiah coming for all nations, prevents them from understanding that the Gentiles are also included in God's redemptive plans. Therefore, they do not undertake the work of prayer for the Gentiles. Instead, the Holy Spirit stirs a Roman centurion named Cornelius to fervent prayer. His prayers open the door for the Father to send the same kind of Holy Spirit wave upon the Gentiles in the home of Cornelius which came upon the Jewish believers at Pentecost. (Acts 10:1-4, Acts 11:15-16)

There are many more examples in the book of Acts. A review of history demonstrates that waves of the Holy Spirit coming in response to Christians' prayers have driven the advancement of the Kingdom of Jesus Christ for the last two thousand years. Jonathan Edwards, the great theologian of British Colonial America, summarizes and confirms this strategic role of prayer in advancing the Kingdom of Jesus Christ.

> It is God's will through His wonderful grace, that the prayers of His saints should be one of the great principal means of carrying on the designs of Christ's kingdom in the world...
>
> When God has something very great to accomplish for His church, it is His will that there should precede it the extraordinary prayers of His people; as is manifest by Ezekiel 36:37... And it is revealed that, when God is about to accomplish great things for His church, He will begin by remarkably pouring out the spirit of grace and supplication (see Zechariah 12:10).[3]

In our present era in the war against Radical Islam, the first role of intercessors is to take part in praying for and participating in these advancing waves of the Holy Spirit which are already converging in Jerusalem.

The secondary, but vitally important undertaking of the intercessors is to cooperate with our Commander-in-Chief Jesus

Christ in deploying the Holy Spirit's strategies and tactics for defeating the demonic strongholds of Satan. If these strongholds are allowed to grow unimpeded to their full terrible flowering, there will be catastrophic consequences for humanity. In addition, God's plans for advancing his Kingdom through these four great waves of the Holy Spirit would also be thwarted for a season—a season in which millions even billions of human beings could be murdered or bound over to satanic bondage through Islam or other forms of demonic deception.

The Focus of this Prayer Strategy
is to Defeat the Stronghold of Radical Islam

In this present epochal era, the Church and the world face threats from many different strongholds. Many divisions in Satan's army are engaged on numerous fronts to destroy God's Kingdom and deceive humanity. The strategies and tactics of prayer and spiritual warfare given in this book will relate to these fronts in God's war against Satan. However, the focus of this prayer strategy remains on defeating the strongholds formed from Islam.

The first reason for this focus is that Radical Islam at this present time in history poses the most dangerous and mortal threat to the Church of Jesus Christ and to humanity. The situation now is analogous to the 1930s and 1940s when the world faced two virulent ideologies Satan was constructing into strongholds to destroy the Christian faith with its Jewish roots and to subjugate humanity: Nazism and Stalinist Communism. Of these two systems of evil, Nazism was at that time the most dangerous to the Church of Jesus Christ and to humanity. In the great fight to destroy Nazism before it prevailed and accomplished Satan's terrible purposes of exterminating the Jews and replacing the Church with Nazi paganism, the Western democracies of Great Britain and the United

States had to join forces and cooperate with the Soviet Union. The battle with the stronghold of Stalinist Communism would await the victory over Nazism.

We are now in a comparable situation with the threat of Radical Islam. Like Nazism, it poses the most virulent threat to God's Kingdom and to those cultures based on Judeo-Christian values as it is daily gaining the military, cultural and spiritual means to accomplish Satan's plans. Yet, other strongholds are also grave threats; one is liberal progressivism. Another is reactionary conservatism in North America, the British Isles, Europe and Russia that moves toward various forms of fascism in reaction to the threats of Radical Islam and Liberal Progressivism. As intercessors, we will face complex challenges as we must keep our eye on defeating the enemy of Radical Islam while simultaneously alert to other strongholds. At times, we must make common cause with those captivated by other strongholds in order to defeat Radical Islam.

The Islamic terrorist attack killing fifty people at the gay nightclub in Orlando on June 12, 2016 brought these dilemmas for intercessors into sharp focus. The attacker had pledged allegiance to the Islamic State and shouted, "Allah Akbar" as he carried out Islam's punishment of homosexuals, which is death.[4] In this case we must make common cause with liberal progressivism to defeat the evil of Radical Islam that not only inflicts death on homosexuals, but also upon Christians and Jews and anyone else who does not submit to their oppression. All who love humanity and cherish freedom must stand together against the evil that is seeking to destroy the free, pluralistic, immensely creative society that our Judeo-Christian values have produced. At stake are a free society in which we can live in peace with people whose theology and behavior are contrary to the Word of God.

This is a time fraught with grave danger and dreadful choices. Ideals may have to give way to practical alliances in which we may be called to make common cause with those with a liberal progressive or even reactionary fascist worldview in defeating this common enemy of Radical Islam which would exterminate or enslave us all, leaving no room for the redemptive work of the Gospel. However, we must simultaneously be engaged in the prayer and spiritual warfare to defeat Satan's plans in the other strongholds seeking to destroy both Western culture and Biblical Christian faith.

The second reason why the primary focus of this prayer strategy is on defeating Radical Islam is that this is what the Lord is doing in this epoch. I believe Father's assault on the demonic deception of Islam is beginning its final phase. In the grand strategy of his plans to fulfill the great commission, these waves of the Holy Spirit converging in Jerusalem, if not thwarted by Satan through our lack of faith and obedience, will soon deluge the Islamic world with the powerful transforming witness to the Gospel. Through the floodtide of the Holy Spirit moving in love, power, and signs and wonders, the Prophet Isa, the Lord Jesus himself, and not the Islamic impostor, will be knocking at the door of every Muslim heart offering freedom from the spiritual, cultural and political tyranny of Islam. Jesus will be extending the invitation to receive him by faith and thus receive the gift of forgiveness of sins and resurrection life.

This great battle is unfolding before us in these present days with Radical Islam's challenge not only to Judeo Christian cultures, but also to all non-Islamic cultures. We are in a vast and deadly clash of civilizations. To turn back the tide of Islam that would enslave all humanity and exterminate Jews and Christians, there will be many actors and countless roles. This will include national governments, militaries, cultural and spiritual leaders. Everyone who is a beneficiary of Western culture, loves humanity and cherishes liberty must contribute to this war effort. We shall address some of these roles later in the book when we deal with the tragic necessity of destroying the human jihadist armies of Islam through military force.

The primary focus of this book and the prayer strategy, however, is upon mobilizing, equipping and deploying the intercessors whom the Lord Jesus is calling to join him in this great battle. Often ignored by the world and discounted as powerless by the powerful, those who pray open the wellsprings of God's actions on earth to shape history by opposing Satan's plans and advancing Jesus' Kingdom.

Who Serve in the Army of Intercessors?

In pouring out the Holy Spirit in these four great waves now converging in Jerusalem, our God has "something very great to accomplish for his church." According to Jonathan Edwards, the method of the Father is to precede his actions in the world by the "extraordinary prayers of his people." This is consistent with how the Lord has decided to work on earth—through human beings created in his own image called and empowered to be his friends and coworkers. For the last one hundred and fifty years, movements of extraordinary prayer have flowed from many springs in Korea, China, North America, the British Isles and in Africa that have formed tributaries, which are now merging, into a great river of prayer.

While the Holy Spirit is praying through all who are born again to sustain and extend his presence and work on earth, the vanguard of this river of prayer, which shapes history, are the intercessors. In this second decade of the 21st century, the Holy Spirit has launched a global mobilization to call and to anoint men and women and even children from all nations to join Jesus' army of intercessors.

How is Jesus Christ Calling You
to Serve in His Army of Intercessors?

The victory in the war with Radical Islam requires the mobilization of all who are counted among God's chosen people—Jews and all who have been born again through faith in Jesus Christ. However, the Holy Spirit is calling only a few as intercessors to the frontlines. All those not on the spiritual frontlines are nonetheless critical for the war effort. These are what I will later be identifying as the Joshua workers through whom our Father will be answering the prayers of the intercessors. While acknowledging that we may be called to various stations in the war, the focus of this prayer strategy is to mobilize, equip and deploy those called to the frontlines of intercession.

Some of you reading this book may not know whether you are called or not, or in what capacity. I urge you to keep reading and seeking the guidance of the Holy Spirit and to let him guide you to your right place in his Kingdom. I know for myself it has been a long process of calling, equipping and stepping into my role as an intercessor. My own call, while unique to me, does point to elements that are similar for all called by Jesus to enter the battle actively.

My Call to Intercession to Defeat Radical Islam

My call to serve in the army of intercession for the Gospel to go into the Muslim world started with my mother and her love for Muslim people. My father served in the US Foreign Service. Besides the Far East, he was stationed in Pakistan and Yemen, with much travel in the Arab world. Nearly everywhere that my father was stationed, my mother crossed over into that culture. She was always working on languages, from Chinese to Arabic, and as an artist was constantly in a state of amazement and appreciation of different cultures. Her heart was so big that no matter where they lived, they brought into our family one or two people who were very close, whom we considered brothers and sisters, and who remained so for decades. A Muslim family calls my parents, Father and Mother. A Palestinian young man who grew up in a refugee camp was educated by my parents and now has a good job. I have a brother from Korea in the Korean diplomatic service and a Chinese brother from Taiwan who manages oilrigs off the Southern US. Above all, my mother was an intercessor constantly engaged in the work of prayer.

After I left home to go to college in the United States, nearly every conversation we had from whatever part of the world where they were living, she was constantly asking me to pray for people. This included many Muslims and Christians under persecution in Muslim lands. That was an open door for me into the Muslim world— - it was through the loving heart of my mother who reflected Jesus' heart.

Behind every intercessor called to pray, is a unique story of preparation to receive the call. This includes the normal growth for a disciple of Jesus Christ. I have found, however, that the more we grow in loving Jesus, the more we will be caught up into the Father's heart for a people group, a nation or an individual. This love is the first step of preparation for becoming an intercessor. So, the first question is, "What is on your heart as a burden?" If you follow that lead, you will arrive at the Father's heart.

The Call to Intercede for President Bush

My mother's love for individual Muslims was the first part of my preparation. The call to the spiritual battle with Radical Islam, however, started in a completely unexpected way—the "hanging chads" on the ballets of the disputed votes in Florida for George W Bush and Al Gore.[1] I had not paid much attention to the presidential campaigns of Al Gore and George W. Bush. I did cast my vote for Bush, but was not enthusiastic about either candidate. Then, after the November 2000 election, amid all the controversy over the vote in Florida, the recounts, and candidate Vice President Al Gore filing a lawsuit for another, the Holy Spirit kept me up all night. I felt him praying through me for the decisions to favor George W. Bush. That night I received the clear and, to me, inexplicable call to become an intercessor for President Bush. This call upon me did not lift until the end of his second term on January 20, 2009. It came as a deep knowing that was to be my burden. There were no mystical moments, just the sure sense in my heart.

I have talked to many intercessors who share that their call also came as a "knowing" that as they followed in obedience to the Holy Spirit and started praying in a specific direction, they were caught up with the Lord on a great adventure. The call to pray for President Bush put me into a sphere of interaction with the Holy Spirit that has led me to this prayer war against Radical Islam. I started walking in obedience, step by step, as the guidance came.

How the Lord Called Me into the Gap as Intercessor

At first, I accepted this guidance to pray for President Bush as part of doing my duty as a Christian citizen of the United Sates. All Christians are commanded to pray for "all who are in authority." (1 Timothy 2:1-2)

Then, on the morning of September 11, 2001, the call suddenly soared into high level intercession and spiritual warfare. I was "called into the gap." (Psalm 106:23)

That morning I woke up earlier than usual with a foreboding of impending evil. The Holy Spirit fell upon me so heavily that I remained in bed praying in tongues, not wanting to move. I did not have any information to help me know what was happening or even how to pray. So, I just welcomed the Holy Spirit to pray through me. Then, emphatic guidance came to pray, in the name of Jesus Christ, to restrain the power of death and evil. The Holy Spirit said, "Pray that God Almighty would thwart Satan from fulfilling all his evil intentions." With this guidance came a vivid mental image of me standing with many others holding our hands up, pushing back against a violent wave like a tsunami about to break. Then the anointing came upon me to pray with the authority of Jesus for President George W. Bush. The Lord specifically told me to pray for the President as at that moment he was anointing him for leadership to fight against great evil and defeat it.

After a while, the heaviness of the anointing lifted enough so that I could get out of bed. I was just having my first cup of tea when the phone rang. It was my mother calling from Washington, DC. She said, "Quick! Turn on the TV! Your sister just called from Manhattan to say that she looked out her apartment window and saw a terrible accident. A jet airplane has just crashed into one of the towers of the World Trade Center. Please pray for your brother! He is on his way to a business meeting at the World Trade Center this morning..." I turned on the TV and sat in horror before it all day. For me it was the beginning of an incredible spiritual engagement of first praying for President Bush, and then engaging in high-level spiritual warfare against the demonic stronghold of Radical Islam, especially as expressed through al-Qaeda and coalesced around Osama bin Laden.

A few weeks after the terrorist attacks of 9/11, I was in

Canada, then in England, and after that in Uganda. In each location, I shared the story of how the Lord had called me into the gap even before the attacks took place. To my amazement, a surprising number of people in each location shared with me that they too were called to intercede before there was any mention of the attacks on the news. I realized then that I had been part of a vast concert of prayer which the Holy Spirit had orchestrated to constrain the powers of evil that day.

Since that powerful experience, I have repeatedly experienced the Holy Spirit calling me into the gap and empowering me to engage both the demonic spirits as well as the people Satan is using to build the strongholds of Radical Islam. Later we shall identify these moments when the Holy Spirit calls us into the gap as *engagements*. It is there, in that point of conflict, that the work of the intercessor takes place in earnest.

However you begin to discern the Lord's call upon you, whether in a gradual knowing to start praying in a particular direction or in a mystical experience that hurls you into the battle, you must walk it out in faith and obedience. So, for those of you who are receiving a general call to pray, walk in obedience and see where it leads. You may find that the Lord will take you more deeply into the gap as an intercessor. It is King Jesus our Commander--in-Chief who recruits us into his army of intercessors. Our role is to discern the calling and then to step forward in obedience and faith.

The Model of Moses and Jesus as Intercessors

This call into the gap as intercessor is modeled for us first by Moses, and then fulfilled in Jesus who by pouring out the Holy Spirit upon us, empowers us to join him in intercession.

Yahweh repeatedly called Moses into the gap to intercede for the Hebrew people as they were liberated from Egypt and headed to the Promised Land. For instance, Exodus 32 records that Moses lingers up on the mountain, meeting with Yahweh for so long that the people give up on him ever coming back down. They abandon their faith in the God who has just brought them out of bondage in Egypt with mighty signs and wonders. At the people's request, Aaron makes for them a golden calf, their god to worship. The wrath of Yahweh is about to consume the people for their sin. However, Moses goes before God to intercede for them.

> [30]The next day Moses said to the people, "You have committed a very serious sin, but now I will go up to the LORD—perhaps I can make atonement on behalf of your sin." [31]So Moses returned to the LORD and said, "Alas, this people has committed a very serious sin, and they have made for themselves gods of gold. [32]But now, if you will forgive their sin…, but if not, wipe me out from your book that you have written." [33]The LORD said to Moses, "Whoever has sinned against me—that person I will wipe out of my book. [34]So now go, lead the people to the place I have spoken to you about. See, my angel will go before you. But on the day that I punish, I will indeed punish them for their sin." (Exodus 32:30-34)

Psalm 106:23 in the King James Version captures this dynamic of intercession as "standing in the gap" and what would constitute, "extraordinary prayer" that opens the door for God's actions that shape human history. [23]*Therefore he said that he would destroy them, had not Moses, his chosen, stood before him in the breach, to turn away his wrath, lest he should destroy them.* Moses had been praying for the people, and in this way, he was an intercessor for them. However, the work of intercession took place when Moses, "stood before Yahweh in the breach." This "standing in the gap" becomes an important concept for us as it is there that we will need to learn the various strategies and tactics of Spirit-led prayer battle.

Jesus Christ is the model intercessor by serving as our mediator and advocate before the Father. While on earth, Jesus often went up the mountain to pray. In John 17 we see him standing in the gap for us, interceding for his disciples and for all who will believe in him through their testimony. His ultimate standing in the breach like Moses came when he went to the cross and allowed himself to be crucified for us. Jesus stood in the gap, taking the wrath of God upon himself for our sins and defeating the power of death and Satan. As Hebrews 7:25 put it, [25]*Consequently he is able for all time to save those who draw near to God through him, since he always lives to make intercession for them.* By going into the Holy of Holies with his own blood, rather than the blood of animals, Jesus fulfills the role of intercessor that is foreshadowed in Moses.

Jesus also calls us as his friends and coworkers to share with him in the work of intercession as is fitting for all born again through faith in him. The type of prayer to which Jesus calls us is well defined by Kenneth Leach.

> Intercessory prayer is not a technique for changing God's mind. Rather, it is a releasing of God's power through placing ourselves in a relationship of cooperation with God. It is an act. Prayer and action should not be opposed to one another for prayer is action. Intercession means literally to stand between, to become involved in the conflict.[2]

Yes! When the Holy Spirit calls us into the gap, we are placed right in the middle of the conflict and join an extraordinary dynamic, cooperating with the Father as well as those through whom the Lord Jesus fights Satan on earth and works his will among human beings.

For both Moses as well as Jesus, the calling and role of intercessor was always on them. But the actual work of intercession took place in those moments when they were stepping into the gap. For Moses, in addition to the episode of the golden calf, there was the battle with Amalek when he stood on the hilltop with his arms upheld by Aaron and Hur as Joshua and his army fought the Amalekites in the valley below. Jesus Christ demonstrated stepping into the gap with the prayer for the disciples and all believers in John 17. The ultimate example is the passion and crucifixion. Now with his resurrection and ascension to the right hand of the Father, Jesus Christ does offer intercession for all times for us. From that place of all authority in heaven and on earth, he has sent to us the Holy Spirit who intercedes for us within us. He links us to Jesus in heaven. This living connection enables us to step into the gap as intercessors and become the means through whom Messiah Jesus accomplishes his will on earth.

The prayer strategy and tactics that I present in this book are to enable each of us to take part of this dynamic of Jesus as intercessor in heaven, working through us, by the Holy Spirit within and upon us on earth. I will be describing these tactics in detail based on my own battlefield experience, but much of what follows will not become comprehensible to you until you say yes to Jesus' call to offer yourself as one through whom the Holy Spirit will be praying.

Facing Fears
Stepping into the Gap May be Costly!

So how is our Father calling you? As you consider whether to say yes, I want to provide one word of caution—not to discourage you from jumping into the battle, but to make sure that you do so fully aware that such a decision will put you in the danger zone. If intercession is stepping into the gap and becoming involved in the conflict, we must face the reality that to say yes to this call may be costly. Being in the gap can be a terrible place in the struggle between the Kingdom of God and Satan's realm. We may take on Jesus' suffering heart for the lost and be subject to Satan's rage as he strikes out at the Kingdom of God, with us in the middle. We shall return to the reality of the costliness of intercession in Chapter 10, but now at the beginning of this book, we must face the potential of danger as we consider whether or not to accept Jesus' call to join his prayer army.

There is always risk in the work of intercession, but in engaging with Jesus Christ in the battle against the strongholds based on Islam, we have not just supernatural enemies to contend with, but human ones as well. Muslims in captivity to the demonic strongholds built from Islam provide Satan a vast human army wielding both spiritual and earthly weapons. This situation may seem to make obedience to the call to intercession especially costly. Actually, it is no more so than the cost of following Jesus as a disciple. Jesus warns us to count the cost!

> [26]If anyone comes to me and does not hate his own father and mother, and wife and children, and brothers and sisters, and even his own life, he cannot be my disciple. [27]Whoever does not carry his own cross and follow me cannot be my disciple. (Luke 14:26-27)

For me, facing the cost of Jesus discipleship came as I was finishing the editing for Book I *Discerning the Times*. I was at the point of approving the final proofs. It was Sunday, and I was attending the church where my son-in-law is pastor. I was watching my five-year-old granddaughter pray at the children's service. As I was watching her, I was flooded with warm happy thoughts of how wonderful it will be to watch her grow up with all the possibilities before her. I could also imagine her going with me on mission trips just like her mother did. She had already asked me when she could go to the mission field and help me tell people about Jesus and the Holy Spirit. I thought too about my other grandchildren. I also imagined their children joining together with Laura my wife celebrating special occasions as one big happy family. These were a grandfather's daydreams while sitting in church. Suddenly, these happy thoughts were intruded upon by the disquieting realization that I am writing two books and offering equipping in high level prayer and spiritual warfare to take on the demonic strongholds of Radical Islam, which could well be putting me right in the bull's eye of Satan and his demonized jihadist agents.

A wave of fear went over me as I thought, "Well, perhaps those books should never be published. We could use them just as study guides at small safe events. Perhaps this whole prayer battle is just too dangerous and I should just quietly go into retirement." Then the Holy Spirit spoke to me, saying, "They will be used for study guides and thousands of intercessors will be raised up all over the world who will help to defeat Satan's plans through Radical Islam. But that will not happen unless you walk in obedience to Jesus. You need to do what he told you to do. Get those books and equipping out to the widest audience possible so that I [the Holy Spirit] can use them to call together the global army of intercessors." I responded with, "Well yes, Lord, but is that not unnecessarily dangerous? Can we not just work this out to be more safe? What if we do this all under a pen name so I can be anonymous? The Holy Spirit responded, "No! What if Rees Howells had remained anonymous? Would I have been able to gather intercessors around someone who was too afraid to be named?"

Then Jesus spoke to me again, "Are you willing to give up all those happy future possibilities with your family and grand- children? Come follow me! Walking with me in my will and calling is the only safe place in the whole universe." I spent the rest of the church service wrestling with God about this. However, by his grace, by the time I got home, I was able to say, "Yes Lord I will follow you and trust you." I accepted the corrected proofs and set in motion the publication process.

How this decision will come to you, I do not know. Just know that you will need to decide. Will you follow Jesus and enter into the dynamic of cooperating with Him as an intercessor, or will you hold back and take yourself out Father's 21st Century kingdom campaigns?

The Blessings of Stepping into the Gap
with Jesus Christ

Having pointed to the possible dangers, I want to tell you of the blessings. We see them in the two greatest intercessors, Moses and Jesus. [11]*The LORD would speak to Moses face to face, the way a person speaks to a friend.* (Exodus 33:11) Jesus Christ as resurrected Lord and eternal Son sits with the Father at his right hand—the place of all power and authority in heaven and on earth. (Mark 16:19)

For those who have counted the cost and join this war, there is not only the promise of Jesus' protection, guidance and empowerment, but there will also be the amazing joy of taking part in the greatest of all adventures of defeating evil and advancing the Kingdom of God. In addition, best of all will be the gift of growing in friendship with the Father, Son and Holy Spirit.

Keep all this—the cost, but also the blessings—in mind as you make your decision.

Cohorts of Intercessors for Defeating Strongholds

Jesus' prayer army will be composed of many units with members having different roles. In this chapter, I cover the role of the Intercessory Prayer Cohort as the unit that is the vanguard in the Lord's battle plans. I will also provide some guidelines to help us determine what our assignment may be. First, we must acknowledge the important role of the pervasive general and continuous work of prayer in sustaining the work of the Father, Son and Holy Spirit on earth.

Everyone who is born again into God's Kingdom is a part of the prayer army. Just as in modern total war, the civilian population of a nation contributes to the war effort. All Christians are part of this prayer and spiritual warfare because everyone who is born again has the Holy Spirit dwelling in them and praying through them.

[26]In the same way, the Spirit helps us in our weakness, for we do not know how we should pray, but the Spirit himself

intercedes for us with inexpressible groanings.[27]And he who searches our hearts knows the mind of the Spirit, because the Spirit intercedes on behalf of the saints according to God's will. (Romans 8:26-27)

This intercession of the Holy Spirit through every Christian whether individually or gathered in prayer groups enables a general work of sustaining prayer and faith, which in turn facilitates the presence and working of our God on earth among us. This pervasive faith and prayer among all believers provides Jesus with a global communication network. The Holy Spirit who is both in heaven at the throne of the Father, and is "sent out into all the earth" makes this network possible. (Revelation 14:6) Human means of communication such as the internet and phone calls complement this global spiritual communication network.

Jesus uses this network to orchestrate vast concerts of prayer. This is what I found was taking place before and during the terror attacks of September 11, 2001; people throughout the world were mobilized directly by the Holy Spirit to pray even before the attacks took place. Later the communications sent through the Holy Spirit's network were both enhanced and confirmed by the human means of text messages, phone calls and the news media. I believe this concert of prayer welcomed the protective actions of God, greatly limiting the number of actual casualties the jihadists had hoped for. When the attacks first took place, there were fears that casualties could be closer to 40,000 people instead of 3,000. We found out later that many strange "coincidences" had taken place that morning that greatly reduced the number of people occupying the Twin Towers at the time of the attacks. One was the commuter train coming in from New Jersey that was late for the first time ever. Others told stories of getting sick or being led not to go to the building that day.[1] The work of prayer may also have prevented the full unleashing of evil that the attack could have had such as hitting other targets like the White House, or releasing demonic spirits to stir up mobs of enraged Americans to attack and destroy mosques and kill innocent Muslims in revenge.

Another result of this general prayer on that terrible day made possible by the indwelling of the Holy Spirit's global communication system was what took place that evening in churches across the nation, and as I found out later, in Canada and the United Kingdom, as well. Without any formal notification or planning, the Holy Spirit sent Christians to their churches for prayer and repentance. That evening I received a strong nudge to go up to the Presbyterian church I usually attend. To my amazement, the sanctuary was already packed with people in prayer. There had been no formal announcement; no one had set up the meeting. Rather the Holy Spirit had issued the call. The people did not pray prayers of revenge, but solemn prayers of confession of our own personal and national sins. The Lord was calling the nation to prayer consistent with his prayer strategy revealed in 2 Chronicles 7:13-14:

> [13]When I close up the sky so that it doesn't rain, or command locusts to devour the land's vegetation, or send a plague among my people, [14]if my people, who belong to me, humble themselves, pray, seek to please me, and repudiate their sinful practices, then I will respond from heaven, forgive their sin, and heal their land.

This repentance plus the work of prayer provided the opening for Almighty God on that day of the attack, and then throughout the Bush administration's war on terror, to constrain and, in some cases, completely defeat the fulfillment of Satan's plans in the powerful demonic stronghold of al Qaeda.

This global spiritual and human communication system connecting the members of the Body of Christ is foundational to the prayer soldiers' one cooperation with one another, and with the

Father, Son and Holy Spirit in his victory over Radical Islam. Full participation in God's global communication grid is a requirement for all who are going to take part in the war against Radical Islam and the mission to advance the Kingdom of God. This involves being born again by faith in Jesus Christ, being baptized with the Holy Spirit for gifts and power, being rooted in the Bible as the Word of God, and being in full participation within a fellowship of believers.

The Strategic Role of Set-apart People and Places for Continuous Focused Prayer

Added to this general work of prayer is another type of important prayer. All through history the Holy Spirit has called together small communities to gather in set apart locations for the ongoing work of prayer that sustains the advancement of the Kingdom of God. The Roman Catholic and Orthodox streams of Christianity are replete with examples. In these traditions, the monastery and the convent have practiced prayer for decades and even centuries. Within the Protestant stream, while the role of the monastic life set apart for the work of prayer was greatly diminished, the Holy Spirit made up for this loss by raising up many prayer centers to sustain the work of missions. One famous example is the 100-year prayer meeting that grew out of the Moravian revival of 1727.[2] The result of this extended period of extraordinary prayer is a global missionary movement which brought many thousands into the Kingdom of God.

In the wake of the devastation of World War II, the Lord raised up many such prayer and worshiping communities for healing and restoration of the war-shattered Church and nations. Some examples are the Taize Community in France, the Evangelical Sisters of Mary in Germany, Iona in Scotland, and L'Abri in Switzerland.

In our present era, since the 1960s with the outpouring of the Holy Spirit in the Charismatic and Third Wave movements, many places of focused, continuous prayer have appeared. One is Jesus Abbey in South Korea, which has sustained the rhythms of prayer on the Benedictine model from its founding in 1966 by Archer Torrey.[3] Another is the International House of Prayer in Kansas City which has maintained 24/7 prayer for years. They have become a university to equip disciples of Jesus Christ within the context of this on-going life of prayer. [4] Another location is the Jerusalem Prayer Tower overlooking the Old City of Jerusalem, which welcomes people to come and pray from all nations.[5] This is a unique expression in that it represents the move of the Holy Spirit among Jews bringing them to faith in Messiah Jesus in fulfillment of the restoration of Israel, as found in Romans 11. In addition to these well-known centers of prayer, there are thousands more the Lord has gathered together as part of his great army of prayer. The Christians of Korea have been in the forefront of this world-wide movement of starting prayer centers. When I have been in Israel, I have been amazed at how many Koreans are there, and how many Korean prayer centers are hidden away in unexpected locations.

This general and continuing work of prayer is all part of the vast global network and communication system of the Holy Spirit. This This army of prayer provides the means for the Holy Spirit to defeat the demonic strongholds of Radical Islam and to sustain the great moves of the Holy Spirit unto the fulfilling the Great Commission.

Cohorts of Intercessors
The Vanguard of God's Prayer Army

Emerging from this general prayer, and often gathered from those taking part in these places set apart for ongoing prayer, is a special configuration of intercessors who form the vanguard of God's prayer army. A good name to describe these special teams is cohorts of intercessors. They are those who are called, equipped and anointed for engagements against the demonic powers behind the human structures of evil. They are the ones through whom Father decisively advances his agenda in the world because they provide the work of "extraordinary prayer," which is how our Father how our Father has chosen to send waves of the Holy Spirit.

Moses, Aaron and Hur
Model the Intercessory Prayer Cohort

A model of a cohort of intercessors is Rees Howells joined by the students of the Bible College of Wales. From 1936 until the end of the war in 1945, this band of intercessors, involving perhaps up to a hundred or more students and faculty led by Rees Howells, were again and again called into the gap. Often these prayer battles would last for days or weeks at a time as the Holy Spirit led them to engage the powers and principalities behind Hitler and the armies of Nazism. We shall constantly return to their example. But to help us grasp the essence of such a band of intercessors, we examine an example with only three people to demonstrate God's strategies for defeating Satan's plans on earth. God put in place the cohort of Moses, Aaron and Hur in the Old Testament battle with Amalek. Amalek came and attacked Israel in Rephidim.

Exodus 17:8-16

[9]So Moses said to Joshua, "Choose some of our men and go out, fight against Amalek. Tomorrow I will stand on top of the hill with the staff of God in my hand." [10]So Joshua fought against Amalek just as Moses had instructed him; and Moses and Aaron and Hur went up to the top of the hill.

Victory O Lord by John Everett Millais — (1829–1896) originally uploaded on en.wikipedia by Paul Barlow (Transferred by lux2545), Public Domain, https://commons.wikimedia.org/w/index.php?cu rid=18811161

[11]Whenever Moses would raise his hands, then Israel prevailed, but whenever he would rest his hands, then Amalek prevailed. [12]When the hands of Moses became heavy, they took a stone and put it under him, and Aaron and Hur held up his hands, one on one side and one on the other, and so his hands were steady until the sun went down. [13]So Joshua destroyed Amalek and his army with the sword. [14]The LORD said to Moses, "Write this as a memorial in the book, and rehearse it in Joshua's hearing; for I will surely wipe out the remembrance of Amalek from under heaven. [15]Moses built an altar, and he called it "The LORD is my Banner," [16]for he said, "For a hand was lifted up to the throne of the LORD — that the LORD will have war with Amalek from generation to generation."

The English pre-Raphaelite artist, John Everett Millais, vividly portrays this model of a cohort of intercessors in action. I love this picture! Artistic imagination may help us learn the following dynamics and roles of an effective prayer team.

Moses, Visionary Leader

It is around the anointed intercessor that the others gather to form the cohort. In Book I, I detailed the process of how a visionary leader is raised up in whom God has planted the DNA of the Kingdom of God. It is around this visionary leader that a group of others coalesce and imbibe the spiritual DNA. This group, the creative minority, joins the leader in implementing the shared vision received from God. Around this core group, a larger social structure forms for doing the work of the Kingdom of God. The key, however, is to recognize the crucial contribution of the visionary leader who, through the dynamic of withdrawal and return, brings back a vision of God's plans and what he intends to accomplish on earth. Thus, the visionary leader may be called by God to be the intercessor standing in the gap.

Moses was a visionary leader whose call included standing in the gap as intercessor. The work of intercession is to be the go-between in the spiritual and human realms through whom the plans of the Lord are fulfilled. In the case of Moses, this included the work of leading the people to the Promised Land as well as revealing to them the Law of Yahweh and the true nature of the God who made covenants with Abraham. Moses' chief labor was to lead. His leadership included intercessory prayer so that these recently liberated Hebrew slaves would fulfill their holy destiny to become a kingdom of priests. Moses stepped into the gap of intercession in order to defeat the forces of evil seeking to block the fulfillment of God's plans. In this case, it is the army of Amalek armed with weapons intent upon killing Yahweh's chosen people.

Rees Howells demonstrates the role of intercessor as visionary leader, given a glimpse of the blueprint of Father's plans and called to pray them into reality. Howells had gone through times of withdrawal in which he received visions from Jesus Christ.

He received the vision of the Bible College of Wales as a missionary equipping center. He articulated his driving mission, birthed from his encounters with God, in the "Every Creature Crusade." Also in the 1930s, Rees Howells shared the vision of the Jewish people returning to their own land and to the Jewish Messiah, Jesus of Nazareth. The Lord called Rees Howells into the gap as intercessor to defeat Satan's plans toto block the advance of the Gospel and to exterminate the Jewish people by use of the strongholds of Fascism and Nazism. Rees Howells and the students of the Bible College had to fight these great battles in the spiritual realm with the Devil in Hitler, but this was always secondary to the true focus of their prayer, which was to advance the Gospel of Jesus Christ.

For us today, in our calling to join the army of Jesus in order to tear down strongholds and to build the Kingdom, the Holy Spirit is raising up many visionary leaders to take on the mantle of Rees Howells a la Moses. Having received God's vision, they will be able to discern the times and take part in the great work of defeating evil and advancing the Kingdom. At the core of every intercessory prayer cohort is the visionary leader, Moses for our day.

Is God Calling You to become a Visionary Prayer Leader?

Could this be you? How would you know if you are called to this Moses visionary leadership role of intercession? Since I have experienced this call myself and have watched others called as well, I offer the following considerations:

1. You can trust the Lord to make the call clear by placing the prayer burden on you. You will, as I described in the last chapter, know that you are supposed to pray for someone or some issue. You may experience a quickening in yourself and the Holy Spirit

may start praying through you. Many people have experienced this as a gift of a prayer language. Or, the Holy Spirit praying through you may take other forms. You may shed tears. You may find yourself crying out in your heart for someone or for something. It may come to you as a deep awareness of the presence of the Holy Spirit. Your call may be confirmed as you live and breathe the Word of God. It can come in a prayer language. For me, I can testify that the words of Jesus have stayed with me, constantly flowing through me like a recurring melody: "I am the way, and the truth, and the life. No one comes to the Father except through me." As you start to pray into the burden and let the Holy Spirit pray through you, you will find the Lord deepening the prayer by giving specific guidance about how to intercede. This guidance will come to you with increasing frequency and clarity as you grow in intimacy with the Father, Son and Holy Spirit, and as a member of the Body of Christ you are integrated into their global communication network. As you walk in faith and obedience to this guidance, you will find the specific work unfolding before you.

One brother associated with PRMI received the guidance several years ago to start praying for persecuted Christians. During a prayer time, he felt led to do an internet search on the subject and found a concise list of attacks by Muslims at the website "The Religion of Peace."[6]

Although the information was very troubling (he found that many believers could not handle the vivid reporting of the atrocities taking place) he began searching for ways to pray into this issue. Each year the *Voice of the Martyrs* produces a map showing the varying degrees of persecution against Christians worldwide. In 2016 the map also included a second map with a list of nine Islamic groups and "how to pray" concerning each group. This information helped him specifically address these various jihadists in prayer; and, as he did, the Holy Spirit kept leading him deeper and deeper into prayers for Christians persecuted by Muslims. This has led him on many calls on many occasions into the gap to pray to defeat the plans of Satan against Christians and Israel. A small cohort of intercessors has now gathered around him and his wife. They meet in person at a secure location, and at the same time over the internet with intercessors from England, Canada, and different parts of the United States. Start with what the Lord is putting on your heart; that is often the doorway into Jesus' heart and the battlespace of intercession.

2. Another way the Holy Spirit may call to intercede a la Moses to intercede a la Moses is by giving you visions of God's Kingdom, as well as glimpses into Satan's opposing work.[7] These visions may be given during times of withdrawal in prayer in which we may be caught up in the heavenly realm. This is what happened to me when I was shown visions of the impending catastrophe if the strongholds of Radical Islam and Liberal Progressivism are not stopped. (I describe the terrible apocalyptic visions in Book I.) On the other hand, it may be more of an intuition or a knowing that is supported by rational analysis of the facts. In whatever way the call comes, the Holy Spirit will open your eyes to see what is going on in the spiritual realm as well as in the natural realm. This will be like the gift of prophetic sight that Elisha exercised and prayed that his servant would also receive.

2 Kings 6:15-17

[15]The prophet's attendant got up early in the morning. When he went outside there was an army surrounding the city, along with horses and chariots. He said to Elisha, "Oh no, my master! What will we do?" [16]He replied, "Don't be afraid, for our side outnumbers them." [17]Then Elisha prayed, "O LORD, open his eyes so he can see." The LORD opened the servant's eyes and he saw that the hill was full of horses and chariots of fire all around Elisha.

This is the type of visionary seeing Moses intercessors must have so they can see clearly into the human and spiritual realms. When such spiritual seeing is given, it must be carefully discerned and confirmed through the facts. This kind of vision from the Holy Spirit will provide the entree entre into the dynamic of intercession led and empowered by the Holy Spirit.

3. You will find yourself actually called into the gap of intercession. Perhaps not as dramatically as Moses or Rees Howells but nonetheless you will find yourself in the battle zone of intercession. You will experience the Lord Jesus Christ directing and empowering you to share with him in his kingdom work. It will be as if you are standing between heaven and earth, yielding yourself to the river of the Holy Spirit flowing through you functioning in the heavenlies or on earth, or both. These engagements may take place while you are alone or with others, and may last from anywhere to a few minutes, to hours or even days or weeks at a time. Thankfully, such opportunities to step into the gap often start small, but they will often grow in length and intensity as you grow in authority and are joined by a supporting team.

This stepping into the gap will confirm that Jesus is indeed calling you as an intercessor.

4. In the times of active intercession in the gap, you may begin to receive glimpses of the whole battlespace and just know what the human and demonic enemies are doing as well as what the Holy Spirit is doing to oppose them. This intuition, which is a combination of spiritual gifting as well as a facility of the human mind, enables you to command and direct the spiritual battles as they connect with earthly conflicts. These are the first steps of battlefield tactical intuition that is the mark of a commander, both in spiritual and earthly warfare.[8] If you find this ability developing

in you along with the anointing of the Holy Spirit and calls into engagements, you can be confident that the Holy Spirit is bidding you take on the mantle of Moses intercession.

5. There is one final sign to mark your call. I write here of the objectively verifiable fruit of your prayer endeavors. First, you will see results from your battles. This confirmation will come when the guidance that you have received is verified by objective results. For instance, my foreboding of evil and the strong call to pray on the morning of September 11th was confirmed through the actual Islamic jihadist attacks on the World Trade Towers. Also, you will find the verifiable fruit in seeing the results of your prayers. Another example in my life is that the Holy Spirit has led me at times to pray that the demonic cloaking protecting a leader in the stronghold of Radical Islam would be pierced. The result is that the person is converted to Lord and Savior Isa, or he becomes exposed to the military and is captured or killed. This has taken place an uncanny number of times. I report on these results in later chapters.

Often in our equipping as intercessors, the Lord will call us into prayer about situations that can easily be confirmed as y taking place in real time. For instance, about eleven in the evening while I was at my desk working on this book, suddenly the name of a friend came into my mind. I knew that there was an issue with his elder daughter because I had prayed with him about this about a month previously, so I started to pray for her again. Then the Holy Spirit came on me in even greater power, but with no clear guidance. So I welcomed the Holy Spirit to pray through me with the gift of tongues. Then the guidance came, "Call Tom right now! Tell him what is happening." Feeling a little foolish, I punched his number into my cell. When he didn't answer, I left a message saying that the Holy Spirit was surging through me and was working somehow in his family. I prayed general prayers of protection and for wisdom and for great overflowing love. The next afternoon Tom called me back and thanked me for the prayers. He told me that one daughter had major dental surgery the next day, and that he was struggling with a decision that he had to make about his older daughter (the one I was praying for) of whether to drop by and see her. As we ended the call, the Holy Spirit led me to break the power of Satan's lies and bondage he had put on the older daughter. In the name of Jesus Christ, I bound the Devil and commanded him or his demons not to interfere with the liberating work the Holy Spirit was doing. I prayed like this until I received a text message from Tom saying, "The police came. She's coming home with me. On the way. More later." There are, of course, many more details, but this is enough to demonstrate that my call to prayer by the Holy Spirit falling upon me had not been a figment of my imagination. I had actually become an agent of Jesus' intervention into a dangerous situation.

Verifiable evidence of the effects of our prayers like this help us to gain confidence that we really are cooperating with the Holy Spirit even when we are dealing with situations when it is difficult or impossible to obtain the verifying evidence. This is often how it works when the Holy Spirit presses us into prayer involving people and circumstances far away or hidden by a veil of secrecy.

I add one more marker to confirm your call. The Holy Spirit ordinarily raises up others around you who share with you in the intercessory prayer work. Moses was joined by Aaron and Hur who helped to keep Moses' arms raised over the battle of Amalek. We can trust the Lord to provide us a similar kind of prayer cohort.

A Cohort of Moses, Aaron and Hur

The anointed intercessor in the gap often receives the public recognition. Rees Howells goes down in history as the great intercessor, but no one remembers the names of the students and faculty of the Bible College who shared with him in the labor of intercession. The role of the visionary Moses-type leader is impossible, however, without the support of those gathered around him or her. Moses needed the help of Aaron and Hur holding up his arms and the staff of God until the setting of the sun when Joshua prevailed. Stepping into the battle space as an intercessor requires a team.

In the picture, we have an artistic presentation of how this could have taken place. In the valley, Joshua and his army are fighting. On the hilltop, Moses is praying. He is joined by Aaron and Hur. Moses is the key intercessor, but Aaron and Hur also bring their own gifts to the prayer battle. This is expressed by holding up Moses' arms. Together they form a cohort for stepping into the gap and doing the spiritual work of prayer, which was supporting Joshua's army fighting in the valley below. To do the work of intercession requires teamwork with others bringing different gifts and playing various roles in the work of prayer. We may use some artistic imagination and see these different roles embodied in Aaron and Hur.

Aaron Embodies the Love and Friendship Upholding the Intercessor Moses

I have always thought that Aaron was on the left holding up Moses' arm, which is holding up the Staff of God. (I do not know what the artist's intention was, but that looks like Aaron to me!) Aaron is standing with Moses, and connecting with Moses, leaning into him and sharing the prayer burden with him. This would be consistent because they are brothers. Together they have fought many battles together learning to function as a team, including facing down the king of Egypt. It is as if Aaron is looking more at Moses and inward to God. Notice too, the tenderness with which he holds up Moses' weary arm.

This is a model of all those who are not called into the battle, but are called to pray for those who are. They support the Moses-type prayer leader with love, friendship and protection. As they stand with the leader, they are indeed in the gap and in the battle, but not on point. This is a critical role that is often very personal, and based on deep spiritual friendship and love in which there is often a heart connection.

Aaron-type intercessors have provided me with the love and friendship to support me in the lonely prayer battles that I have fought. Often the Holy Spirit notified them to pray for me even before I have a chance to call them. They often have felt within themselves the battles in the spiritual realm and received in their own bodies the agonies of earnest prayer or the assaults by demonic spirits. They have served as a shield, providing the space for me to focus entirely on the battle without having to worry about my back or the flanks.

Is the Holy Spirit drawing your heart to the intercessor on the frontlines rather than toward the battle? If you consistently receive guidance to provide cover for someone who is an intercessor, then this may be your call. Take this nudging by the Holy Spirit very seriously because without you, the intercessor will be unable to stand in the gap without getting hurt. Your role in this war with Satan's strongholds of Radical Islam is to understand the tactics well enough to be able to support the intercessor as they are in the spiritual battle space.

Hur Provides, Strength, and Actionable Intelligence

The other figure in the biblical story and the painting is Hur, the one clothed in red. Hur is also supporting Moses by holding up his other arm. Notice Hur's strong muscular arm and his erect posture like steel, standing unmovable in the spiritual battle. His will is set on upholding Moses' arms with all his massive strength until winning the victory. He seems to be looking outward toward the battle. Perhaps his outward gaze is all the way to the Promised Land where he sees the strategic role of the battle in fulfilling God's plans of getting them there. Hur's engagement is very different from Aaron's. Now, of course, I am using the interpretation of the artist and my own projections onto the painting based on my own study of scripture and experience with this work of being an intercessor. However, these serve to illustrate these different roles in the cohort.

I suspect that Hur's role is to report to Moses what is happening with Joshua in the battle. He is assessing the situation and passing on information that may consist of guidance from the Spirit of God, but also from an assessment of the situation on the ground. This is another critically important function—getting intelligence to know how to pray. In this picture, Hur does not seem engaged either in the prayer battle or in compassionate support of Moses. He is more objective! He has to be so that he can get good intelligence, reflect on it, and pass it on to Moses who is totally engaged.

Intercessors like Hur, who stand firm in their faith in Jesus Christ, upholding me through the strength of their faith, have immensely blessed me. They have also joined in the fight by receiving guidance from the Holy Spirit as to the ebb and flow of the battle and how God is calling me to pray. Others have served as intelligent officers who are not called into the gap themselves, but are listening to the Holy Spirit and assessing the news reports and gathering intelligence, which they are constantly passing on to me.

You may find yourself drawn not so much to the intercessor, but to the battle. If you are being given the guidance needed to discern what Satan is doing and how Jesus is also at work, but you have not received the call or anointing to actually step into the gap, then your role may be similar to that of Hur. You may be finding in yourself a steadfast faith and total trust in Jesus Christ for the victory. This is a calling to stand firm and support the lead intercessor when their faith is shaken or they are blinded by their struggles with Satan. Your task as the more objective participant will be to master the tactics and strategies of intercession so you may provide guidance to those in the Moses role when they are in the heat of conflict.

Others Roles in the Cohort

Not included in the three models of Moses, Aaron and Hur are other roles needed for the full functioning of the intercessory prayer cohort. These will be unique to the individuals called and their spiritual gifting, personalities and experience. One that is not included in the Old Testament example is the networker and communicator. This is the person involved in the prayer work, but is also gifted at including others in the process. This requires great communication skills that can grasp the essence of what is going on in the spiritual realm and communicate it to others, often over the internet in writing so that they can join in the discernment and in the actual prayer engagements.

For instance, a gifted communicator (name withheld for security reasons) accompanied me on our Jerusalem Prayer Endeavor in 2016. There, we as a team were often called into the gap at specific locations in Jerusalem, which are at the epicenter of Satan's plans to replace Judaism and Christianity with the deception of Islam.

This intercessor undertook the dual burden of engaging in the intercession and bringing in other intercessors from around the world into our cohort on site. This required constant communication and the ability to articulate the spiritual dimensions of the prayer engagements. This took place on

Facebook as well as by e-mails and videos that we posted.

The challenge is to move past the travelogue mode of reporting on places and activities into bringing others into the actual discernment process of the working of the Devil and the countering tactics of the Holy Spirit. For instance, our intercessor did a masterful job describing the spiritual dynamics of Satan's deceptions on the Temple Mount where Islam is seeking to eradicate three thousand years of Jewish history. The result was that our intercessory prayer cohort of fourteen located on site in Jerusalem, expanded to about thirty—others praying concurrently from England, Canada and the United States.

We can expect to be surprised by the joy of witnessing Jesus' extraordinary work of forming cohorts around visionary, intercessory prayer leaders, from around the world in order to accomplish the prayer work he deems necessary at the time.

The Key to Effectiveness is the Cohort Functioning as a Cohesive Unit

The cohort is the smallest unit in the prayer army, comparable to the platoon in the United States Army or a Police Special Weapons and Tactics Team (SWAT), which, being small, is nimble and able to respond quickly to constantly changing situations on the battlefield. The number of people in the cohort may vary according to the mission. This could be two or three and, in special cases, up to about a hundred and fifty which seems to be the natural limit of the number of meaningful relationships a person can have. [9] The cohort, just as an army platoon, must be an integrated part of the rest of the army, the Body of Jesus Christ.

Each cohort may consist of one or two Moses type intercessors, but can have many others in support roles similar to those of Aaron and Hur. I have also found that in actual practice these roles may be fluid as the anointing of the Holy Spirit shifts from one person to another. I have, on a few occasions, been called to step back from the engagement when another person is anointed to step in. Then, I move to the support position of Aaron or Hur.

The key to implementing the guidance of the Holy Spirit during the battle is the team having developed seamless communication and an appreciation for one another's gifts. They must learn to function as a team to implement the tactics and strategies that are required to cooperate with Jesus Christ in defeating strongholds in order to advance the Kingdom of God.

How is Jesus Calling You?

These three spheres or areas of prayer—the Holy Spirit praying through all Christians, those called to take part in fellowships where focused and continual prayer is taking place, and those called to cohorts of intercessors—have interconnected and supportive purposes in this war against Satan.

The Holy Spirit may call few believers to the frontlines, be sure that all Christians must serve in the war. While not all will be empowered to implement the prayer strategies and tactics described in this book, all will need to understand the dynamics of the warfare so they may provide the support to those on the frontlines.

It is critical for the victory of Jesus Christ over Satan's schemes that each of us who is born again into the Kingdom of God discerns our call and steps into our place in the army of Jesus. Jesus depends upon each of us as his friends and coworkers for doing his work on earth.

Opposing War Aims of the Lord and of Satan

Now on to the war. All the work of discerning the times, gathering intelligence into demonic strongholds, exposing Satan's goals, and revealing God's master strategy for redemption, is to prepare us to enter the battlefield.

We must turn all this intelligence into clear battle plans for gaining the victory over Satan and his plans through Islam for replacement of God's way of salvation, genocide of Jews and Christians and imposing slavery to Sharia law.

This war is being waged simultaneously on multidimensional spiritual and earthly battlefields. To express this complex reality, I will start using the term "battlespace" which has replaced the term battlefield in recent US Army and Marine Training manuals. As we prepare for our role as intercessors and spiritual warriors, it will help to introduce a few traditional military terms. These definitions are based on the Prussian General Carl von Clausewitz's (1780–1831) great work, *On War*.

Defining the War

Clausewitz gives what has become the classic definition of war:

Essentially war is fighting, for fighting is the only effective principle in the manifold activities generally designated as war. Fighting, in turn, is a trial of moral and physical forces through the medium of the latter. Naturally moral strength must not be excluded, for psychological forces exert a decisive influence on the elements involved in war.[1]

Essentially, the art of war is the art of using the given means in combat; there is no better term for it than the *conduct of war*. To be sure in its wider sense the art of war includes all activities that exist for the sake of war, such as the creation of the fighting forces, their raising, armament, equipment, and training.[2]

This focuses our attention on the reality that this war with Satan and his strongholds on earth will involve us in fighting against the powers of darkness and his deceived human agents. This implies a conflict, a clash between two Kingdoms–Satan's and God's—and between the human beings and institutions aligned with Satan or God.

Paul warns us of this in Ephesians 6:12 when he writes of our struggle. The weapons of our warfare will be spiritual, and given to us by the Holy Spirit. Our specific weapons suited to this spiritual combat will be many and varied, but will include prayer and worship under the authority of the name of Jesus Christ and directed by the Holy Spirit. Jesus Christ gives to His disciples authority over the Devil and power to build the Kingdom of God. We will deal with weapons as we address the topic of tactics in later chapters.

It is important to note that the *spiritual* nature of our weapons does not imply that there is no real conflict or casualties in the human realm. There will be! While this war for us intercessors is primarily spiritual, it does involve earthly armed clashes. Jesus will call us to pray for and support those through whom God is destroying the human and military components of these strongholds. This warfare will take place on two dimensions at once. Clausewitz's definition starts with the human dimension and fighting with earthly weapons; the Bible starts with the spiritual dimension and fighting with spiritual weapons. However, both dimensions converge in God's war against Satan's strongholds of Radical Islam

The same is true for our adversaries; they are fighting the Kingdom of God and humanity armed with earthly and spiritual weapons.

God's War Aims

Clausewitz is famous for his maxim: "War is merely the continuation of policy by other means." He elaborates this truth in the following paragraph drawing conclusions:

> We see, therefore, that war is not merely an act of policy but a true political instrument, a continuation of political intercourse, carried on with other means. What remains peculiar to war is simply the peculiar nature of its means. The political object is the goal, war is the means of reaching it, and means can never be considered in isolation from their purpose.[3]

God's war aims as revealed in the Bible are the fulfillment of the Great Commission in which the Gospel of Jesus Christ goes forth to all the nations of the earth. The ultimate goal is that, [10]at the name of Jesus every knee will bow—in heaven and on earth and under the earth—[11]and every tongue confesses that Jesus Christ is Lord to the glory of God the Father. (Philippians 2:10-11)

This is what it means when we pray, "Father, thy Kingdom come, Thy will be done on earth as it is in heaven." (Matthew 6:10) The Holy Spirit prophetically shows us this victory in Revelation 21:3, And I heard a loud voice from the throne saying: "Look! The residence of God is among human beings. He will live among them, and they will be his people, and God himself will be with them."

In this war through Jesus Christ, the Father has chosen to make this a war not to impose his will upon humanity, but to create the context for human freedom where human beings have a free choice to choose love, life, truth and, on their own volition, seek to be in a relationship with God. Cultures based on Judeo-Christian values such as the sacredness of human life, the freedom to own property, the rule of law, and other individual freedoms such as religious liberty enable a maximum of human freedom. A core value is the essential equality of all human beings based on the truth that every person is created in the image of God. Another truth is that human sinfulness requires checks to limit all expressions of human power which left unconstrained always lead to tyranny. Additionally, it is God and not government who has given every human being certain "unalienable" rights. The purpose of human government is to protect these rights. These foundational values and consequences for human life are expressed in the preamble of the American Declaration of Independence.

We hold these truths to be self-evident, that all men are created equal, that they are endowed by their Creator with certain unalienable Rights, that among these are Life, Liberty and the pursuit of Happiness. —That to secure these rights, Governments are instituted among Men, deriving their just powers from the consent of the governed — That whenever any Form of Government becomes destructive of these ends, it is the Right of the People to alter or to abolish it, and to institute new Government, laying its foundation on such principles and organizing its powers in such form, as to them shall seem most likely to effect their Safety and Happiness. [4]

Islam, in its essence, is completely contrary to this culture of human liberty and equality, and is dedicated to the destruction of both this culture and to the foundational values upon which it is based.

This war is to defend these cultures of freedom in which humanity is free to believe or not to believe. This is consistent with the means chosen to implement this vision—love for humanity and respect for the human will. These create the context for the freedom of choice. This is in stark contrast to Islam's Allah who demands submission and imposes his creed by the coercion of the sword and subjugation.

As we must fight in this war, we must never forget the Father's aims as it determines the means he gives us to win the victory. The means must be in accord with the end. For example, in dealing with Islamists who shout, "Death to America, and death to Israel," Jesus tells us that we cannot curse them back with death, but must pray blessing upon them. To curse back is to work for Satan's ends, not God's. We cannot force compliance with our Christian beliefs on anyone, but must defeat all forms of tyranny that enslaves the human will and destroys human creativity to shape reality.

Satan's War Aims Through Muhammad

Satan's goal for this campaign launched through Muhammad, is the replacement of God's way of salvation through the Jewish people and the Jewish Messiah—Jesus Christ. Satan's servant Muhammad embodied the means that Satan has chosen to accomplish this policy of replacement: deception, subjection, and extermination. Satan is waging his war with other nonviolent means as well. However, violent means are the distinctive means, which Muhammad and those who follow him have chosen. The strongholds of Radical Islam have been built to carry out these means.

To use Clausewitz's terms, both God and Satan have political goals of establishing their kingdoms on earth, one bringing life and freedom, the other bringing death and tyranny. Satan has chosen the means of war through Radical Islam to establish his political goals. Therefore, our Father, through the Church and the common grace structures of governments, has chosen his own kind of warfare as the means to oppose Satan and fulfill his Kingdom on earth.

Radical Islam's Concept of War

The definition of war and the purpose of war given by Clausewitz grows out of our Western Culture with its deep roots in our Judeo-Christian values. Islam has an entirely different framework for understanding war, which we must understand if we are to develop the battle strategies and tactics for defeating the strongholds based on Islam. Dr. Sebastian Gorka acknowledges these profound differences in his book *Defeating Jihad: The Winnable War.* The first difference is that unlike the Western military doctrine which sees warfare as the means of advancing national policy by other means, for the jihad, "war serves only one purpose: the realization of Allah's sovereignty here on earth."[5] This means that we face an adversary whose motives for waging war are not only contrary to our own, but often incomprehensible within our secular Western worldview.

Islam also provides a completely different approach to the means of waging war than that of the West. Our approach is to assess the enemies' strengths and war making capabilities and then target those assets for destruction in order to force surrender. For Islam, however, the goal and the means for war are entirely different. Sabastian Gorka provides analysis of the Islamic counter parts to Clausewitz who affirms that, "there is only one target of importance in war: the soul of the enemy. The infidel foe must be converted to Islam or crushed."[6] This has many consequences for how the Islamic jihadists wage war. For instance, terrorism seeks to destroy the Western soul and belief system rather than directly attacking our military power.[7]

Both these Islamic concepts of the nature and means of waging war help us grasp why the Radical Islamic jihad is so formidable an enemy with whom there can be no appeasement and no coexistence. It also confirms to us why Satan finds the religion and ideology of Islam so useful in building the strongholds necessary to accomplish his goals.

Defining Campaigns

To accomplish his goals of the war against Satan, the Father has launched a number of campaigns. A campaign is a connected series of engagements or military operations which form a distinct phase of a war and bring about a specific result.

In the Bible and throughout history, we find many specific

campaigns to advance the Kingdom of God on earth. Each of these has been led by a leader, or cluster of leaders[8] who embody God's plans and launch his work on earth. Each campaign has distinct objectives. The length of the campaign may be months, years, decades or generations.

From the spiritual warfare perspective, we may understand campaigns as movements of the Holy Spirit to advance the Kingdom of God in specific ways with clearly defined objectives. In the Old Testament, these campaigns often had a military dimension, as did the campaign to bring the people out of bondage in Egypt. In the book of Acts, there are several overarching campaigns to advance the Kingdom. Each of these movements are associated with an anointed person. In one, Philip takes the Gospel to the Samaritans and into Ethiopia through the baptism of the high official from the court of Candace, queen of the Ethiopians. (Acts 8:4-40) In another, Paul and his team extend the Kingdom of God into the Greco-Roman world. The history of the Church since Pentecost is the story of one campaign after another in the war to set humanity free from Satan's kingdom and to advance the Kingdom of God.

King Jesus' Five Campaigns in this Epoch

In this present age at the end of the 20th and beginning of the 21st century, King Jesus has launched four interconnected but distinct campaigns to advance his Kingdom.

1. The first campaign is to bring the Islamic world to saving faith in Jesus Christ.

God's intent in fulfilling the Great Commission encompasses all nations on earth, including Satan's enslaved people in the fortress nations of Islam. This campaign is embodied in the mission work of the Church, the witness of Christian martyrs, and a major movement of the Holy Spirit inside Islam itself, with signs and wonders, dreams and visions, bringing Muslims to faith in Jesus Christ.

2. The second campaign is to restore the Jews to the land of Israel and to faith in Jesus of Nazareth as their Messiah.

In this campaign, the Father is restoring the original unity between the Jews and Gentiles by the power of the Cross. (Eph. 2:12-20) The Holy Spirit is working this miracle of unity through faith in Jesus Christ. The Father's master plan for bringing his Kingdom to the whole world depends on this unity of the Body of Jesus Christ.

3. The third campaign is set to raise up a vast army of "people of the chopsticks."

Those peoples of Confucian culture (Chinese, Koreans and Japanese, primarily) are being called to complete the Great Commission by spreading the Gospel into Muslim nations back to Jerusalem.

The Father is mobilizing, equipping and now deploying this vast army of Asian witnesses in his overarching campaign to bring the Gospel not just to the Muslim world, but to the whole world.

4. The fourth campaign is poised to renew and ignite waves of the Holy Spirit in the Christian Church.

At present, there are great moments of the Holy Spirit taking place within all branches of the Christian Church which are moving beyond renewal of faith to empowerment for participation in fulfilling the Great Commission. These outpourings of the Holy

Spirit are taking place especially in the United States, Canada, The United Kingdom, the former British sphere of influence in Africa and in Latin America.

5. **The fifth campaign is to defeat Satan's demonic strongholds of radical/militant Islam.**

This fifth campaign is required because Radical Islam has declared and is aggressively prosecuting a war of terror, subjugation and extermination of Jews and Christians. This is total war against the "nations of the Cross" and against Western culture molded through Judeo-Christian faith and values. This campaign is a "just war" to thwart Satan's plans of genocide and the replacement of God's way of salvation by the deception of Islam.

We must fling ourselves into the gap as intercessors and join the spiritual conflict to defeat the strongholds of Radical Islam. Prevailing in this war against Satan will require a ferocious focus and total commitment of the spiritual warriors and intercessors called as the vanguard of God's army. However, in the severity of the battle we must not forget these other campaigns of Jesus Christ as they represent the true aims of the war—advancing the Kingdom of God.

These campaigns connecting with the outpourings of the Holy Spirit are all part of the Father's master strategy for fulfilling the Great Commission which will include the defeat of fortress Islam and the Gospel of Jesus Christ going to the entire Muslim world.

Into the Gap
Engagements with the Enemy

Stepping into the gap is the way the work of intercession was defined in Chapter 2. This is the actual point when the intercessors join the conflict and are the means through whom the Lord is working in heaven and on earth to implement his tactics for defeating Satan and advancing the Kingdom of God. In this chapter, we will expand our understanding of what it means to step into the gap, by defining these events taking place in the spiritual and earthly battlespace as "engagements."

Defining an Engagement

Carl Von Clausewitz in *On War* gives the following summary of the conduct of the campaigns that comprise war:

The conduct of war then consists in the planning and

conduct of fighting. If fighting consisted of a single act, no further subdivisions would be needed. However, it consists of a greater or lesser number of single acts, each complete in itself, which as we pointed out in Chapter 1 of Book I, are called "engagements" and which form new entities. This gives rise to the completely different activity of planning and executing these engagements, and of coordinating each of them with the others in order to further the object of the war. One has been called tactics, and the other strategy.[1]

In Clausewitz's single paragraph, we see three terms that provide a way to organize our cooperating with the Holy Spirit in the campaigns to defeat Radical Islam and advance the Kingdom of God: engagements, strategy and tactics.

Within each campaign are a number of engagements. An engagement from our spiritual perspective consists of a conflict that takes place both in the heavenly and earthly realms. People, demons, angels, the Holy Spirit are all involved. These conflicts are usually limited to a specific period of time during which victory is either won for the Kingdom or lost to Satan.

Paul's Engagement in Philippi

An example of one such engagement reported in Acts 16:11-40 took place over a few weeks in Philippi. First Paul baptized Lydia and her whole household. Then Satan counter attacked through the demonized slave girl. She harasses Paul and Silas for many days until Paul cast the demons out of the enslaved girl, robbing her owners of financial gain. This led to a riot. The city officials had Paul and Silas beaten and thrown into prison. God dramatically intervened by sending an earthquake and opening all the doors of the prison. The Holy Spirit brought the jailer and his entire household to faith in Jesus Christ. Paul baptized them. Paul and Silas returned to Lydia's home where they encouraged the believers visiting Lydia's home. Then they continued on their journey, which took them to Thessalonica. Acts Chapter 17 then describes another series of engagements.

We may characterize an engagement as being preceded by a time of preparation which includes gathering one's forces and getting into place. Then, the actual conflict with Satan or actions advancing the Kingdom of God can occur. This involves both prayer as well as evangelism and confronting demonic strongholds. The engagement involves the intercessory prayer cohort as well as many different people in different roles working together and cooperating with the Holy Spirit.

Usually the engagement is followed by a phase of stepping back from the conflict for a time of rest and preparation for the next engagement. It is important to understand that in any campaign, these engagements are not isolated events, but each is linked to the next in a series that leads to the fulfillment of the goals of the campaign. Clausewitz summarizes the results of this principle as follows:

> By looking on each engagement as part of a series, at least insofar as events are predictable, the commander is always on the high road to his goal. The forces gather momentum, and intentions and actions develop with a vigor that is commensurate with the occasion, and impervious to outside influences.[2]

This linking of engagements is evident in the book of Acts. Each is connected and moving toward the goal of advancing the Gospel, *"in Jerusalem, and in all Judea and Samaria, and to the farthest parts of the earth."* (Acts 1:8) As Jesus Christ deploys us as intercessors and spiritual warriors in his campaigns to defeat Radical Islam and advance the Gospel, we can look forward to many series of engagements.

An Example of an Engagement

An example of one engagement was praying that the Holy Spirit would silence the radical American cleric who was calling for the killing of Americans. This engagement was prepared for by weeks of intercession and listening to the Holy Spirit about how to defeat the strongholds of Radical Islam. Every morning I read the *Wall Street Journal*. On November 8, 2010, the following headline and picture arrested my attention:

"Cleric Issues Call to Kill Americans", by Evan Perez, updated Nov. 8, 2010, 12:01 a.m. ET

WASHINGTON—Yemeni-American cleric Anwar al-Awlaki issued a renewed call for jihad against Americans in a video released Monday, as his father's lawyers went before a U.S. judge to argue that Washington can't legally order him killed.   In Mr. Awlaki's latest sermon to surface on jihadi internet forums, he sits, bespectacled and dressed in white, with a traditional Yemeni dagger showing from behind a glass-topped desk. Speaking in Arabic, he argues in the 23-minute video that jihadists don't need to seek permission from clerics to kill Americans and others he said were enemies of Muslims. "Killing the devil doesn't need any fatwa," Mr. Awlaki said. He also lashed out against Israelis and Iranians, whose Shiite regime he said is seeking to dominate Sunni Muslims....[3]

As I read this, I found within myself the moving of the Holy

Spirit. He whispered, "I need you to begin the work of intercession *now*, so that I can begin the work of breaking the curses he is speaking which Satan is using to build a stronghold of death." I did some research and found that Satan was coalescing a group of jihadists around Anwar al-Awlaki. This launched me into an intensive period of intercession.

Then over a period of several days the Holy Spirit led me up the mountain to pray that this man's power would be broken. After a season of prayer, the Holy Spirit said, "The deceived servant of Satan al-Awlaki spoke these curses calling for death to Americans over video published over the internet. I am calling you to make a video breaking these curses and blessing al-Awlaki in my name. You must also publish this over the internet." So I did. Next, the Lord clearly said, "Call other intercessors into this engagement in my Name." On November 9, 2010, I sent out a letter to our intercessory prayer network and the cohort who were joining me in the prayer. I called for a "Crusade of Prayer" for Anwar al-Awlaki.

I then provided some suggestions of how to pray based on the guidance I had received while praying on the mountain.

1. Jesus tells us, [27]"But I tell you who hear me: Love your enemies, do good to those who hate you, [28]bless those who curse you, pray for those who mistreat you." (Luke 6:27-28 NIV)

In the name of Jesus Christ, we pray that you will bless Anwar al-Awlaki. Let him know your forgiveness for the evil that he is doing. Lead him to paradise with the river of life which is only found through faith in you, Lord Jesus.

In your name, Jesus Christ, we break the power of his death curses that have been spoken against Americans."

2. Jesus says, [18]"I tell you the truth, whatever you bind on earth will be bound in heaven, and whatever you loose on

earth will be loosed in heaven." (Matthew 18:18 NIV)

In the Name of Jesus Christ, we bind the demonic spirits of hatred, murder, deception and any others by whatever name, that are using his words to accomplish their purposes.

We also, in the name of Jesus Christ, block this man from further evil intent, in the realm of the spirit and on earth, and we remove any favor he may have.

This prayer alert stirred up considerable response with many people over the next few weeks joining in this prayer work. The Holy Spirit led us over the next few weeks to know how to pray and how to pray together.

When the intensity of the prayer lessened and we stopped receiving guidance, we all knew that the engagement was over. In this case, there was no clear evidence that anything had happened. We just trusted that the Father had worked what he needed to through us in his campaign. We all entered a time of rest in preparation for the next engagement.

For months after this engagement and even while being called into others, I kept an eye out for news reports. I may have missed it, but Awlaki did not seem to make any more widely circulated pronouncements calling Muslims to kill Americans. Then eleven months later, I read in Al Jazeera that on September 30, 2011,

A government statement released to the media on Friday said Awlaki was hunted down by Yemeni forces, but did not elaborate on the circumstances of his death. He was wanted by both the US and Yemen.[4]

The actual prayer engagement had taken place over a few weeks, but the Holy Spirit had used our prayers and actions to set in motion a complicated series of events with consequences in both the spiritual and human realms. These led to the removal of al-Awlaki as Satan's tool to build a section of the stronghold of Radical Islam. This engagement was preceded and followed by others that were all part of that phase in the campaign to defeat the demonic stronghold of al Qaeda. Each of the engagements were connected and built upon each other and together served to defeat Satan's plans.

This concept of engagements provides a way to describe the call into the gap to start the work of intercession. We also must understand that each engagement is part of a series that constitute the entire campaign orchestrated by the Holy Spirit.

The Holy Spirit's
Strategy and Tactics

How are these engagements linked together to accomplish God's purposes? What happens when we enter these engagements? This leads us to the concepts of strategy and tactics.

Defining Strategy

Clausewitz again gives the classic definition of strategy:

Strategy is the use of the engagement for the purpose of the war. The strategist must therefore define an aim for the entire operational side of the war that will be in accordance with its purpose. In other words, he will draft the plan of the war, and the aim will determine the series of actions intended to achieve it: he will, in fact, shape the individual campaigns and, within these, decide on the individual engagements.[1]

For those of us called into the army of the Lord, it is Jesus Christ through the Holy Spirit guiding who is the master strategist. In order to fulfill the overarching goals of the Great Commission, he will reveal to us the strategies that will determine the engagements.

The book of Acts demonstrates the strategies that Jesus Christ is implementing in order to initiate the engagements with human beings and demonic powers, which advance the Kingdom. For instance, one of these strategies is calling, anointing and sending a man uniquely equipped to witness to both Jews and Gentiles–the Apostle Paul. Another strategy is to gather believers together into fellowships, which serve as beachheads for the Kingdom. These fellowships provide the support for sending out witnesses like St. Paul, and for assimilating and growing disciples. They also provide a concentration of worship and prayer power to sustain the mission. A third strategy revealed in the book of Acts is sending waves of the Holy Spirit to advance the Kingdom of God.

This is not a book on the theory of spiritual warfare. Therefore, we will limit our attention to the specific strategies and tactics that King Jesus implements to achieve the goals of his campaigns to defeat Radical Islam and advance the Gospel of Jesus Christ into the hearts of Muslims.

Defining Tactics

According to Clausewitz, "Tactics teaches the use of armed forces in the engagement." For us this will be the specific ways that the Holy Spirit will be leading us in the engagements to defeat Satan and to advance the Gospel. The Acts of the Apostles are a historical record of the many engagements the disciples had as they were taking part in the Holy Spirit's campaign to establish the Church of

Jesus Christ. Each of these engagements is a part of the Holy Spirit's overall strategy. Within each engagement, the Holy Spirit called the disciples to use various tactics.

For instance, the Holy Spirit led St. Paul to use the following tactics in the engagement at Philippi. First Paul discerned that a good starting place would be the place of prayer beside the river. There he started to talk about the Gospel to the women who had gathered there. Preaching was the tactic. Another tactic was commanding the demonic spirit in the name of Jesus Christ to leave the slave girl. Then, when Paul and Silas were in prison suffering from the severe beating and with their feet in the stocks, the Holy Spirit empowered them to deploy the tactic of verbally offering prayer and praise to God. The result of using these tactics during this engagement was that the Holy Spirit pushed back the reign of Satan in order to establish a beachhead of the Kingdom of God.

In our example of the prayer engagement to break Satan's power to speak death curses against Americans through Anwar al-Awlaki, we see how both strategy and tactics work. The overall strategy was to remove those empowered by Satan to build demonic strongholds. The Holy Spirit called us to use the following tactics to achieve that strategy:

First, the Holy Spirit called and anointed me to counter these curses spoken by al-Awlaki over the same medium he had spoken them—a video released over the internet. Second, the Holy Spirit led us, in the name of Jesus Christ, to bless the man who was cursing us.

Third, we expressed the authority that we have in the name of Jesus Christ to bind the demonic spirits that were working through this servant of Satan.

The tactics which the Holy Spirit led and empowered us to deploy achieved the goal of the strategy, that is, to remove those through whom Satan was building a stronghold. Before leaving this example, we must note that these prayer tactics are not dealing with human beings, but are instead, our steps of cooperation with the Holy Spirit as he deals with the demonic spirits who are working in and behind Satan's human agents. For instance, the tactic of speaking the blessings on a video over the internet is not so that Anwar al-Awlaki can hear and see us blessing him. Rather my publicly spoken words of blessing are giving the Holy Spirit what he needs to break the curses. We cover this dynamic in chapter twelve on breaking curses.

You may wonder if this really accomplishes anything in the earthly realm. A sign that it does is that each time I have been led to break the curses spoken by Islamists over the internet, immediately afterwards our web pages have been hit with cyber-attacks. We have also experienced demonic attacks against the intercessors. Finally, we have later—sometimes months later—had an objectively verifiable confirmation that the Lord used our prayer work to remove the leader.

Strategies and Tactics Provide a Useful Framework

To recap, we focus in this book on Jesus' four campaigns for defeating Satan's strongholds of Radical Islam and bringing the Gospel to the entire Muslim world. Achieving the goals of these campaigns will require specific strategies, which in turn will involve us as intercessors and spiritual warriors in a number of engagements. Accomplishing the Holy Spirit's purpose for each engagement will require the use of the tactics he will direct and empower us to use.

This framework of "strategies" with specific "tactics" will provide the way to organize the prayer and spiritual warfare to defeat the stronghold of Radical Islam. The task of the rest of the book will be to bring you as intercessor and spiritual warrior into a fully anointed participation with Jesus Christ in gaining this victory.

Intelligence Preparation of the Battlespace

A critical part of war planning is the "Intelligence Preparation of the Battlefield/Battlespace." The US Army manual on doctrine defines this as:

> Intelligence Preparation of the Battlefield (IPB) is the systematic process of analyzing the mission variables of enemy, terrain, weather, and civil considerations in an area of interest to determine their effect on operations.

> Intelligence Preparation of the Battlespace (IPB) is the systematic, continuous process of analyzing the threat and environment in a specific geographic area. [1]

When we add the spiritual dimension of the battlespace, then these definitions may apply to the work of prayer and spiritual warfare. For us in spiritual warfare, the task of discernment and gathering intelligence is to know what Satan is doing. Book I *Discerning the Times: Exposing Satan's Plans in Radical Islam*, contains information needed for the intelligence preparation of the battlespace. This intelligence provides the basis for the development of the necessary prayer strategies and tactics.

In this chapter, we will summarize the following intelligence that was gathered in Book I:

- The four schemes that Satan is implementing through Radical Islam.
- Naming the archon (high level demonic spirits) through whom Satan is building the strongholds of Radical Islam
- The map of the strongholds of Radical Islam with a focus on ISIS.
- Definitions of the three battlespaces where we are called to cooperate with Jesus to defeat Satan's plans.

For the details, history, and analysis of the present situation, and the documentation confirming these summary conclusions, you will need to refer back to Book I.

The Four Schemes of Satan
Being Implemented through Islam

In any warfare, whether human or spiritual, one must know what the true intentions of the enemy are in order to prevail. Without this basic intelligence, we will lack an interpretative framework to understand the enemy's actions. Misjudging or misunderstanding the enemy's true intentions and long-term goals results in choosing the wrong strategies and tactics. This will lead to defeat.

Our warfare is not primarily with flesh and blood, but with Satan and his legions. Therefore, we must ask, "What are Satan's goals and long range plans that he is seeking to accomplish through the religion of Islam and the present-day strongholds of Radical Islam?" I believe the Holy Spirit has revealed to us that Satan has four basic schemes, which if allowed to come to fruition, will have disastrous implications for the Church and humanity.

Satan's First Scheme
Replace God's Way of Salvation
with the Deception of Islam

Satan's ultimate goal through the religion and cultural system of Islam is the complete replacement of Yahweh's Way of redemption with the totalitarian system of militant Islam. Satan's plan is:

- To replace the Jewish patriarchs, and prophets, Jesus Christ and the Apostles with the false prophet Muhammad,
- To replace the Old and New Testaments with the deception of the Quran and the Hadith,
- To replace the Kingdom of God with the totalitarian spiritual, cultural, and political bondage of Sharia law,
- To replace the worship of God in spirit and in truth with submission ("Islam") to Allah,
- To replace the true God—Father, Son and Holy Spirit— revealed in the Bible and through nature with "Allah"— Satan himself disguised as the moon god worshiped at Mecca,
- To replace the Gospel of the Kingdom of God (salvation by faith in Jesus Christ) with works righteousness leading to eternal death,
- To replace the promise of eternal life with the Father, Son and Holy Spirit, with the delusion of eternity with the

"houris," the dark-eyed ones (virgins who minister to Allah's warriors).

Satan's Second Scheme
Exterminate Jews and Christians
to Negate Yahweh's Covenants

Islam has always been a tool for Satan to subjugate Jews and replace the Church of Jesus Christ. Go to Jerusalem today and you will notice that virtually every holy Jewish or Christian site, cherished by the Lord's covenant people, has a mosque built directly on top of it or next to it. The purpose is not to establish "another religion." It is to *replace* Yahweh's covenant people by either absorbing them into Satan's new system, or getting rid of them. Now, as Satan realizes that his time is short, he is intensifying his plans to nullify Yahweh's covenants by exterminating Jews and Christians. He intends to expunge all evidence from history of the existence of any reality to counter the great deception foisted on the world through the false prophet Muhammad—the fraud of the Quran and the Hadith.

Satan has constructed the near perfect killing machine in the strongholds of Radical Islam to murder billions of people.

Satan's Third Scheme
Strangle the Winds of the Holy Spirit
Blowing in the House of Islam

The Holy Spirit is bringing more Muslims to faith in Jesus Christ than at any other time in history.[2] This movement is well documented in *A Wind in the House of Islam: How God is Drawing Muslims around the World to Faith in Jesus Christ* by David Garrison.

Satan is intent upon using the demonic stronghold of Radical Islam both to restrain the Holy Spirit from drawing Muslims to

Christ, and to choke movements toward moderation. Satan is using the sword and all means of social-political coercion to enforce the Wahhabis' interpretative framework of the sacred texts of Islam and the tyrannical rule of Sharia law. This is done through the rigorous and brutal implementation of the Sharia laws against blasphemy and apostasy.

Satan's Fourth Scheme
Establish a Radical Islamic Caliphate
from which to Wage Offensive Jihad

The Caliphate is the full, mature expression towards which the demonic stronghold of Radical Islam is—unless stopped— inexorably growing.

The Caliphate gives Satan the human, spiritual, cultural, political, economic, and above all the military means of a slave army and a slave state to accomplish the three aims above and to coerce the global hegemony of Islam.

The Gathering of the Archons to Form the Strongholds

We have discerned that at this season in history there is a gathering of high-level demonic spirits. In Ephesians 6:12, St. Paul calls these *rulers*, or *principalities*, from the Greek word *archon*. They seem to be the highest level of demonic beings, above another level of beings called the *world rulers*, or in Greek, the *kosmokrator* (Αρχας Κοσμοκρατορας.)

A further way of confirming that these are the actual demonic entities in Radical Islam is that they bring the talents needed to accomplish Satan's plans of replacement of Christianity, genocide and world subjugation. They are listed by their biblical names.

I believe these are the same high level demonic beings that Satan gathered to build and implement his nearly identical plans in the stronghold of Nazism.

Gog (Ezekiel 38; Revelation 20:7-10)

Gog, a high-level archon of tyrannical oppression and totalitarian government, destroys liberal, pluralistic, and democratic societies where human freedom flourishes.

Gog is working through the Wahhabi interpretation of the Islamic texts to create the stronghold of radical, political Islam set on imposing Sharia law on all people. This includes the coercion to accept the Islamic creed through the sword and subjugation. Once people are enslaved in this system of both spiritual and political oppression, they are held there by all the forms of coercion instituted by the Islamic totalitarian state.

This is affirmed by President George W. Bush in his declaration of war on terror which identifies the true nature of the demonic stronghold based on Islam. In this particular battle, the stronghold was al Qaeda:

> We are not deceived by their pretenses to piety. We have seen their kind before. They are the heirs of all the murderous ideologies of the 20th century. By sacrificing human life to serve their radical visions—by abandoning every value except the will to power—they follow in the path of fascism, and Nazism, and totalitarianism. And they will follow that path all the way, to where it ends: in history's unmarked grave of discarded lies.[3]

President Bush, of course, does not use the term archons or high level evil spirits in his address to Congress, but he does identify the very same characteristics of the stronghold of al Qaeda that are found in Nazism. The same identification may be made with ISIS and the Islamic Republic of Iran, both of which reflect the character of Gog which is totalitarianism.

There are other strongholds in the world where the archon Gog is gaining power and influence, as in North Korea, China and Russia. There is also evidence of this demon gaining power wherever socialism (collectivism) takes hold and moves toward totalitarian government. This is presently happening in the USA with the coercion to conformity to the left's moral and political agenda. See *The Road to Serfdom* by F.A Hayek for warnings of liberalism's tendency toward tyranny.

Moloch (Jeremiah 32:35; Acts 7:43)

Moloch, the archon of death who murders children, thrives on the death of the innocent and consumes life, especially through fire. Wherever the choice is made to champion death and not life, Moloch is able and ready.

When ISIS shows videos of burning people alive, Christian children being shot or beheaded, or the mass murder of apostate Muslims, all the while chanting "Allah Akbar! God is greater!" they reveal that they are listening to Moloch and to Satan himself, who is a "murderer from the beginning."

The Spirit of Lawlessness (2 Thessalonians 2:1-12)

This archon brings lawlessness and anarchy that opens the door for the imposition of tyranny—a paved road of welcome to Satan and his archons to construct strongholds to grow and gain the power to accomplish their purposes. This demon is very much at work generating murder and chaos through ISIS, which intends to usher in the Mahdi. In the Shia Iranian version, this is the hoped for 12th Imam. His coming is being prepared for by Iranian terrorist activities and the obtaining of nuclear weapons with which to wreak chaos and destruction on a vast and terrible scale.

The Spirit of the Many Antichrists (1 John 2:18)

Both Sunni and Shia apocalyptic versions see Islamic jihad-induced anarchy leading to the coming of a messianic figure who bears a striking resemblance to the Beast and the Antichrist of the book of Revelation.

One version even includes the return of an Islamic Jesus Christ who is the opposite of the true Jesus Christ of the Bible. "He will fight the people for Islam, breaking the cross, killing the swine, and abolishing the poll tax. In this time, [Allah] will destroy every religious community except Islam. He will destroy the Deceiving Messiah."

The final outcome of this twisted vision is Islamic domination and the tyranny of Sharia law over all humankind. This clearly fits the role of the Antichrist as an archon who specifically opposes the spread of the Gospel of the Kingdom of Yeshua.

The Islamic version of Jesus Christ, however, is completely opposed to the true Jesus Christ as revealed to us in the Bible and the universal creeds of the Church. Indeed, the Islamic Jesus Christ is actually the anti-Christ revealed in the Bible.[4]

The Demonic Spirit of the Amalekites (Exodus 17:16)

Exodus 17:16, ...for he (Moses) said, "For a hand was lifted up to the throne of the LORD—that the LORD will have war with Amalek from generation to generation."

Here our God declared war against Amalek for all generations because this archon is committed to blocking God's Kingdom on earth and either to subjugate or to exterminate Yahweh's chosen and redeemed people, both Jews and Christians. We see it at work especially in Islam's enduring hatred of Jews and Radical Islam's stated intentions to destroy Israel and exterminate the Jewish people.

This archon bringing death to God's chosen people, first found an open door in the heart of Muhammad, and then has been passed down through generations of Muslims. The most recent pathway is through the Ottoman Caliphate/Occult German genocide of Armenian, Assyrian and Greek Christians. This evil spirit has now been transferred to modern Radical Islam through the Nazi/Islamist stronghold to exterminate the Jewish people and replace Christianity through genocide and subjugation.

Leviathan Holding these Archons Together

Leviathan is described as a sea monster in Job 41 and Ezekiel 32. This is more than a description. It is depiction of a principality. In Psalm 74:13-14 we read: *[13]You split the sea by your strength and smashed the sea monsters. [14]You crushed the heads of Leviathan and let the desert animals eat him.*

Leviathan has many "heads" which suggests that he is an evil spirit of great power and authority. Leviathan is a principality that controls cultures against God and His people. The root word for Leviathan is "twisted" or "coiled." Leviathan is a sea monster or dragon that coils itself around the victim in order to twist the life out of him.

This is the tactic and strategy of this archon—to coil itself around the people of God and twist things until there is no life. Note the leviathan strategy employed in the Garden of Eden. He twisted God's words so that Eve doubted God's goodness and his intentions toward Adam.

In gathering these five archons and melding them together under Leviathan, Satan has assembled a formidable team. They are uniquely suited to fulfill his aims of the genocide of billions and the imposition of global Islamic tyranny.

They have each proven themselves from Old Testament times up to the recent history of Nazism. In the present Islamic State

Caliphate, they are demonstrating their aptitude by the extermination of Christians and Muslim infidels and the brutal imposition of the Wahhabi interpretation of Sharia law. These archons—Gog, Moloch, the demonic spirit of the Amalekites, the Spirit of Lawlessness and the Anti-Christ—under the coordinated leadership of Leviathan, when given the means of deceived human beings, are deadly, formidable adversaries.

The Diagram of the Strongholds of Radical Islam – with a Focus on ISIS

The following diagram visualizes the intelligence gathered and presented in Book I concerning the structure of the demonic stronghold of ISIS and Radical Islam. This will provide the starting point for developing the strategies and tactics for defeating these strongholds and thwarting Satan's plans.

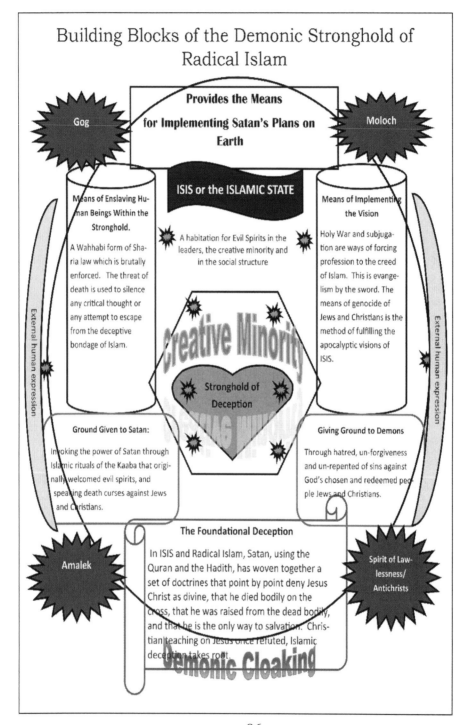

Building Blocks of the Demonic Stronghold of Radical Islam

Provides the Means for Implementing Satan's Plans on Earth

Gog

Moloch

ISIS or the ISLAMIC STATE

Means of Enslaving Human Beings Within the Stronghold.

A Wahhabi form of Sharia law which is brutally enforced. The threat of death is used to silence any critical thought or any attempt to escape from the deceptive bondage of Islam.

A habitation for Evil Spirits in the leaders, the creative minority and in the social structure

Means of Implementing the Vision

Holy War and subjugation are ways of forcing profession to the creed of Islam. This is evangelism by the sword. The means of genocide of Jews and Christians is the method of fulfilling the apocalyptic visions of ISIS.

External human expression

External human expression

Creative Minority

Stronghold of Deception

Ground Given to Satan:

Invoking the power of Satan through Islamic rituals of the Kaaba that originally welcomed evil spirits, and speaking death curses against Jews and Christians.

Giving Ground to Demons

Through hatred, un-forgiveness and un-repented of sins against God's chosen and redeemed people Jews and Christians.

The Foundational Deception

In ISIS and Radical Islam, Satan, using the Quran and the Hadith, has woven together a set of doctrines that point by point deny Jesus Christ as divine, that he died bodily on the cross, that he was raised from the dead bodily, and that he is the only way to salvation. Christian teaching on Jesus once refuted, Islamic deception takes root.

Amalek

Spirit of Lawlessness/ Antichrists

Demonic Cloaking

A Summary of the Building Blocks of the Stronghold of ISIS

1. The Stronghold of Deception within the Mind and Heart of the Leader

All strongholds start in the human heart and mind and consist of ideas and systems of thought planted by Satan that oppose God's truth as revealed through natural and biblical revelation. (See II Corinthians 10:14.)

In Radical Islam, the source of deception is the Wahhabi interpretative framework, which reforms Islam by returning to Satan's original deception of Muhammad through whom was given the revelations that formed the Quran. Next in authority is the compilation of the reports of what Muhammad said and did, along with commentary, which form the Ahadith. From the vast and varied material of the Quran and the Hadith, Satan has chosen a particular set of texts to form a worldview consistent with his goals.

Specifically, these are the reports and stories from the time when Muhammad and his band of followers had to withdraw to Medina—these have become known as the "sword verses." This stronghold of deception is both conceptual and emotional. That is, ideas and feelings such as hatred of Jews and Christians are fused together. This stronghold of deception gives ground to demonic spirits who may take root in the leader's heart, intensifying the lies and the emotions. The ideas, emotions, and demons coalesce to form the stronghold, which is comparable to DNA that may be passed on to others.

2. The "Creative Minority" who Gather Around the Leader

A small core group with complementary personalities, talents, similar thoughts and attitudes forms around the leader. The stronghold of deception carried by the leader infects this core group. The core may also be demonized or possessed by demons, which gives them power and authority. This group may be called the "creative minority," those who embody the reality around which Satan coalesces the larger social, political and cultural reality that forms the fully mature stronghold. This process follows well-established principles of the social construction of reality.[5] Shared deceptions and evil spirits hold together this core group.

The basis for the present-day stronghold of Radical Islam is the original creative minority—the companions—who formed around Muhammad which is enshrined in the Quran and Hadith. In the present-day stronghold of ISIS which has formed around their imitation of this original creative minority, a set of deceptions exist that Satan has constructed from many sources, but especially from the Quran and the Hadith refracted by the Wahhabi interpretive framework. In addition, in both the Sunni version and the Shia version, apocalyptic expectations have been added.

The ideology of the genocide of Christians (rather than subjugating them) is added from the Ottoman Caliphate/Occult German genocide of Armenian, Assyrian and Greek Christians. The racial ideology, hatred, goals of exterminating the Jewish people, and replacing the Church of Jesus Christ with Islamic/Nazi ideology—all these are grafted onto this Islamic root and carried into the present by the al-Husseini/Adolph Hitler embodiment of these ideals.

These have all formed a coherent system of ideas, beliefs and attitudes which form the ground for the stronghold of Radical Islam. This coherent system is first held by the core leaders and the creative minority, and then infused throughout the entire social organization that constitutes the stronghold known by its own particular name.

3. Demonic Spirits Exert Control over the Leaders and the Core Group

Demonic spirits are welcomed both into individuals as well as into the social fabric of the stronghold through Satan's deceptions, unconfessed sins such as murder and hatred, and through intentional invocation by prayer, religious rituals, and worship of false gods. The attachment of these demonic spirits enables the stronghold to become a human-demonic, intermingled entity.

In Radical Islam, these demons have also been passed down through the generations starting with Satan's original deception of Muhammad. More recent open doors to demons are the unconfessed sins of the Ottoman Caliphate/German Occult Nationalist genocide of Armenian, Assyrian and Greek Christians. A second pathway for demons into the present stronghold is Muslim unconfessed complicity in the extermination of the Jewish people under al-Husseini.

Implications for Battle Strategy and Tactics

Since the leader and the creative minority form the core around which the entire stronghold coalesces, they must be removed in order to prevent the stronghold from reaching its full maturity. At many points in the development of the stronghold, the removal of the leader and the creative minority will result in the stronghold coming unraveled and ceasing to be a threat.

For intercessors, this will begin in the spiritual realm. It will include such tactics as praying that the Holy Spirit will penetrate their hearts and bring the truth of Jesus Christ to overcome the Satan's lies forming the stronghold of deception. This work in the heavenlies will also involve binding the demons that may have gotten into them. In some cases, this may involve high-level engagements with the archons that are working through them to exert control over the entire stronghold. These engagements with the demons working through the core leaders will require many different tactics of binding evil spirits, or breaking the curses being spoken through them. Under the right circumstances, the tactic of dividing Satan's kingdom that is behind these human organizations can be employed. The battle tactics for removing these leaders depends upon identifying them, discerning their roles in Satan's work, and then seeking the guidance of the Holy Spirit as to how we are called to cooperate with Him in removing them.

If the human leaders of the core of the stronghold are not removed or neutralized by either being converted or cut off from the demons who empower them, then they may need to be removed from the core of the stronghold through other means.

The tactics used to remove the leaders depend on the type of system that the leaders and creative minority have created. Radical Islam, like Nazism or Stalinism, has chosen the means of death and a totalitarian oppression. So, the tactics for removing them by necessity become more drastic. This may take place by praying for their friends to turn against them. In some cases, this removal may require military intervention as it did with the removal of Osama bin Laden by Seal Team Six. In all these options, the role of the intercessor is to cooperate with the Holy Spirit to become the means through whom Jesus works out his plans in the human sphere.

4. The Human Name Given to the Demonic Stronghold

ISIS

This is the outward expression of the words, curses, and lies that Satan used to speak into "the hour of the power of darkness" that when received in "faith" by human beings, plants in their minds and hearts the seeds for forming the demonic stronghold itself.[6] (See Luke 22:53.) Around the key leaders and the creative minority, the larger organization, movement, and the political and military structure are built. This human component of the stronghold is given a distinctive name such as the, "Ku Klux Klan," "Nazi Party," "ISIS," or "The Islamic Republic of Iran." It maintains cohesiveness and dynamism through the following:

1. The inspiration of the ideas and worldview of the foundational deception.
2. The presence of evil spirits and the power of Satan.
3. The "routinization" [7] of the vision through enforced imitation of the ideas and behaviors of the creative minority.
4. Systems of coercion that enforce compliance and eradicate through death, enslavement and intimidation, any deviance from the inner and external reality of the stronghold.

Discerning the names that Satan is using to speak to Muslim hearts and minds to construct the strongholds is daunting. To those not steeped in Arabic language and history, a term like "Islamic Caliphate" has little meaning or power. But for those enslaved within Islam's system of deception, the "Caliphate" is a term rich with meaning and demands the absolute allegiance of all Muslims worldwide. The proclamation of the caliphate releases a vortex of demonic power that draws Muslim "true believers" into the stronghold far beyond the creative minority.

Keep in mind that using the name of ISIS or the Islamic State is to illustrate the general principles of the formation of a category of strongholds based on Islam that have purposes similar to Satan's four purposes. In 2016, ISIS is a major threat; but in the future, this could well change and a new name may emerge that will be a more accurate description of the stronghold Satan is using. Most likely this will be from the Shia branch of Radical Islam embodied in the Islamic Republic of Iran. I believe this outcome has been insured by the Obama administration's appeasement of the Mullahs in the nuclear deal.

In this war against Radical Islam, as in any war, clearly naming our enemy is essential for developing a realistic battle plan for victory. This is consistent with Sun Tzu's wisdom, "If you know the enemy and know yourself, you need not fear the result of a hundred battles. If you know yourself but not the enemy, for every victory gained you will also suffer a defeat. If you know neither the enemy nor yourself, you will succumb in every battle."[8] Book I, *Discerning the Times* in the series of *A Prayer Strategy for Jesus' Victory over Radical Islam* provided the basis for knowing and being able to name the enemy. Having named the enemy as the demonic strongholds based on Islam, with the intentions of carrying out Satan's fourfold plan; we now have a basis for developing this prayer strategy.

As Winston Churchill once observed, "Out of intense complexities, intense simplicities emerge."[9] This has happened to me as I have struggled with all the complexity of this enemy and the multidimensional war we are called to fight. However, as I have persisted in this process, the intense simplicity emerges—which is that this enemy named Radical Islam must be vanquished using all spiritual and human weapons that have been given us.

5. Means of Implementing the Vision

These are the methods chosen for fulfilling the vision, specifically, for bringing the world under submission to the creed of Islam and under the rule of Sharia law.

> **Means of Implementing the Vision**
>
> Holy War and subjugation are ways of forcing profession to the creed of Islam. This is evangelism by the sword. The means of genocide of Jews and Christians is the method of fulfilling the apocalyptic visions of ISIS.

In the case of ISIS and other expressions based on the specific Islamic texts of the Quran and the Hadith crafted by Satan to form the stronghold of Radical Islam, the means chosen are Holy War and subjugation.

Radical Islam of the 21st century is the direct spiritual and ideological successor of the Ottoman Caliphate, which launched the genocide of Armenian, Greek and Assyrian Christians. It is also the successor of al-Husseini and Adolph Hitler who launched a genocide of the Jewish people and the replacement of the Church of Jesus Christ.

These means of genocide and coerced inclusion into the bondage of Islam are the methods chosen by ISIS and other expressions of Radical Islam. This is evangelism by the sword. The means of murder is chosen for all Muslims who have departed from the true faith as defined by the Wahhabi interpretation of the Islamic text. They have become "infidels" or "apostates."

These means chosen by ISIS are intended to fulfill its apocalyptic visions of the Caliphate, the coming of the Mahdi, and the establishment of worldwide Islamic hegemony.

6. Means of Enslaving Human Beings Within the Stronghold

Means of Enslaving Human Beings within the Stronghold.

A Wahhabi form of Sharia law which is brutally enforced. The threat of death is used to silence any critical thought or any attempt to escape from the deceptive bondage of Islam.

Once people become ensnared in a stronghold, Satan uses various tools to enslave them and prevent their escape. In the strongholds of Radical Islam, the first means is through a Wahhabi form of Sharia law which is brutally enforced. The threat of death silences any critical thought or attempt to escape from the deceptive bondage of Islam.

All societies and movements implement elements of coercion that keep people within the established norms of the movement. These may be peer pressure, shame, intimidation or laws whose violation requires punishment. But the stronghold of Radical Islam, like Nazism, Stalinism and other tyrannical forms of government, has chosen the most extreme form of coercion—death to all those who seek freedom from bondage.

Implications for Battle Strategy and Tactics

The means chosen to implement the vision and to enslave human beings in the stronghold has profound implications for dealing with the human political, cultural and military aspects of the stronghold. This choice of means—which in the case of Radical Islam is genocide and subjugation—must guide all our strategies and tactics for defeating them. As amply demonstrated by Ambassador Morgenthau and Prime Minister Neville Chamberlain, well-intentioned attempts to seek diplomatic solutions with regimes supported by demonic strongholds committed to the means of genocide prove futile. In the case of Chamberlin, his efforts amounted to appeasement, which actually bought time for strengthening the stronghold of Nazism. Military defeat, not diplomacy stopped the genocides.

Our role model in wining this war over Radical Islam must be Winston Churchill. He had a grim realistic assessment of the nature of Nazism, and an awareness of the means that they had chosen. This led him not only to discern the times, but also to clearly and decisively name the evil. This led to the development of an overall strategy for defeating Nazism. He knew that with an enemy who had chosen death as its means and was committed to the destruction of what he called, "Christian civilization" [10] there could be no appeasement, no negotiation, only a total commitment to total victory over the evil of Nazism. This victorious strategy, based on naming and rightly understanding the enemy, is summed up in Churchill's famous speech of June 22, 1941 when the Nazis invaded the Soviet Union.

> We have but one aim and one single irrevocable purpose. We are resolved to destroy Hitler and every vestige of the Nazi regime. From this nothing will turn us. Nothing. We will never parley; we will never negotiate with Hitler or any of his gag. We shall fight him by land; we shall fight him by sea; we shall fight him in the air, until, with God's help we have rid the earth of his shadow and liberated its peoples from his yoke. Any man or State who fights on against Nazism will have our aid. Any man or State who marches with Hitler is our foe.[11]

In dealing with the stronghold of Radical Islam and developing the strategy for its defeat, we must have the same moral clarity as Winston Churchill in defeating Nazism. All our intelligence gained from discerning the times has revealed to us that the strongholds of

Radical Islam share the identical satanic goals and means as Nazism. To defeat this nearly identical evil, Churchill's approach to Nazism must guide us as we develop our strategy based on reality rather than on our hopes for an ideal world.

It will be our task as intercessors to "stand in the gap" to break through Satan's defenses into the heart of the stronghold to expose the means chosen and to take part in preventing their fulfillment. The Holy Spirit also calls us to pray for government and military leaders who name the enemy and develop plans for victory on the military and cultural battlespaces.

7. Ground Given to Satan

Ground Given to Satan

Invoking the power of Satan through Islamic rituals of the Kaaba that originally welcomed evil spirits, and by speaking death curses against Jews and Christians.

The ground is the legal right granted to Satan and demonic powers to have a claim on a person's mind and heart. Invoking the power and presence of Satan through Islamic rituals grants this legal right of occupation. Death curses spoken against God's chosen people and redeemed people—Jews and Christians—also invoke the power of Satan who is a "murderer from the beginning." Muhammad did not do away with the pagan rituals of Mecca and the Kaaba that invoked evil spirits, but made them obligatory for all Muslims. Each time Muslims prostrate themselves in rote prayers toward Mecca, they are in fact invoking evil spirits and are opening doors for demonization.

These prayers and rituals include the invocation of a false god named Allah whose attributes, as revealed in the Quran and attested to by his servants and recorded in the Hadith, are not those of the one true God, the Creator of heaven and earth, revealed in the Torah, the Old and New Testaments, and in Jesus Christ.

When death curses are ritualistically incanted against God's chosen and redeemed people, they open a door for demons to enter both individual human hearts and corporate organizations by bringing curses down upon themselves. (cf. Genesis 12:1-3) So when Muslims chant "death to America" and "death to Israel," intending in their hearts and minds to kill Jews and Christians, they are in fact welcoming demonic spirits to enter their own hearts.

8. Ground Given to Demons

Giving Ground to Demons

Through hatred, un-forgiveness and un-repentance of sins against God's chosen and redeemed people, Jews and Christians.

This is similar to the legal right given to Satan to have control over a person's mind and heart. This giving ground to demons to harass and to become attached to a person is due to specific sins committed that are not confessed, repented of and forgiven. The Ten Commandments given by Yahweh to Moses provide the universal categories of His law that when trespassed, open the person or a human social organization to the affliction by demonic spirits. This affliction starts from without, but may move into deeper levels of attachment within the person's psyche. In extreme situations, this attachment may reach the level of possession or total control by the demonic spirits. Possession, however, cannot happen to born again Christian because the Holy Spirit indwelling the person is a shield against compete control. For non-Christians, because they were created in the image of God, I believe there is a general protection against the occupation of evil spirits if they have followed their conscience which keeps people within the parameters of God's Law for human life.[12]

Individuals deceived by Satan's lies spoken and acted on by Muhammad are especially vulnerable to attachment and possession by evil spirits. The reason: Islam is not a religion of grace and forgiveness. So, anger and hurts are held on to and allowed to turn to hatred.

Ground to demons has been given through centuries of cursing, oppressing, and murdering God's chosen and redeemed people, Jews and Christians. Stratum upon stratum of unconfessed sins against Jews and Christians has allowed these demons to be passed down through the generations to the present.

Today's Islamists' refusal to forgive the atrocities committed against Muslims by crusaders hundreds of years ago, nor to forgive the more recent alleged or real offenses of Westerners against Islam, compound Muhammad's lack of forgiveness.

Regardless of how justified one's hatred or refusal to forgive may be, it is spiritually necessary to do so. Unforgiveness always opens doors for demons to strengthen their control over human hearts and minds by blocking a person from receiving the Father's forgiveness. Jesus taught, [14]"For if you forgive others their sins, your heavenly Father will also forgive you. [15]But if you do not forgive others, your Father will not forgive you your sins." (Matthew 6:14-15) This applies to all human beings regardless of their faith because it is based on the way we are created in God's image.

Additionally, the commands of Muhammad given in the Quran and the Hadith that allows such evil treatment of women, especially captive women, demonstrated in the Armenian genocide and the present actions of ISIS, are direct violations of God's law and thus an invitation to demonic spirits to occupy and possess those who commit these atrocities and condone them. When these evil practices become ingrained in an entire cultural system as they have in Radical Islam, then ground is provided for the demonization and possession of individuals, their culture, and their organizations.

9. The Foundational Deception

The Foundational Deception
In ISIS and Radical Islam, Satan, using the Quran and the Hadith, has woven together a set of doctrines that point by point deny Jesus Christ as divine, that he died bodily on the cross, that he was raised from the dead bodily, and that he is the only way to salvation. Christian teaching on Jesus once refuted, Islamic deception takes root.

The religious, political, and legal system of Islam and the strongholds of ISIS and Radical Islam are built upon this deception. The foundational deception was conceived first in the heart of Muhammad, transferred to his companions, and is now rooted in the hearts of the present-day leaders and creative minority. This foundational deception provides the conceptual framework which enables the social organization of the stronghold to adhere as one.

I define deception as any false ideology or concept concerning the nature of God, human nature, or God's covenant promises and commandments as revealed in the Old and New Testaments. In ISIS and Radical Islam, Satan has used the Quran and the Hadith to weave a set of doctrines that point by point deny and replace Jesus Christ as divine, as actually having died on the cross, as having been raised from the dead, and as the only way to salvation.

This foundational deception provides the legal right for Satan to exercise control over the hearts and minds of all those within the stronghold.

10. Archons, High Level Demonic Spirits

The archons, or high level demonic spirits, are generally located in the heavenly realm above the earthy human sphere. (Ephesians 6:12) Usually archons accomplish their purposes  through the stronghold by the demons under their command. There are times, however, when an archon works directly in the stronghold by possessing the leader or the leaders around whom the stronghold has coalesced. Whatever the case, the archon expresses its unique evil attributes through the medium of the demonic/human organization of the stronghold.

Five high level demonic spirits are operating within and through Radical Islam, especially in the present form of ISIS. The biblical names of these spirits are Gog (Ezekiel 38, Revelation 20:7-10), Moloch (Jeremiah 32:35, Acts 7:43), the Spirit of Lawlessness (2 Thessalonians 2:1-12), The Spirit of the Antichrist (1 John 2:18, 4:3), and the Demonic spirit of the Amalekites (Exodus 17:16). Each of these archons has unique functions and spheres of authority that together, under the coercive rule of Leviathan (who may well be Satan himself) are both building the stronghold of Radical Islam and expressing their natures through it.

Implications for Battle Strategy and Tactics

In summary, the building blocks of the stronghold provide the interface between the human and demonic and enable Satan to control human hearts. The tactics for dealing with all strongholds thus begin in the realm of the spirit. The Holy Spirit may call us to become the means through whom Jesus actually engages and defeats the archon. This will lead us into the tactics of spiritual warfare which will be addressed in chapters nine and ten.

In addition, victories in the spiritual realms over high level demons removes Satan's blocks to the great moves of the Holy Spirit converging on the city of Jerusalem. These waves of the Holy Spirit are together fulfilling the Father's strategy of overcoming the "Foundational Deception" of Islam with the truth of Jesus Christ. This leads us into the strategies for cooperating with the Holy Spirit in the work of missions and evangelism of Muslims worldwide.

11. Demonic Cloaking Protects and Holds the Entire Stronghold Together

This cloaking is complex and works both within and outside of the stronghold. Within, it functions like a "strong delusion" in which Satan darkens people's minds to prevent them from seeing. The cloaking is also maintained within the culture of the stronghold by attitudes and prohibitions that prevent any critical thought or 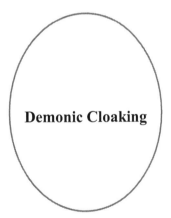 criticism of Satan's woven structure of deception. The delusion and prohibitions are reinforced by harsh, institutionalized methods of silencing anyone who violates these taboos.

Outside the stronghold, the cloaking works to prevent the true purposes, goals, means, and actions of the stronghold from being seen and understood by those who are either it's intended victims or those who may have the power to expose, destroy, or prevent the stronghold from accomplishing Satan's purposes. Satan utilizes a diverse arsenal to provide the cloaking. Secrecy and distortion of the facts by those within the stronghold keep it hidden. A worldview held by those outside the stronghold that cannot imagine the evil that Satan is intending or who dismiss the role of religious faith also keeps people blinded.

This demonic cloaking is essential to the formation of Satan's strongholds, especially in the beginning stages of their construction before they have obtained the earthly power for either self-defense or to impose their view of reality upon others.

Implications for Battle Strategy and Tactics

Having reliable intelligence is essential for cooperating with the Holy Spirit in Jesus' war to defeat Radical Islam. A first task in our warfare is to understand the nature of Satan's cloaking. This will lead us to implement our first prayer strategy: to pray for the Holy Spirit to pierce the cloaking so that we may see clearly Satan's methods and plans.

12. The External Human Expression of the Demonic Stronghold

This chart of the demonic stronghold of Radical Islam, and ISIS depicts the internal human and demonic realities fused together to form the core of the stronghold. Around this core, like an external shell, is the human, political, cultural, and military organizational aspects, together with the many individuals who form the outward and earthly expression of the stronghold. It may help to understand this with the image of the Old Testament model of the human heart, in which the mind, soul, and spirit (this last being the dwelling place of the Holy Spirit in believers) are completely fused with and expressed through the physical biological part of us, our body. So, we are both spiritual and material. Likewise, a demonic stronghold has both spiritual as well as material dimensions. Just like our physical bodies, the external physical, human expression provides means for both the spiritual demonic entities as well as our own ideas and visions to be expressed in the physical and human world.

The Three Battlespaces

To bring order to this bewilderingly complex situation, we will organize the strategies and tactics for defeating the stronghold of Radical Islam into three battlespaces. In actual battle, they will all be interwoven. However, for the sake of clarity and to provide a way of organizing the different prayer strategies and tactics, it is useful to break them out into the following categories.

The First Battlespace—Engaging the Demonic Powers

A stronghold is a human and demonic organization. This implies that interfacing with the human beings and working through the culture and organization of the stronghold is a hierarchy of demonic beings. In centralized structures, such as ISIS or Hezbollah, the human hierarchy may correspond to the demonic hierarchy. Hell is a totalitarian dictatorship; so it is not surprising that Satan duplicates totalitarian structures on earth. The highest level demonic beings possess and work through the highest level of human beings who have the most authority and power. From the top down, there will be myriads of demons interfacing with every level of the human organization.

The first battlespace we as intercessors and spiritual warriors are called to engage with will be this hierarchy of demons behind the human beings and their human structures. Our calling will be to cooperate with the Holy Spirit and in the authority of Jesus Christ break the power of the demons to ultimately divide the kingdom of Satan.

The Second Battlespace—the Demonized Leaders of the Stronghold

The second battlespace is the visionary leader along with the creative minority who have formed around him. In addition to the strongholds in the mind and the hearts of the leaders and the creative minority are the high-level demons directly attached to the individuals. These leaders and the human organization and culture give these demonic powers access and influence to the minds of all those in the stronghold. In this second battlespace, our calling will be to implement the strategies and tactics for removing the core leaders and dispersing the creative minority so they are no longer Satan's seeds for growing strongholds.

The hope is that if these leaders forming the core of the stronghold are removed in time, the strongholds will come unraveled and lose their authority to gather others.

The Third Battlespace—External Human Organizations and the Material Means of the Stronghold

This is the outward human organizational aspects of the stronghold. These are the many human beings who have been enslaved in the system and willingly or unwillingly have become the means through whom Satan is now carrying out his purposes. These are the jihadist armies carrying out Satan's plans. While the hope is that they may be converted to faith in Christ or deradicalized and turned away from their evil, in many cases they must be destroyed through military means.

In this battlespace, the role of the intercessor and the spiritual warrior will most commonly not be engagement in military operations, but will be praying in support of those whom God has called into this role.

Only Jesus Christ
can Prevail over Satan in Radical Islam

When we realize that the stronghold of Radical Islam has its roots in the human heart through deceptions planted by Satan, we are led to the conclusion that only the victory of Jesus Christ over Satan on all fronts—the spiritual and the material—can prevail against this stronghold. God's grand strategy for victory is that those in bondage to Islam may be set free by accepting Jesus Christ as Lord and Savior. Only then can the lies of Satan planted in their hearts through Islam be overturned by the indwelling Holy Spirit who bears witness to the truth. The implication for us is that spiritual warfare and earthly military warfare will be taking place simultaneously in this war to defeat the strongholds of Islam. Tactics and strategies for victory over both the Devil and his Islamic slaves who have declared war on us must be developed that take into account this interwoven demonic/spiritual and human/earthly nature of our adversary.

The keys to defeating Radical Islam and to bringing the Gospel to the entire Muslim world are contained in the intelligence summarized in the map of the demonic stronghold of ISIS. This reveals an adversary that is a demonic and human fused structure. This implies that spiritual and earthly means will both be required to prevail over it.

It will be left to those in the military, cultural and political arenas to develop the military, political and cultural strategies for defeating and destroying the human dimensions of Radical Islam. For those of us called as intercessors, our role will not only be in support of these human efforts, but will also take us into the spiritual dimension of engaging the demons behind the human beings. We will be called into the spiritual battlespaces that are behind the earthly battlespaces.

.

Part II
The First Battlespace

Engaging the Demonic Powers

Tactics for Piercing the Demonic Cloaking

Satan is the master deceiver and has developed many methods of cloaking or hiding his intentions in the stronghold. In Book I *Discerning the Times*, the various ways this cloaking is formed is covered extensively. Here we must move right into the prayer tactics the Holy Spirit is calling us to use to pierce through the cloaking.

It is imperative for our warfare that Satan's cloaking be broken if we are to have reliable intelligence as to his aims and methods. We must also break through this cloaking to see into the true motivations, agendas and tactics of Satan's human agents. Without this knowledge of our enemy, we will have no firm basis in fact to do our part in cooperating with Jesus in this battle. The prayer strategy for piercing the cloaking of the demonic stronghold will require four tactics.

Tactic #1
Praying for the Holy Spirit to Expand our Worldview to be Able to See with Biblical Eyes

To engage effectively in this war of many dimensions, we must have a worldview that enables us to see and appreciate all the different aspects of reality. There are many routes to obtaining such a worldview: travel to different cultures, extensive reading of the great classics, and being open to a wide range of experiences. All human beings, because we are created in the image of God, have a general awareness of the spiritual realm, of good and evil that may be cultivated.

This awareness is universal to humankind. Many non-Christian cultures have a worldview that contains the best of human wisdom as well as an awareness of supernatural evil.

However, seeing and experiencing the working of God in human history springs from true *enlightenment* by the Spirit of God. Likewise, an understanding of supernatural evil embodied in Satan and in human sinfulness depends on the Spirit's revelation anchored in God's word. To live life with a biblical worldview, we must be grounded in the Old and New Testaments. To obtain this worldview not only requires study of the Bible and God working in human history, but also asking the Holy Spirit to expand our vision to see reality as God sees it. This biblical worldview includes the reality of evil entities that are at work in the world opposing God's Kingdom and seeking to enslave human beings. A biblical worldview will enable us to see with terrifying clarity the evil Satan is planning in Radical Islam and the depths of human depravity that willingly embrace this evil.

Many Western Christians with a scientific or humanistic worldview may need to ask the Holy Spirit to expand their worldview to include the reality of sin, of the Holy Spirit, and of evil spirits. I suspect that there will be many parts of this prayer strategy that will be beyond our comfort zone. It has been for me!

We may expand our worldview to include biblical concepts of reality in the following ways:

1) Read and study the Bible! Let the Holy Spirit open our eyes through the Word of God!

2) Read the testimonies of the great intercessors who have gone before us. My favorite is *Rees Howells: Intercessor* by Norman Grubb. This book expands our worldview and shows us the power of prayer. Another is *Love on its Knees* by Dick Simmons. Another is *The Believers Guide to Spiritual Warfare* by Tom White, my teacher in the work of dealing with demons.

3) Reading the reports of others is a good beginning place, but often our worldview does not change to include realities revealed in the Bible until we experience them ourselves. One way to have such experiences is to place oneself in a context where the Holy Spirit is at work bringing the "manifest" or real presence of Jesus Christ.[1]

4) I have found that being around people who are both anointed for prayer and intercession and who have worldviews expanded to see into spiritual realities is a good way to see my own worldview stretched.

An Encounter with a High Level Demonic Spirit
Expanded my Worldview

I grew up with a biblical worldview that came from my parents who were faithful Christians. However, I had no place in my worldview for high level demonic spirits working through human organizations. In my elementary school years, I had looked into evil by seeing pictures of the Nazi concentration camps and reading Elie Wiesel's book *Night*. I could see the terrible inhumanity that human beings were capable of. I suspected that the Devil was at work in this human evil, but this was a theory based on the words of Jesus and Paul rather than on my own firsthand experience. Further, I had, without even knowing it, imbibed deeply our Western materialistic worldview that excluded Satan and evil spirits as actual personal entities capable of operating through human beings as instigators behind human evil. I accepted as true biblical statement that "our struggle is...against the world rulers of this darkness, against the spiritual forces of evil in the heavens," (Ephesians 6:12) but I did not really believe it.

Then I had a worldview expansion experience. This happened while I was at Jesus Abbey in South Korea. Archer Torrey, a greatly empowered intercessor, directed this prayer community located in the rugged mountains of the Korean East Coast. On this evening, the group of Koreans who lived at the Abbey and fifteen pastors that I had brought from Taiwan were called into an engagement with the high-level demons of North Korea. There had been an incident at the DMZ[1] where the North Koreans were threatening to attack South Korea. Archer was leading the prayer in Korean, and then in English, which I translated into Chinese. We were praying that the powers of evil would be contained and not able to escalate the tensions to lead to war.

There came a time when the Holy Spirit brought us all into the presence of Jesus Christ with singing in the Spirit followed by a deep silence full of the glory of God. Then in our own languages, in the name of Jesus Christ, we commanded the powers of evil that were seeking to stir up war to retreat. The prayer time ended and we concluded with praise. Everyone went off to bed, but I lingered with Archer to debrief the evening. Suddenly we knew that we were not alone; there was a malevolent force pressing in from outside the prayer chapel. Archer smiled! He turned to me and said, "It looks like the Holy Spirit has used our prayers to stir up the Devil and now he is attacking back." Then he shouted, "Hallelujah! The Lord is telling us to step outside and do battle!"

Frankly, I thought Archer had lost his mind! As I hesitated, he bounded up to the altar, snatched up the large wooden cross, and rushed out the door into the bitter cold moonlit night. As I followed him, I stepped into a different dimension of reality. Archer pointed down the mountain valley, saying, "There! Do you see it?" And yes, to my amazement I could see it—a black shape extinguishing all light. At one moment, it seemed to tower over us and take up the whole valley, the next it seemed to be just a point from which emanated intense, life-engulfing evil. Around this presence, like the eye of a tornado, swirled demonic spirits. I knew that I was in the presence of a being with the will to destroy the prayer community, and indeed all the churches in Korea.

I should have been paralyzed by terror. Instead, I was surprised and heartened to find within myself a steadfastness and a burst of joy at the battle. I started to pray in tongues at the top of my voice. Archer, holding high the cross, speaking with words filled with Christ's supernatural authority, commanded the demon to come no further. There was a moment of struggle; like a blast of a hostile wind that nearly knocked us both down, and then, suddenly like snapping awake after a nightmare, it was gone. Archer put down the cross, lifted his hands shouting praise to Jesus Christ for defeating the powers and principalities by his death on the cross.

Archer was so full of joy; it was as if he were a little giddy or even drunk. I was too stunned to say or do anything. As we walked back inside, Archer's comment was, "I just love it when Jesus lets us go with Him into battle!" All I could do was to stammer, "What the hell was that?" Archer replied, "You got that right! It was right from hell! No doubt an archon. It may have been Gog, the high-level demon of tyranny; he must have left his headquarters in North Korea and came down here to try to shut down our prayers, but Jesus defeated him."[2]

This engagement profoundly shaped my worldview, altering my concept of reality and my practice of cooperating with Jesus Christ in defeating Satan's kingdom.

The Realization of the
Power and Authority of Jesus Christ

This was a high-level demon attacking us directly and unmediated through human or natural agency. I knew without doubt that this entity was terrifyingly real and wicked. More important than the reality of the archon was the experience of seeing the authority and power of Jesus Christ expressed through this fellow human being Archer Torrey. My worldview expanded to include the reality that Jesus Christ has given us believers today the same authority he gave his first disciples.

> [17]Then the seventy-two returned with joy, saying, "Lord, even the demons submit to us in your name!" [18]So he said to them, "I saw Satan fall like lightning from heaven. [19]Look, I have given you authority to tread on snakes and scorpions and on the full force of the enemy, and nothing will hurt you. [20]Nevertheless, do not rejoice that the spirits submit to you, but rejoice that your names stand written in

heaven." (Luke 10:17-20)

These verses must become part of our worldview if we are to name the enemy and to use Jesus' authority to defeat him. My suggestion to you is to first ask the Holy Spirit to sear in your heart through personal experience the reality of the Devil and the vast authority we have in Jesus.

Ask the Holy Spirit to bring you to someone you trust who has such a worldview as well as the anointing for this battle, and then ask that one to mentor you. Usually it is in the context of a relationship of love and deep trust that we take the risk of letting the Holy Spirit expand our worldview to include the reality of both the demonic and Jesus' authority.

We Must Be Willing to Let the Holy Spirit Expand Our Worldview

In this battle, we must be willing to let the Holy Spirit expand our worldview to include all that the Bible tells us is real. The will plays an important role in determining whether we will see spiritual reality or not. We may decide to see or not to see. The decision of "not to see" often comes from spiritual pride.

In the story of the rich man and Lazarus, Jesus warned that there would be those who would not be willing to believe God's words and actions whether in prophecy or in miracles. *31He said to them, "If they do not hear Moses and the prophets, neither will they be convinced if someone should rise from the dead."* (Luke 16:31) The Pharisees "saw" evidence that Jesus was the Son of God, but refused to acknowledge it. They wanted to know about Jesus, but were unwilling to obey Him. When they challenged Jesus as to the source of his teaching, he answered them: *17"...If any man's will is to do His will, he shall know whether the teaching is from God or whether I am speaking on my own authority."* (John 7:17) The implication is that having our worldview expanded to include the reality of the supernatural is directly related to our willingness to obey God and do his will.

Willingly stepping out in obedience to the Holy Spirit puts us in the context of experiencing the reality of both God and the Devil. Therefore, if Jesus calls you into this prayer battle to defeat demonic strongholds, then follow Jesus in obedience. Once on the spiritual battlefield, it will not be long before you will have firsthand experiences of both God and the powers of evil. There is no substitute for firsthand experience that comes from following Jesus. As I have done that, I find that my worldview is transformed to see with God's eyes both the human and spiritual realms. Also, my faith and dependence on Jesus Christ as our commander in this great war deepens, resulting in guidance and authority to engage.

Tactic #2
Praying for the Lord to Raise up Those who are Especially Equipped to Pierce the Demonic Cloaking Shielding Radical Islam

I am not a scholar of Islam; I do not read Arabic; I have read the Quran as well as the life of Muhammad, but I am not an expert. Most of us who read this will not be experts either. So, we must pray that the Lord will raise up those who *are* experts, who have the experience, knowledge and courage to expose cloaking and smash through it.

One of these credible witnesses is Abraham Nhial, an Anglican Bishop from South Sudan. He was one of the "lost boys" of Sudan who experienced firsthand the truth of everything we are warning you of concerning Satan's evil intentions through Islam. When Abraham hears Islam called a religion of peace, he is incredulous.

He says, "Tell that to the thousands of Sudanese Christians who have been murdered and enslaved through fifty years of Islamic jihad."[3]

Yet despite all the suffering he and his people have endured, he has no malice towards Muslims; instead, he has a deep love. He is passionate about fulfilling the call to share with them the Gospel of Jesus Christ as the only way out of their bondage to Satan and eternal death. Personal friendships with people like this have corroborated what I am learning from other formal sources.[4]

Our prayer is that the Holy Spirit will enable us to connect with and hear the words of those whom God has raised up to pierce the cloaking hiding the evils of Islam. We must also pray for their protection by being hidden in Christ as they are risking their own lives to be the means of the Holy Spirit revealing this vital information to us.

Tactic # 3
Praying for the Holy Spirit to Open our Eyes and Grant us the Gift of Discernment

When we are working in the various dimensions of reality—whether human or spiritual—our reason, intuitions, and rational analysis will always play a role. These essential tools for exercising dominion were given when we were created in God's image. We must, however, recognize that these natural gifts must be complemented by the supernatural gifts of the Holy Spirit to see into the spiritual realm. The gifts of discerning of spirits, words of knowledge, wisdom, and prophetic vision are essential for piercing the lies and webs of deception Satan spins to cloak his strongholds and obscure his true intentions.

We must pray for these gifts. As we read in the news about terrible atrocities committed by Islamists, or read of the movement of armies, or listen to the words of either terrorist leaders or our own political leaders, we must ask, "Lord, reveal to us what is really taking place. Show us what we need to know so as not to be deceived. Lord, reveal the demons that are at work here, and the lies being told as a piece of Satan's cloaking."

As we pray for Father to reveal the deep plans of Satan or the hidden motives and agendas of human beings, we can expect the Holy Spirit to reveal to us what we need to know to cooperate with him.

It may be of help in receiving such discernment to recognize that each of us will often receive this guidance in ways unique to our own personalities. For some it will be through rational analysis of the facts. For others, insight will come through visions, dreams, or intuitions.

The important point here for us as intercessors is to first learn how God speaks and reveals things to us. Secondly, as we pray to receive the gift of discernment, the Lord expects us to be a part of a vital Christian community that is centered in Jesus Christ, grounded in the Bible as the Word of God, and open to the guidance of the Holy Spirit. This is the type of fellowship envisioned by St. Paul in I Corinthians chapters 12-14 where all of the gifts of the Holy Spirit are present and are wrapped in the love of Jesus Christ.

An Engagement Illustrating these Tactics
to Pierce the Devil's Cloaking

One engagement, which is still underway as I write this chapter, will help to illustrate these tactics. The Holy Spirit called me into the engagement when I read these headlines in *The Wall Street Journal* online, November 14, 2015, "Paris Attacks Leave More Than 100 Dead: Gunmen hit crowds in nightlife district and set off blasts outside soccer stadium in France"[5] This was the beginning of a series of attacks by ISIS. French President Hollande called them an "act of war by the Islamic State."

The dust had hardly settled in Paris when on November 20 another Islamic jihadist attacked in Mali.[6] A Russian airliner that exploded as it was flying out of Egypt, killing all aboard on November 2, had preceded these attacks.[7] The terror bombings in Beirut were on the 20th.

A continuous stream of news media reports followed. French police caught most of those responsible for the Paris attack. The French and Russian air forces unleashed massive bombing campaigns against ISIS targets in Syria. A heated debate was taking place in the United States about how to defeat ISIS. In the midst of all this welter of information and strongly expressed opinions, I was praying, "Lord, pierce the cloaking and reveal what the Devil is doing. Lord, how am I to pray, and call others to pray, to prevent further evil?" The answers came in phases and involved other intercessors whom the Holy Spirit had formed into a cohort.

The anointing fell on me on the next Saturday morning, and the Lord led me into the thick of the engagement. I was reading the *Wall Street Journal* and pondering the sequence of attacks, when I felt the Holy Spirit say, "Remember what Jesus said when they came to get him in the garden!" So I read the passage in Luke 22:52-53, [52]Then Jesus said to the chief priests, the officers of the temple guard, and the elders who had come out to get him, "Have you come out with swords and clubs like you would against an outlaw? [53]Day after day when I was with you in the temple courts, you did not arrest me. *But this is your hour, and that of the power of darkness!"*

I felt in myself the dread of growing evil. Following the outbreak and triumph of evil in the Paris murders by Islamic jihadists, we had entered the reality of, *an hour of the power of darkness.* This is analogous to a Holy Spirit given *kairos moment* when the Lord is ready to work. Except, this is when the conditions are aligned for Satan to empower his demonized human agents to accomplish his plans in greater measure. This is when these evil actions have an amplifying and multiplying cycle of more evil and destruction.[8]

The news reports of this recent series of atrocities disclosed the initial stages of this unleashing of death that can take place in the *hour of the power of darkness*. Once unleashed, how can these powers of evil be constrained? In the human realm, law enforcement and the military aggressively seeking out and apprehending or killing Satan's human agents may stop them before they work their mischief. However, this requires that the police know whom they are looking for. This is no easy task as human cunning and demonic cloaking will be conspiring to hide the people and their plans.

The guidance that I received was to get an email out to our PRMI intercessors, calling them into prayer to block Satan's work during this *hour of the power of darkness*. But how to pray? I knew we had to pray for the piercing of the demonic cloaking. I felt a great urgency about this, but no guidance yet as to the tactics we were called to deploy.

The second phase happened on Saturday morning as I was having breakfast with my wife, Laura. She asked why my phone vibrated so early in the morning. It had awakened her much too early. I checked the phone. It was a text message from Jon at 4:33 am: "I woke up to a vision of a Maersk shipping container and the words, 'major destruction.' It may have been New York, but I am not positive about that. I think it's something we need to bind!"

The moment I saw this, I witnessed to it. Yes, we need to step in and bind the demons working in radical Islamic agents to accomplish their plans for major destruction. Then when I told Laura the message, she told me about the prayer meeting at her church on Friday night where they had been praying against evil. The first guidance that came to one of the intercessors was that, "Christians would have ears to hear." That is the tactic of praying for open eyes and for discernment. The group prayed along those lines for a while, and then they went on to other prayer concerns. The Holy Spirit, however, answered these prayers right away by opening the spiritual ears of my wife and then Jon in the dream. Laura told me that as the group was praying for something else, a rhyme popped into her head.

> For want of a nail the shoe was lost,
> For want of a shoe the horse was lost,
> For want of a horse the rider was lost,
> For want of a rider the battle was lost,
> For want of a battle the kingdom was lost,
> And all for want of a horseshoe-nail.[9]

The Lord impressed upon Laura to pray, "Lord! Act now to hide or destroy the nail that is the key to the implementation of their plans for evil."

That was the guidance! The moment I heard it, I saw a vision of the long chains of events that Satan was putting together to cause "major destruction." I knew then our task as intercessors was to pray to break these links and thwart the plans. I also knew we needed to pray for the Holy Spirit to reveal to us what the specific metaphorical horseshoe nail would be.

As of this writing at 1:05 am on Monday morning November 23, 2015, this prayer engagement is still actively taking place. I have personally not received any guidance about what this horseshoe nail is. So, I am praying mostly in the Spirit that Satan's plans for destruction will be thwarted. It may be that other intercessors have received specific guidance as to what the link in the chain of events is and have already broken it in the name of Jesus Christ.

Now whether this is about the shipping container that Jon saw in the dream, we do not know yet. We may never know what may have been prevented. But I just checked Fox news online again—I check the news constantly while on a prayer engagement as a way of confirming guidance in the spiritual realm—and the urgent news is: "Officials announced Sunday that Brussels would remain on the highest state of alert into Monday due to a 'serious and imminent' threat. Brussels, the Belgian capital where several of the Paris terrorists had connections, is on a heightened state of alert since the French attacks."[10] Something is indeed happening in the spiritual and human realm. (The results were that the leaders were all apprehended and their plans for another attack were thwarted.) [11]

Tactic #4
Commanding the Demons Embedded in the Stronghold to Reveal their Presence and Intentions

The problem we always face when moving from the human realm into the invisible spiritual realm is discerning whether we are in fact dealing with high level demons hidden behind the human actors.

This becomes an important question as it relates to the strategies and tactics that we use to overcome what may just be a human organization and human sinfulness. Alternatively, we may be dealing with a demonic stronghold that includes the human organization. Even with a movement as overtly evil as ISIS, we may not be dealing directly with supernatural evil, but only with fallen human beings whose motives and actions result in evil.

The tactics required for dealing with human actions that are evil and are in line with Satan's plans are different than when fighting against the direct agency of evil spirits working and manifesting evil through human beings. We must be sophisticated in our discernment and nuanced in our prayer strategies. We must resist the tendency to see everything as demonic or everything as merely human.

One prayer tactic for piercing the cloaking and discerning whether we are actually dealing with high level demonic spirits is to command them to manifest their presence and reveal their intentions. This approach grows out of experience with personal deliverance and exorcism. I have done this many times. I look right into the eyes of the person I am praying for and in the name of Jesus Christ command the demons that may be attached to them to reveal their presence. When this is done in faith and at the direction of the Holy Spirit, if there are demons attached, they will reveal their presence either through subtle or sometimes violent manifestations. As one keeps pressing in on the demons in the authority of Jesus Christ, an unmistakable separation will often take place in which one is no longer dealing with the human person, but an alien demonic entity.

Once the demon has shown itself, I will then command it to tell me why it is present and what its purpose is. After the evil spirit's hold on the person has been weakened through removing the reasons for its attachment, I will then cast it out in the name of Jesus. If there are no demons present but only emotional wounding, mental illness, or other human issues, then there will be no separation, and engagement with an evil spirit. The outcome of this testing approach provides the intelligence needed to pray for Jesus to set the person free. The experience gained from doing personal deliverance may provide guidance in piercing the cloaking in a corporate entity like ISIS or Boko Haram that is geographically distant and far more dangerous.

Commanding the Demons Behind ISIS to Reveal Their Presence

When the scourge of ISIS started to break out in the Middle East, I asked the Holy Spirit to give me the gift of discernment. I prayed for the Lord to expose the evil spirits energizing this movement. I also asked the Lord to show me whether ISIS is a demonic stronghold built on the sacred text of Islam, or if ISIS is an Arab nationalistic movement against Western imperialism, driven by concern for Israeli injustices against Palestinians.

The Holy Spirit led me with other intercessors in the cohort to speak the following commands, "In the name of Jesus Christ, I command you evil spirits working through ISIS to manifest your presence. I command you by the authority given me in Jesus Christ to expose to the whole world your intentions and plans. You cannot hide, but you will reveal for the entire world to see whether or not you are rooted in the Quran and the example of Muhammad as the means of building this demonic stronghold of Radical Islam."

I did this under the strong anointing of the Holy Spirit and in unity and agreement with others in the name of Jesus Christ. I was aware that Jesus Christ himself was granting me the authority to make these commands in his holy Name. As I spoke these commands under the anointing, I could feel ripples of power moving in the spiritual realm and reaching all the way to the Middle East. I could feel demons fighting back, seeking to stay hidden in the hearts and minds of the ISIS fighters. I could see hosts of angels carrying flaming swords driving them from hiding.

When this prayer battle was over, I was exhausted but invigorated. I was expectant that something would happen quickly for the entire world to see, and it did—in a horrible fashion. The news reported a series of terrible atrocities. (Some of these atrocities had taken place months before, but were just now being released to the news media.) Christian children were beheaded, Christians crucified, women raped and sold as sex slaves, and apostate Muslims shot *en masse*. I think the worst were the images of the Jordanian fighter pilot being put in a steel cage and burned alive. Though later this horror was superseded with the videos and news report that, "19 Yazidi girls burned alive for refusing to have sex with their ISIS captors."[12] All this was revealed to us by ISIS itself through gruesome videos accompanied by the chanting of verses from the Quran and the Hadith, and the shouts of "Allah Akbar!" (Allah is greater!) The Islamic roots and inspiration of this movement were there for all to see. We could see the demons of death and lust fully at work in the men who often with laughter and smiles committed these atrocities.

What confirmed to me that ISIS really was a demonic stronghold was that I felt the demons in ISIS that Jesus Christ had forced into exposing their presence then come raging against me. I dealt with waves of fear coming over me. Worse was that these demons were stirring up all my own sinful tendencies to follow those smiling Islamic fanatics doing the will of Allah in an orgy of blood lust. These attacks lasted for weeks. The news reports and these direct attacks of demons against me all convinced me that ISIS is a demonic stronghold, and that it is based on selected verses of the Quran and the Hadith. Further study and analysis has confirmed this to be true.

Now, am I saying that my prayers were what provoked these atrocities? No, I do not think so, but somehow I do think I was sharing in Jesus' vast Kingdom plans, which include exposing to the entire world the true evil of Radical Islam. With this intentional piercing of the demonic cloaking in the authority of the name of Jesus Christ, commanding the demons to manifest their presence and character, I knew positively that we were in a battle not with flesh and blood, but with the Devil. I also knew without doubt that Satan was building this virulent stronghold of death based on the Islamic texts of the Quran and the Hadith. The soul of ISIS and Radical Islam is indeed Islam. It is not some perversion of Islam! It is the Islam embodied in Muhammad and his companions in its original 7th century form.

As we engage in these battles to defeat Radical Islam, the Holy Spirit will call us repeatedly to deploy these tactics for piercing the cloaking that hides Satan's actions and plans. I recommend that the moment you become aware of the Holy Spirit leading you into a time of battle, start putting on the armor of God and asking for the covering and protection of Jesus Christ. Then ask the Lord for directions as to what he is calling you to do. He will often lead you into these tactics for piercing Satan's cloaking so you can have the actionable intelligence to know the next steps in the engagement.

Are Intercessors Authorized to Engage the Archons?

Before moving to the tactics for defeating high level evil spirits, we must first address two questions of considerable controversy within the Christian community. First, when we discern the existence of high level demonic spirits, is there anything we as human beings are called to do about them? Is it God's role to defeat these entities, or do we participate with him? I address the question in this chapter.

A second related question, which will be dealt with more fully in the next chapter, concerns counterattacks. Sometimes intercessors or those close to them experience spiritual and physical counterattacks. The assumption often made is that counterattacks against intercessors take place because the intercessors have somehow stepped out beyond their authority by engaging higher level demons. Is it the intercessor's fault when bad things happen to them?

The two questions are related, and should not be separated. Let me illustrate. Several of our team members including myself have experienced intense counterattacks as Jesus has repeatedly called us into engagements against demons working in the stronghold of Radical Islam. For instance, while praying with a prayer group, I had the experience of being hit in the back by a demonic force, which others felt moving through the room. The result was that for months I experienced constant, and at times nearly debilitating, back pain. An MRI revealed a disk protruding into a nerve. Only after months of prayer, medication and physical therapy was I pain free.

A Canadian Presbyterian pastor (name withheld for security reasons), a fellow prayer warrior in these frontline engagements, was taken out of the prayer battle because his wife became seriously ill with inflammation of the pancreas. Months after these initial episodes, she was diagnosed with pancreatic cancer and, after a terrible ordeal, she died.

When these attacks started coming against us, I sent out an e-mail asking our support team to intensify their prayer covering. I received back the following from some intercessors in Michigan, who were very concerned for the safety of those of us engaged in this battle.

> Caution people against directly engaging powers and principalities—something which sometimes stems from pride and places us outside of God's protection, and call people instead, to call on God to uproot/tear down the powers and principalities that are being discerned. Call people to engage God, not demonic powers/principalities. Perhaps even encourage intercessors to read John Paul Jackson's book, *Needless Casualties of War*. It is short, and yet contains much wisdom.

Is it always true that we are to "engage God and not demonic powers/principalities"? Part of this comes from the assumption that Jesus' crucifixion and atonement on the cross defeated Satan and the forces of evil in the heavenly realm, and therefore it is not our sphere of activity. A biblical basis for this is Colossians 2:15, *Disarming the rulers and authorities, he has made a public disgrace of them, triumphing over them by the cross.*

Let me make explicit my assumptions so that those called into this battle will not be beset with doubts or unjustified fears that we are stepping out of the bounds of God's will and authority.

Christ did defeat Satan, but on Earth
Our Cooperation is Required

On the cross Jesus Christ did indeed defeat the powers of Satan. This is clear from Colossians 2:15. This disarming the rulers and authorities by the power of the cross was complete in heaven as we see in Revelation 12:9: *So that huge dragon — the ancient serpent, the one called the devil and Satan, who deceives the whole world — was thrown down to the earth, and his angels along with him.* However, on the earth, because of human sinfulness, the battle still rages. The Kingdom of God, established on earth through Jesus Christ, will be completely fulfilled only with his second coming. Until then Paul warns us in Ephesians 6:11-12 that we must put on the full armor of God, that our battle is not with flesh and blood, but with the Devil and those demonic powers aligned with him. Jesus Christ has delegated authority to us as his representatives to engage in the battle with these defeated but still powerful foes who are desperately holding ground on earth.

While the battle is the Lord's and the victory is in Jesus Christ, God has chosen to work this victory out on earth through his children, born again in his Son Jesus, who are in God's Kingdom and are called and anointed as Jesus' friends and coworkers. In this battle we will play our role of speaking and acting in kairos moments of opportunity. We will be praying and asking Jesus Christ to defeat the powers of Satan, to root up and tear down strongholds. But in turn, the Holy Spirit will call for our faith and obedience as the means through whom he will be working to root up and tear down the strongholds. Jesus expresses his power and authority through us, the people of God.

This holds true not just in defeating strongholds, but for almost all of God's work on earth. God's usual way of working will be mediated. However, because he is Lord, he has the authority to bypass us and work directly. An example of this dynamic is the Old Testament battle of Jericho. (Joshua 6) God knocked down the walls, but the people had to do their part of marching around the city and blowing the shofar and shouting. The victory was the Lord's, but he worked with his people acting in faith and obedience. We see this same dynamic when Jesus sent his disciples and later the 72 as his witnesses; they came back amazed, saying, *"Lord, even the demons submit to us in your name!"* (Luke 10:17-20) This power and authority was all from Jesus, but the disciples had to go out in obedience. Jesus cast out the demons, but He did it through his disciples. This principle of God working on earth through us is a fundamental principle for understanding the nature of spiritual warfare, and explains why we must be involved even though Jesus has defeated Satan on the cross.

Adam and Eve Granted Dominion on Earth

What is the extent of our sphere of authority in spiritual warfare? Jesus clearly gives us his disciples authority over demons that are attached to people in the human sphere on earth. Does our authority include higher level demons? From my understanding,

Jesus may call us as his coworkers to be the means through whom he is working to express his authority over not just demons afflicting individuals, but also high level demons, even the arch demon Satan. To come to this conclusion means taking seriously not just particular verses of scripture, but the biblical framework of how God has decided to include us both in advancing His Kingdom as well as in the governance of the Kingdom.

In Gen 1:26-28 God gave Adam and Eve dominion on the earth. How far this dominion extended beyond the earth sphere is not revealed to us in the Genesis story. What is clear is that dominion carries great authority and freedom limited only by God's command that they not eat of the tree of the knowledge of good and evil. (Genesis 2:16-17) This fellowship of divine-human cooperation in dominion was shattered by our first parents falling into sin. We were alienated from God, his image within us warped, and the human expression of dominion became twisted toward evil. Human sin now gave Satan and evil spirits a foothold in the earthly and human realms. From the ancient witness of the book of Job, Satan seems to have had free access not only to earth, but all the way to the heavenly realms.[1] Later in Revelation 12:7-9, there is war in heaven when Satan and his fallen angels are cast out and come down to earth to enslave humanity and wage war against the Church of Jesus Christ.

The Location of Evil Spirits

These demonic entities that invaded earth represent an empire of evil that is located on earth, clinging to the ground given them in the hearts of sinful human beings. This, as Paul suggests, includes the spiritual realms that seem to reflect higher orders of demonic beings with greater spheres of authority. *For our struggle is not against flesh and blood, but against the rulers, against the powers, against the world rulers of this darkness, against the spiritual forces of evil in the heavens.* (Ephesians 6:12) These are located in the spiritual realms or in the heavens. But just where is this? Paul has spoken of being caught up into the third heaven, which he equates to Paradise. (2 Corinthians 12:2-4) There he encountered God and received divine revelation.[2] Demonic entities cannot be in this place that Paul called the third heaven or Paradise because that is where God the Father, the Son, and the Holy Spirit are. In the book of Revelation, John is given a glimpse of God in Three Persons in the throne room in the highest of heavens. The Holy Spirit is located both in the heavenly throne room and in the earthly sphere mediating the Father and the Son on earth.[3] God cast the Devil and his fallen angels out of this heaven. Jesus saw *"Satan fall like lighting from heaven."* (Luke 10:18)

This suggests that there is some other spiritual realm between the human/earthly sphere and the dwelling place of God. It is this spiritual realm that Satan and the higher level evil spirits (what St. Paul has called "rulers" or in Greek "archons") inhabit and from which they extend their power and influence toward earth. Somewhere between the material world and reaching to the location of the dwelling place of God, these demonic spirits have made their base of operations from which to attack the earthly and human sphere.

The Christian's Sphere of Dominion

In Genesis, our sphere of dominion seems restricted to the earth and to the created order of the plant and animal kingdoms. When we are born again through faith in Jesus Christ, the original authority for dominion over the earth is restored, and with it the original vision of human and divine cooperation, which now includes earth, the human sphere, and extends to the heavenly realms.

We find this in the words of Jesus in Acts 1:4-8. I quote Acts 1:8 here, *"But you will receive power when the Holy Spirit has come upon you, and you will be my witnesses in Jerusalem, and in all Judea and Samaria, and to the farthest parts of the earth."* This includes the entire human and earthly spheres. The Great Commission makes it clear that this includes all the nations of the world.

Further, in sending out his disciples, Jesus clarifies that our restored dominion in the Kingdom includes authority over demonic spirits that are holding people captive.[4] (Mark 6:7) This authority includes the heavenly realm where Jesus Christ sits with his Father. Paul tells us when we are born again, *that Jesus has raised us up with him and seated us with him in the heavenly places, in Christ Jesus.* (Ephesians 2:6 NAS) Where is Christ? He must be in the third heaven where he is above all the powers and principalities. He is sitting above the powers and principalities both in terms of authority and in terms of location. Therefore, when we are sitting with Jesus Christ in the heavenly places, our delegated authority includes authority over these powers in whatever other heavenly realms where they have their base of operation.

It must be clear that we never engage these entities (regardless of what sphere they are in) on our own initiative. It is always in the authority of Jesus Christ and at the direction of the Holy Spirit. Paul affirms that our battle is not with flesh and blood, and not just with demons located in the earthly and human sphere, but includes those in the heavenly places. (Ephesians 6:12) It is from heaven to earth that Jesus calls us to work with him as his coworkers and friends, empowered and directed by the Holy Spirit and receiving his authority over these high level demonic entities. After his ascension to the right hand of the Father, Jesus Christ now delegates to us, his born-again friends and coworkers, his work as prophet, priest and king to advance the Kingdom of God on earth all the way to heaven.

The implication is that the Holy Spirit working through us will bind, attack, cast out and destroy the demonic strongholds and these demonic entities at any place in the battlespace. This battlespace includes the earth and human spheres, but will also reach into the heavenly realms of wickedness.

Piercing the Demonic Cloaking Hiding al-Zarqawi

This interface between the earthly and spiritual battle spaces is demonstrated when the intercessory prayer cohort gathered around me was called to engage the demons cloaking the terrorist leader al-Zarqawi.

 In May of 2006 I saw a picture of al-Zarqawi, the leader of al-Qaeda in Iraq who was responsible for some of the worst terrorist bombings and atrocities. The Holy Spirit spoke, "This man is the one through whom Satan is building the stronghold of death in Iraq. Pray now that the cloaking hiding him will be removed." I shared this guidance with the intercessors in the cohort. An intensive season of praying for a breakthrough followed. One of the intercessors had the guidance that the Lord was working through a close associate of al-Zarqawi to make him disgusted with the carnage. The intercessor had an image in his imagination of seeing this associate sneaking away and revealing to the American military al-Zarqawi's hiding place. We all prayed into this image.

In the name of Jesus Christ, we bound the evil spirits providing protection. We were not sure of the names of the demons, but they all seemed to be providing a shield of protection around al-Zarqawi, even to the extent of exposing to him any plots that others may have hatched against him. We also besought the Lord to negate this man's effective work of casting al-Qaeda's vision of death and subjugation over the internet. Satan was effectively using these images as curses to draw more young men into the stronghold and to spread fear over Iraq. We prayed in the name of Jesus that the demons providing the shield of cloaking would be bound and disconnected so that they could no longer provide covering for al-Zarqawi. As we prayed in this way, even though the person involved was half a world away, in the spiritual realm the battle was immediate and intense. Some of us in the cohort experienced spiritual attacks that brought waves of confusion. It seemed that Satan was trying to scramble our discernment into his realm. Others on the cohort including me felt wave upon wave of violent, sadistic images of tortured bodies. It was like we were being given a glimpse into this man's soul and the demons who were occupying and controlling him. This battle was taking place in earthy and spiritual space, it included us as well. It was as if the spirits of murder were seeking to invade us, our own souls. The battle to expose al-Zarqawi became a battle to prevent those demons from attacking us and bringing us into their sphere of his evil influence. We persisted in the battle until these demonic attacks ceased. Then suddenly the Holy Spirit lifted from us, and the engagement that had lasted for about a week was over.

Then about two weeks later we read in the news:

Al-Qaida Leader in Iraq Dead After Air Strike - By PATRICK QUINN, AP BAGHDAD, Iraq (June 8, 2006) –

Abu Musab al-Zarqawi, the al-Qaida leader in Iraq who waged a bloody campaign of suicide bombings and beheadings of hostages, has been killed in a precision airstrike, U.S. and Iraqi officials said Thursday. It was a long-sought victory in the war in Iraq.

At the White House, President Bush hailed the killing as "a severe blow to al-Qaida and it is a significant victory in the war on terror." But he cautioned: "We have tough days ahead of us in Iraq that will require the continuing patience of the American people."

Gen. George Casey, the top U.S. commander in Iraq, said the hunt for al-Zarqawi began two weeks ago, ...He said tips and intelligence from senior leaders of al-Zarqawi's network led U.S. forces to al-Zarqawi as he was meeting with some of his associates. Casey also said Iraqi police were first on the scene after the airstrike.[5]

This example illustrates that if we are moving in the authority of Jesus Christ and at the direction of the Holy Spirit, we will see results in the human sphere of our battles with the ground level and high level demonic spirits.

However, apart from Jesus we lack authority and will place ourselves in grave spiritual and physical danger. With Jesus, we share in his vast authority as he calls us to take part in advancing the Kingdom of God.

The Intercessor Standing Between
Heaven and Earth

This chapter, like the last one, is a necessary stepping back from our engagement with demonic powers to address hindrances to our whole-hearted participation in this war. We may be puzzled by a related question: Where are these battles taking place? Are they on earth or in the spiritual realm? Or both? Those who have been in this type of warfare may know exactly what I am talking about. For others, this may be alien to their experience or worldview. However, exploring this topic may help us prepare for the battles Jesus calls us into.

An example from the desert father Saint Anthony (3rd – 4th century), though extreme, will help us focus on our question. St. Athanasius, bishop of Alexandria, records one of Anthony's battles with demons.[1]

One day Saint Anthony, then aged 35, decided to spend the night alone in an abandoned tomb. A great multitude of demons came and started beating him, wounding him all over. He lay on the ground as if dead. The claws of the demons prevented him from getting up. According to the hermit the suffering caused by this demonic torture was comparable to no other. The next day, by the Providence of God, a friend came to visit him and carried him on his shoulders to the nearest village for treatment. Anthony came to himself and begged his friend to bring him back to the tomb. Upon arriving there, Saint Anthony exclaimed: "Here is Anthony. I do not flee your beatings nor pain, nor torture; nothing can separate me from the love of God.

The demons made such a racket that the whole place was shaken, knocking over the four walls of the tomb; they came in droves, taking the form of all kinds of monstrous beasts and hideous reptiles. And the whole place was filled with lions, bears, leopards, bulls, wolves, asps, scorpions. The lions roared, ready to attack; bulls seemed to threaten him with their horns; snakes advanced, crawling on the ground, seeking a place of attack, and wolves prowled around him. They all were making a terrible noise. Groaning in pain, St. Anthony faced the demons, laughing: "If you had any power, only one of you would be enough to kill me; but the Lord has taken away your strength, so you want to frighten me by your number. The proof of your powerlessness is that you are reduced to taking the form of senseless animals. If you have any power against me, come on, attack me! But if you cannot do anything, why torment yourselves unnecessarily? My faith in God is my defense against you." But all of a sudden a bright light illuminated the tomb; at that moment, the demons vanished. The pains ceased. When he realized that God was coming to his aid, he asked: "Where were you, Lord? Why did you not stop this suffering earlier?" God answered him, "Anthony, I was present at your side. But I waited, observing your fight. And since you have resisted so bravely, I will now always be at your side, and I will make your name famous throughout the world." Having heard the words of the Lord, the monk stood up and prayed. He then received such strength that he felt in his body an even greater vigor than before.[2]

Where was this experience taking place? Was this in the realm of the spirit perceived in the vivid imagination of Saint Anthony? Or was the supernatural intersecting with the physical, earthly sphere? St. Athanasius records, "When we visited St. Anthony in the ruins where he lived, we heard a commotion, thousands of voices and the clash of arms. Also, at night, wild beasts would come, and the saint fought them off with prayer."[3] That Athanasius and others also saw and experienced these strange phenomena confirms that this battle was taking place in both the spiritual and material realms.

Many intercessors have had similar experiences that bridge the spiritual and earthly realms. They are physically assaulted by spiritual beings. My mentor in the work of prayer, Archer Torrey, told me the following:

The life of intercession is dangerous. It can be dangerous to your health, and if the Enemy gets wind of it, he can send his assassins after you. I just read in a missionary prayer bulletin about Muslim fanatics going into a Far East Broadcasting Company studio in the Philippines and shooting three of the broadcasters dead. 'Live dangerously.' Being an intercessor is one way.[4]

I observed this myself one afternoon at Jesus Abbey when

Archer Torrey staggered in late to teatime looking like he had taken a bad fall down a rocky slope. We jumped up and asked what had happened. He said, "Just pray. It has been a real prayer battle."

We asked, "Were you on the mountain? Did you fall down?"

"Oh yes, I was on the mountain, but I never left the prayer chapel." He refused to say any more, but just asked for cleansing prayer. It took a few days for him to recover physically.[5]

My other great teacher of intercession, Rees Howells, endured terrible struggles both in the physical and in the spiritual during prayer battles to hold back the onslaught of the Nazis. One must read between the lines of the prayer journals kept during these battles to find hints of what intercessors were experiencing within themselves. One such moment was during the battle of Dunkirk. May, 1940 was a month of near constant intercession as Hitler's army smashed through Holland and Belgium and then pushed the retreating French, Belgian and British troops to Dunkirk with their backs to the English Channel. Not only was the army about to be destroyed, but an invasion of the British Isles seemed inevitable. As the defeat of the British army seemed certain, the students at the Bible College were all in prayer. This note is in his prayer journal:

> From the night of May 22-25 Mr. Howells no longer came to the meetings; other members of the staff took them. He went away alone with God to battle through, and, as others have testified, the crushing burden of those days broke his body. He literally laid down his life.
>
> The 26th was a public day of prayer with prayer meetings at Westminster Abbey and throughout Great Britain. Winston Churchill spoke and Rees Howells attended. On the 28th, Rees Howells was again alone with God. This prayer work continued until the great miracle happened: nearly all the soldiers were evacuated and the nation was delivered. The battle took place not only on land and sea,

but also in the hearts and bodies of the intercessors.[6]

I have had similar experiences that have left me spiritually and physically exhausted and pummeled as if by invisible fists. After one particularly difficult high level engagement, my fellow prayer warrior, living in Canada, told me, "As you were binding the archon in Osama bin Laden, a host of wicked looking grasshopper-like demons were invading my study. I jumped up from my desk and in the name of Jesus Christ fought them off with the sword of the spirit. I felt like large hailstones were pounding me. Then they started to throw me around the study. It hurt like hell! But in the mighty name of Jesus, I unleashed counter attacks against them. They left, about the time you finished binding those demons."

Stories like this may be multiplied many times over by those who have been in such battles and are not afraid to share them. Many may be skeptical and suspect these are forms of mental illness or just imaginary events. Others may reject them on theological grounds. They object, "But If Jesus has done it all on the cross, why do we Christians get attacked? Why do we suffer in this battle? Can't we just proclaim Christ's victory and then step back and watch Christ and His angels do all the work?"

Many seem to think that based on Jesus' victory over Satan, which has already taken place; our role in spiritual warfare is like US Air Force drone pilots located a continent away in secure, air-conditioned offices releasing guided munitions against terrorist strongholds in the Middle East. This seems to be the image of spiritual warfare assumed by many. The battle has been completely and totally won in Jesus Christ, so there will not be any satanic counterattacks against us the intercessors. In this view, if there are any casualties, then it must be due to the intercessor's own sin or stepping beyond our authority.

The Reasons for Casualties in Spiritual Warfare

There is, of course, an element of truth in this assessment of the cause of counterattacks from Satan. Unconfessed sin and wrong attitudes such as hatred do indeed open up the intercessor to attacks which can be serious. In addition, moving into battle without sufficient prayer protection, or moving in presumption, can put a person outside of God's protection—there can be disastrous results. Most of us as intercessors, in our zeal to defeat Satan, have learned these lessons the hard way through our own folly and suffering.

I learned this the hard way! While serving as a missionary in Taiwan, I had invited a well-known teacher on spiritual warfare to do an equipping event at the Lay Training Center. This is on the campus of the Presbyterian Bible College in Hsinchu which is at the foot of a mountain. Up on the mountain above us are many Buddhist and shamanistic temples. These are all very active with many worshippers by the bus loads making visits.

After hearing teaching on the power of Jesus Christ to overcome the territorial spirits, the group of about a hundred, mostly Taiwanese pastors, enthusiastically decided to give it a go. One group led by our famous teacher set out for the seven story Idol on the top of the mountain overlooking the entire city. Thankfully I was not led to go on any of these sorties. So I do not know exactly happened. But I did witness that they all came back shattered. The group who had taken on the demon in the temple received a severe physical and spiritual thrashing by the demons. Our famous speaker whose name I have withheld for security reasons, who led the charge, spent the next number of months in such mental and spiritual anguish and torment by demons that he feared for his life. We have both written about this experience and others like it, relating what the Lord has taught us of the terrible consequences of going beyond Jesus' call and protection.

Nevertheless, it is still possible, even when doing everything right, and staying within the guidance, anointing and protection of the Lord, to experience the consequences of the battle within our spiritual and physical being. We may even suffer terrible counterattacks within ourselves or in our loved ones.

How do we account for this? It has to do with the nature of the battle itself and the role of the intercessor stepping into the gap and joining the conflict. Jesus Christ himself, our paradigm of an intercessor, models this. The battles in the heavenlies took place within him as our advocate. Jesus' human nature, like ours, is made in the image of God, and so he is the link between the heavenly realms and the earthly human realms. He is the nexus or the meeting place between heaven and earth. The result is that these battles that he was fighting took a spiritual and physical toll upon him. Jesus was famished in the wilderness after fasting for 40 days. He was so physically, emotionally and perhaps even spiritually exhausted from the intensity of ministry that he could sleep in a boat being thrashed by a violent storm. In the garden of Gethsemane, Jesus was in such a colossal struggle with whether or not to go to the cross that, 44And in his anguish he prayed more earnestly, and his sweat was like drops of blood falling to the ground. (Luke 22:44) We know for sure that this struggle was within him, but it may also have been with tormenting evil spirits. Then he endured the unimaginable pain of physical torture in his own body by being scourged and then nailed to the cross.

However, that may have been small compared to the inner spiritual torment he must have undergone during those endless hours dying on the cross while feeling abandoned by the Father. Those who witnessed the crucifixion reported that, *Around three o'clock Jesus cried out with a loud voice, "Eloi, Eloi, lama sabachthani?" which means, "My God, my God, why have you forsaken me?"* (Mark 15:34) This physical and inward spiritual side of Jesus stepping into the gap for our sins is expressed in the affirmation of the Apostles' Creed, ...*Suffered under Pontius Pilate; was crucified, died, and was buried. He descended into hell...*

Jesus' Call to Share with Him in the Battle

With the call to step in the gap just as Jesus did, we may well bear within ourselves some of the struggle and the pain as he did. Of course, we do not have to duplicate his sacrifice on the cross; but we, as his royal priesthood, become mediators between heaven and earth. This means that as Jesus' coworkers, he will express his authority and victory over Satan won on the cross through us in the conflicts with Satan on earth. Spiritual and material reality are all co-mingled in us, and so there are times when the spiritual battles may well take place in us.

Romans 8:26, *In the same way, the Spirit helps us in our weakness, for we do not know how we should pray, but the Spirit himself intercedes for us with inexpressible groanings.* When this happens to us, there may be physical and emotional manifestations in our minds, bodies and spirits as we are the interface or nexus between the spiritual and human worlds through whom the Holy Spirit is praying and working. When this intercessory prayer involves the Holy Spirit guiding us to use the authority of Jesus Christ to bind evil spirits, or when he guides us to join the battle when angels are actually fighting with demons, this battle may have a physical and emotional impact upon us.

A Mystical Encounter with Jesus Defeating Satan

I experienced the role of the intercessor as the nexus between heaven and earth in a mystical experience. This took place on Saturday night of a PRMI Missions and Evangelism Conference,

March 21, 1998, in Montreat, North Carolina.[7] This was a defining moment in my life, when the Holy Spirit caught me up into the presence of the glorified Jesus sitting next to the Father. Jesus gave me a personal call to advance the Gospel of life and advance the Kingdom of God to the ends of the earth in the power of the Holy Spirit. It was a long, mystical encounter, which I have recorded elsewhere. Here I narrate the part that led me to understand this concept of us becoming the nexus between heaven and earth and the means through which Jesus will wage war against Satan.

I had gone outside into the wintry night accompanied by two participants in the conference, Bill Emrich and Carolyn Ederman. We were walking up the road by the stream. As I was sipping a cup of hot tea, I began to feel the Holy Spirit rushing through me. Suddenly, I was no longer on earth beside the mountain stream or my two companions, but in some other spiritual realm. With the eye of the Spirit, I saw in front of me vast hordes of demons, distorted horrible shapes, howling blasphemies and filled with hate. In their midst were structures, like dark, hideous cities, tangled, rusted, steel girders all interlaced, holding people captive. Instantly the attack was upon me and I felt the demonic power like a wave crashing against me. It seemed like the battle was taking place in my own body. I cried out to Jesus. I forget the exact words, but it was something like, "Move forward, move forward, Jesus! Jesus! Jesus, move forward! Jesus!! Push back the darkness! Jesus, push back the darkness; push back the darkness!"

All this was striking my own body, and I was tossed, turned, and knocked down by the battle raging in the realm of the spirit. I think I may have fallen in the middle of the road had I not been held up by Bill and Carolyn. The realm of the spirit was so real that I could not see them, but only felt their strong hands and prayers holding me up. I was thankful they were there standing with me in this demonic assault. The battle seemed to last a long time with the outcome undecided. Finally, as I persisted in speaking Jesus' victory over them, I saw the armies of God, a vast angelic host, advancing forward, enabled by my prayers and pushing back the darkness as in the hymn, "Let all Mortal Flesh Keep Silent."

Rank on rank the host of heaven
Spreads its vanguard on the way,
As the Light of light descendeth
From the realms of endless day,
That the powers of hell may vanish
As the darkness clears away. [8]:

I was seeing this happening before me. The battle was taking place in my own soul, but transcending it to include the spiritual realms. As the Kingdom of Light advanced, I saw the black evil structures collapsing and being swept away. Emerging from the collapsing strongholds, Jesus was liberating millions of people to come into the Kingdom of God. Festive crowds from all nations and races were running, leaping, and dancing, coming to Jesus and joining the great feast of the Lamb. It was like they were running through me into the welcoming arms of Jesus.

That was what I was experiencing from the inside. Bill Emrich reported what he saw, standing next to me: "We hadn't walked too far when suddenly the Styrofoam cup flew out of Brad's hands, he doubled over, and I tried as best I could to discern what was happening and what I should do. Although I did not know specifically what was happening, I could discern that this was a spiritual attack. As I prayed in the Spirit, Brad described what was happening. He said that we could not see what was happening because the attack was upon him. He cried out to Jesus, and I believe said something like, 'Put your cross between me and this horrible darkness.' The struggle continued for what seemed like hours, but really was only a few minutes. Finally, Brad said that it was over. He physically straightened up once again, and we continued our walk up Greybeard Road."

The Intercessor as the Nexus between the Earthly and Spiritual Realms

I realize that this was the call to stand in the gap like a Moses or a Rees Howells. This experience was my call to intercession, to spiritual warfare to defeat the demonic strongholds that are holding people in bondage away from the light of Jesus Christ. What this experience demonstrated is that while this battle was taking place in the heavenly realms, God was calling me on earth to step into the gap between heaven and earth. I realized that I was becoming a nexus between heaven and earth, and that God had chosen to express His authority through me in His battle to defeat Satan and set the captives free.

When Jesus calls us to share with Him in the role of intercessor between heaven and earth, the reality is that the battles may take place in us, and we will experience the effect of the battle within our own bodies and souls. In addition, when Satan counterattacks, we may well be caught in the crossfire. As God's friends and His chosen means of working within the world, Satan will do everything he can to destroy us.

The very moment we step out in obedience, even if we are under complete covering of the armor of God as well as strong prayer protection, nevertheless we step out into the battlefield where Satan may hit us back. Satan is impotent against God, so he turns his rage against Jesus' friends and coworkers.

Living in the Battle Zone of
the Kingdom of God Having Come but Not Yet Fulfilled

We live in the battle zone, in a fallen world in which the Kingdom of God has come in Jesus Christ, but will not be fully actualized until Christ returns. This means that our walking in obedience to Jesus Christ to engage the Devil's strongholds may entail a high cost. The reality is also that while our "justification" in Christ is complete; our sanctification is a process that will not be completed until we meet Jesus face to face. So, no matter how well we prepare, we will always have some sin in us that will give some ground for Satan to attack us. The best we can do in this battle zone of life in a fallen world is to "abide in Jesus Christ." And not to be afraid, but to go boldly into battle as Jesus directs us, trusting his authority and the guidance of the Holy Spirit. To join this battle, we must have certain knowledge that our lives are hidden in Christ, which provides the only real protection against the powers of death and evil.

Martin Luther in his great hymn "A Mighty Fortress is our God" describes both our hope and the battle in which we are engaged where there may be casualties.

A mighty fortress is our God, A bulwark never failing;
Our helper He, amid the flood Of mortal ills prevailing.
For still our ancient foe, Doth seek to work us woe;
His craft and power are great, And, armed with cruel hate,
On earth is not his equal.

Did we in our own strength confide, Our striving would be losing, Were not the right Man on our side, The Man of God's own choosing:

Dost ask who that may be? Christ Jesus, it is He; Lord Sabaoth, His Name, From age to age the same, And He must win the battle.

And though this world, with devils filled, Should threaten to undo us, We will not fear, for God hath willed His truth to triumph through us:

The Prince of Darkness grim, We tremble not for him;
His rage we can endure, For lo, his doom is sure,
One little word shall fell him.

That word above all earthly powers, No thanks to them, abideth; The Spirit and the gifts are ours
Through Him Who with us sideth:

Let goods and kindred go, This mortal life also;
The body they may kill: God's truth abideth still,
His kingdom is forever.[9]

Ask the Holy Spirit to seal those words in your heart, or better still, the Bible verses behind them, so you may not be afraid to fling yourself into this Jesus-led campaign against the amassing armies of Satan in the strongholds of Radical Islam.

Binding the Demons at Work in the Leaders

The last chapter was a necessary digression into the sphere of the intercessor's authority and why we may have to endure the effects of these battles within ourselves. The two points are opposite sides of the same coin. We wouldn't have to deal with negative side effects and spiritual assault if our authority in prayer weren't a genuine threat to Satan's malevolent kingdom.

Now that we are assured of our authority in Jesus Christ, we turn to the implementation of Prayer Strategy B: Engaging the demonic powers behind human leaders and organizations of the strongholds of Radical Islam.

These high-level demons were identified by their Biblical names: Gog, Moloch, The Spirit of Lawlessness and the Antichrists, and the Demonic Spirit of the Amalekites. Above these four archons is "Leviathan," possibly Satan himself, galvanizing them into a supernatural "Axis of Evil."[1] Beneath these archons in chains of command are innumerable demons that are interfacing with individual humans and inhabiting human social structures forming strongholds. This demonic empire fused with its human structure is a formidable foe. It appears to be an impregnable fortress, protected by Satan's cloaking, preventing spiritual warriors from devising any plan of attack. The tactical challenge that often appears insurmountable is engaging these well-defended supernatural enemies hidden within the human social structures.

Rees Howells
An Example of the Holy Spirit's Plan of Attack

Rees Howells and the students at the Bible College of Wales provide a model of how the Holy Spirit may meet these tactical challenges of engaging the demons behind the leaders. Rees Howells was among the very few who saw clearly the mortal danger in the growth of Nazism.

However, dealing with demonic strongholds was not the focus of their prayers. They were in earnest prayer for the *Every Creature Commission* work of world evangelism. When the Italian dictator Mussolini launched the invasion of Ethiopia in 1935, they had to step into the gap to pray against this major block to evangelism. In 1936, the year of tipping points in the growth of the stronghold of Nazism, their prayer focus shifted again. On March 7, the German army marched unopposed into the Rhineland breaking the Locarno Treaties.[2] At the Berlin Summer Olympics, the world was treated to the spectacle of a new muscular, vital, and growing Germany, where all their athletes were championed as triumphs of a Nazi controlled society.

With the invasion of the Rhineland, the Holy Spirit called Rees Howells to a sharp focus on Adolph Hitler, a call that remained until the Allied victory over Nazi Germany in 1945. Now looking back, when we know the history and the critical role Hitler was to play in world events, this focus seems completely obvious. At the time, however, Hitler was only one among a whole cast of villains. Norman Grubb reports the following rationale for Rees Howells's concentration on Hitler:

> It was in March 1936, that Mr. Howells began to see clearly that Hitler was Satan's agent for preventing the gospel going to every creature. As he said later, "In fighting Hitler we have always said that we were not up against man, but the devil. Mussolini is a man, but Hitler is different. He can tell the day this 'spirit' came into him." For several years Mr. Howells stressed the fact that God must destroy him, if the vision of the Gospel to every creature was to be fulfilled.[3]

Rees Howells established the reason for this focus because in dealing with Hitler, unlike Mussolini, Christian intercessors were actually fighting the Devil. The Devil, of course, was working through many other people who were part of the Nazi death machine, but the focus of the intercessor must be to discern the person or group of persons who are the gateway through whom Satan and the high-level archons are directing the entire stronghold. The Holy Spirit revealed to Rees Howells that Hitler was the gateway through whom Satan had built a command and control system for demons to have power over millions of people. Hitler provided the focal point for the intercessors to engage these high-level demons whose base of operations was in the spiritual realm. Many prayer engagements followed. Norman Grubb reports:

> The first battle of prayer on this international scale was in 1936 when Germany sent her soldiers into the Rhineland, and broke the Locarno Treaty. "We knew that France would be on fire in a day," said Mr. Howells, "and it meant

nothing less than a European war, and the consequent hindrance to the spread of the Gospel. Only those who were in the College can realize the burden the Holy Spirit put on us. 'Prevail against Hitler,' He said to me, and it meant three weeks of prayer and fasting."[4]

In this battle the call to pray was for the Lord to "prevail against Hitler." In the summer of 1938 during the Munich crisis, the call was, "Lord, bend Hitler." These commands taking authority over Hitler were the means of taking authority over the Devil and the archons working through Hitler. This is not just my interpretation of what was happening. The intercessors demonstrated in their own words that they were called by Jesus Christ to engage in a battle against the Devil. This is clear from a description of the prayer battle during the Munich Crisis when Neville Chamberlain, the British Prime Minister, was in negotiations with Hitler to give him Czechoslovakia in exchange for the promise of peace:

We now know that the Voice Hitler followed, which coincided with the advice of some of his trusted advisors, was urging him to attack while Britain was still totally unprepared. War seemed inescapable, and the leaders of the nation called for a day of prayer. God made the challenge very real to the College, and for days the conflict was bitter. It was essentially a clash of spiritual forces—a test of strength between the devil in Hitler and the Holy Ghost in His army of intercessors.

At the height of the battle the one prayer that the Holy Ghost gave to the College through His servant [Rees Howells] was, "Lord, bend Hitler." A point came when that cry of travail changed into a shout of victory. The devil had to give way.[5]

While they celebrated a great victory won in the spiritual realm, on earth there seemed to be nothing but a series of disasters as Hitler's armies surged into Czechoslovakia. However, Hitler did not attack an unprepared England. Later, it became known that Hitler had not obeyed "His Voice" that, along with his human military advisors, had been urging him to attack England that October before she could mobilize for war.[6]

There were many more amazing prayer battles involving Hitler that were engagements with the archons behind the man and the Nazi movement he embodied. Satan must work on earth through human beings created in the image of God, so there is often a blurring of the lines between the human and demonic—the natural and the supernatural. The important principle of spiritual warfare is that Jesus' victories, won at this high level over both human and demonic leadership, will have the greatest strategic impact for entire campaigns.

The Call to Engage the Archon by Engaging the Leaders of Radical Islam

The Holy Spirit is calling us to use the same tactics as Rees Howells in cooperating with Jesus Christ to defeat our present-day nemesis, Radical Islam. The Holy Spirit's battle plan calls for us as intercessors to focus our primary attack on the high level demonic spirits who are working through the leaders around whom the stronghold has coalesced.

During the many engagements that are part of the campaign to defeat the stronghold of Radical Islam, God may call us to engage many levels of demons. For instance, being led to bind the demons in an individual jihadist whose picture we have seen cutting off the heads of Christians. The Holy Spirit may direct us to pray for confusion among the demons at work in launching a terrorist attack, or we may need to deal with the spirits over a specific location. The Holy Spirit will lead us to the appropriate level where he needs us. However, we must keep in mind that our primary battle will be at the highest levels of the interface between high level demons and those human beings who have the greatest authority in the stronghold. It is at this high level—the command and control level—that our Holy Spirit led prayers will have the most impact. At this level, Jesus may use our prayers to unravel an entire stronghold or thwart Satan's strategic plans.

A Visitation of the Holy Spirit Needed before Engaging High Level Evil Spirits

Caution! Never engage at this level or any level for that matter, unless Jesus first empowers you with the Holy Spirit, gives you this authority, and then specifically calls you into the engagement.

Rees Howells and the Bible College students teach us about this need for preparation for high level spiritual warfare. Before the prayer conflict of 1938 during the Munich crisis, they experienced a remarkable visitation of the Holy Spirit. Several key events which preceded the visitation are also critical for our preparation for high level intercession.

During the engagement in March, in 1936 when Hitler sent his army into the Rhineland, the Holy Spirit issued a call through Rees Howells for intercessors. "God is calling for intercessors—men and women who will lay their lives on the altar to fight the devil, as really as they would have to fight the enemy on the western front."[7] Many students responded to this call.

The call to commitment to intercession, "lay their lives on the altar to fight the devil" is as essential for us today as it was for them. Without this total commitment to Jesus Christ and the battle with

Satan, we will not be able fully to receive God's provision needed for the battle.

In the Christmas vacation of 1936, they spent considerable time in prayer. Then the divine visitation began:

> As we approached the New Year of 1937 there was an increasing consciousness of God's presence. The first outward sign that He was working in a new way was when one of the staff broke down in prayer, confessing her sense of need and crying to the Holy Spirit to meet her. Then we heard how the Holy Ghost had so manifested Himself in the Glory of His Divine Person to some of the girl students, that they wept before Him for hours—broken at the corruption of their own hearts revealed in the light of His holiness. An awful sense of God's nearness began to steal over the whole College...[8]

The rest of the account is truly amazing. It was Pentecost, and the Holy Spirit was present at the College in his empowering and sanctifying work.

> He did not come like a rushing mighty wind. But gradually the Person of the Holy Ghost filled all our thoughts, His Presence filled all the place, and His light seemed to penetrate all the hidden recesses of our hearts. He was speaking through the Director in every meeting, but it was in the quiet of our own rooms that He revealed Himself to many of us. We felt the Holy Spirit had been a real Person to us before; as far as we knew we had received Him; and some of us had known much of His operations in and through our lives. But now the revelation of His Person was so tremendous that all our previous experiences seemed as nothing. There was no visible apparition, but He

made Himself so real to our spiritual eyes that it was a "face to face" experience. And when we saw Him, we knew we had never really seen Him before. We said like Job, "I have heard of Thee by the hearing of the ear; but now mine eye seeth Thee"; and like him we cried, "Wherefore I abhor myself and repent in dust and ashes..." [9]

This visitation of the Holy Spirit prepared the faculty, staff and students of the Bible College for the prayer battles that were ahead. The Spirit was upon them giving the spiritual gifts and power needed for the intercession and spiritual warfare. The Holy Spirit was also filling their hearts with his presence to bind them together into a fellowship of prayer, an intercessory prayer cohort that was of one heart and mind in a living relationship with Jesus Christ. With this outpouring, they were given the authority and guidance to cooperate with God in defeating the high-level demons that were making war on the Church and humanity through Nazism. This visitation was the greatest of the outpourings of the Holy Spirit that took place during these long terrible years of battling with the powers and principalities.

Mr. Howells repeatedly called his community to offer themselves to the Lord in intercession and even martyrdom for the advancement of the Gospel.[10] At these moments, they repented of their sins and stepped out in obedience to pray. These human actions were followed by the divine actions of an outpouring of the Holy Spirit granting the power, authority, and guidance to engage in battle. This is consistent with God's pattern of working in the book of Acts where, in response to the confessions and prayers of his people, he sends outpourings of the Holy Spirit equipping them for the work ahead.

We as intercessors are called to engage with the high-level demons behind the leaders of Radical Islam, but we must also pray for and welcome such visitations of the Holy Spirit. We must be "walking in the light," willing to repent of our sins as the Holy Spirit points them out. We must be committed to sacrifice all for the Gospel. In addition, we must constantly be prepared to move out into these engagements as the Holy Spirit gives the call. To do this we must live as Jesus said: [5]*"I am the vine; you are the branches. The one who remains in me—and I in him—bears much fruit, because apart from me you can accomplish nothing."* (John 15:5)

Discerning Which Leaders have High Level Demons behind Them

Our task in this mission is to focus our prayers for Jesus Christ to prevail over Satan, or in the name of Jesus Christ to bind the archon who is working in a particular leader around whom the strongholds are coalescing. Jesus will often call us—like Rees Howells—to fight the few Hitlers rather than the many Mussolinis. The Mussolinis may be carrying out the Devil's work, but they are not strategic gateways. As for the many human beings in bondage to the stronghold, we shall see later that it will be by evangelism that they are converted to Jesus Christ and set free, or by tragic necessity will need to be killed through military force.

In the often-bewildering unfolding of present events and the morphing of leadership structures of Radical Islam, discerning who the Hitlers are is no easy task. Rather than listing off the leaders whom we have presently discerned to be the focus of our prayers, I think it best to provide you with some guidelines for discernment so you can come to your own conclusions. Besides, our list will most likely be obsolete by the time you are reading this. The following four guidelines may help us discern the leaders through whom the demons are working.

Four Guidelines for Discerning the Key Leaders
Through Whom the Devil is Working

1) We must recognize that Satan will do everything possible to hide the identity of his true leaders who are carrying the DNA for the stronghold. Smoke-screens and diversions will be plentiful. We will need to depend heavily on supernatural revelation.

The first step is to ask the Holy Spirit to reveal whom to focus prayers upon. I have found this guidance is given as I have kept up with the news. The Holy Spirit may highlight one name mentioned among many others. Sometimes the guidance will come as a direct command to pray for that individual.

On the other hand, after praying that Satan's schemes and people will be revealed, I have seen a reference in the news to someone and suddenly the Holy Spirit says, "That's him! Focus on him!"

2) Second, we need to confirm this guidance wherever possible by the rational evaluation of the information received through news media. Pay special attention to those news outlets you have learned to trust, who have access to information that you may not have, and who bring gifts of discernment.

The "Hitler" leaders will give themselves away because they are the ones casting Satan's vision. Look for the vision casters and there is a good chance that either they are themselves strategic in Satan's plans, or they will lead you to the person who is. Also, look for those at the center of a creative minority, giving them the means of implementing their plans.

3) The third step, getting to the demons who are working behind a leader, is more difficult. Again, ask the Holy Spirit to reveal to you who these demons are. You may also command the demons to reveal their presence by their actions. It may happen that you will receive this guidance through the leaders themselves as they are

casting vision or initiating some action that reveals their intentions.

4) Fourth, usually it is during events taking place in the natural realm that we can begin to identify both the leaders and the nature of the demons at work. There will be "revelatory" events that expose the true intentions of both the human and demonic actors involved.

When you receive revelation about both the leader and the demonic power at work through him or her, what you do next depends on the specific guidance of the Holy Spirit for the particular engagement.

Receiving Authority and Power from Jesus Christ to Bind Satan's Demonic and Human Agents

In many cases, the Holy Spirit calls the intercessor to bind the evil spirits working in the leader to prevent the actions they are taking through him. Again, the Lord Jesus gives us authority over evil spirits. We see this in the following promises of Jesus:

> [17]Then the seventy-two returned with joy, saying, "Lord, even the demons submit to us in your name!" [18]So he said to them, "I saw Satan fall like lightning from heaven. Look, [19]I have given you authority to tread on snakes and scorpions and on the full force of the enemy, and nothing will hurt you. [20]Nevertheless, do not rejoice that the spirits submit to you, but rejoice that your names stand written in heaven." (Luke 10:17-20)

This tactic of "treading on snakes and scorpions and the full force of the enemy" is based on the authority that Jesus himself has over Satan and has given to us.

Some have argued that this authority was just for the 72 sent out by Jesus. This is true. It was a special anointing for those Jesus commissioned for that unique mission. However, after Pentecost Jesus gives all his disciples the promise of the power and authority of the Holy Spirit. This is the meaning of Acts 1:8. [8]*"But you will receive power when the Holy Spirit has come upon you, and you will be my witnesses in Jerusalem, and in all Judea and Samaria, and to the farthest parts of the earth."* This empowerment to witness to Jesus Christ includes binding and removing evil spirits that oppose the advancement of the Gospel.

Jesus also assures us of our authority to undertake this work in the following promise:

> [18] "I tell you the truth, whatever you bind on earth will have been bound in heaven, and whatever you release on earth will have been released in heaven. [19]Again, I tell you the truth, if two of you on earth agree about whatever you ask, my Father in heaven will do it for you. [20]For where two or three are assembled in my name, I am there among them." (Matthew 18:18-20)

This authority to ask in the name of Jesus Christ for God to bind Satan and block his plans is based on Jesus' victory over Satan on the Cross.

We must understand the nature of Jesus defeating Satan on the Cross. It was there that Satan's authority in the world was indeed overcome. Nevertheless, he still has great power; and—where humans grant him access—he exercises authority on earth. On the cross of Jesus Christ, Satan lost no power; he lost authority. Likewise, Satan did not gain power at the fall, he gained man's authority to rule in the earth. [11] Jesus did not dispute Satan's authority to hand him kingdoms during the temptation in the wilderness. (Luke 4:6)

After the resurrection, Jesus tells us, "all authority has been given to me in heaven and in earth." He did not say "all power." The reason Satan can still afflict us is that he still has power. Our power in and of ourselves by comparison is small and weak. However, not only does our relationship with Jesus Christ restore our original authority of dominion, but also we have received the Holy Spirit. The power that we receive as we obey in faith is not ours, but the power of the Holy Spirit working through us, just as we were promised in Acts 1:4-8.

We have the critical role in the dynamic of God working on earth of asking in faith and obeying the guidance of the Holy Spirit to accomplish the Father's will. We are in the thick of the battle; we are the means through whom the victory of the Cross is now applied. The Father gives us both the Holy Spirit's power and Jesus' authority to defeat Satan's power on earth and in the spiritual realms.

The Prayer Battle to Bind the Demons Behind Iranian President Mahmoud Ahmadinejad

An example from our prayer engagements with high level demonic spirits involving the Shia Islamic stronghold in Iran will illustrate this approach. In 2006 the Holy Spirit called us intercessors to heightened vigilance concerning Iran and the Islamic radicals' quest for nuclear weapons. It was during this time that I became aware that many of those in the Iranian regime including then President Ahmadinejad were fanatical "Twelvers"; that is, they believed in the immediate return of the 12th or hidden Imam.[12] Most dangerous of all, these Islamic fanatics believe they are called to actively bring about the Mahdi's return by aggressively causing cataclysmic events, making good on their often-chanted threat of, "Death to America, and Death to Israel."[13]

We had been praying intensely for months about this threat, asking for specific guidance about how to bind the demons working in all this. Everything was ambiguous until I read an opinion piece by Bernard Lewis in the August 8, 2006 issue of the *Wall Street Journal* entitled simply "August 22."[14] In this article, Bernard Lewis warns that the deterrent of "Mutually Assured Destruction" (MAD)[15] that worked so well to deter the United States and the Soviet Union in the Cold War would not work with radical Islamists who see the death of millions of their own population as an opportunity for martyrdom and a quick pass to paradise.

I paid great attention to this article because Bernard Lewis, a world-renowned expert on Islam, wrote it. However, there was more! Lewis is Jewish. I have learned to pay attention to Jewish voices who have learned firsthand to take seriously those who say that they want you and your people dead. In the article, Lewis gives specific dates, confirming that Ahmadinejad was a key person in these plans of launching a genocidal attack on Israel or America.

In Islam, as in Judaism and Christianity, there are certain beliefs concerning the cosmic struggle at the end of time—Gog and Magog, anti-Christ, Armageddon, and, for Shiite Muslims, the long-awaited return of the hidden Imam, ending in the final victory of the forces of good over evil. Mr. Ahmadinejad and his followers clearly believe that this time is now, and that the terminal struggle has already begun and is indeed well advanced. It may even have a date, indicated by several references by the Iranian president to giving his final answer to the U.S. about nuclear development by Aug. 22, 2006. This was at first reported as "by the end of August," but Mr. Ahmadinejad's statement was more precise.

"What is the significance of Aug. 22? This year, Aug. 22 corresponds, in the Islamic calendar, to the 27th day of the month of Rajab of the year 1427. This, by tradition, is the night when many Muslims commemorate the night flight of the prophet Muhammad on the winged horse Buraq, first to 'the farthest mosque,' usually identified with Jerusalem, and then to heaven and back" (c.f., Koran XVII.1). This might well be deemed an appropriate date for the apocalyptic ending of Israel and if necessary of the world. It is far from certain that Mr. Ahmadinejad plans any such cataclysmic events precisely for Aug. 22. But it would be wise to bear the possibility in mind.[16]

When I read this the Lord said, "Bind the demons of destruction working in Ahmadinejad. He is the gateway."

Reports that I read online confirmed this guidance. "[Ahmadinejad] was the founder and main political leader of the Alliance of Builders of Islamic Iran,[17] a coalition of conservative political groups in the country."[18] This group may have been the "creative minority" that provided the core of the stronghold based on the Twelfth Imam apocalyptic expectation that Satan was building around Ahmadinejad. There were also allegations that Ahmadinejad had been one of the radicals who took part in the 1979 hostage crisis in Revolutionary Iran.[19] While most of the facts were obscure, we had enough to conclude that the Holy Spirit knew what he was doing in telling us that Ahmadinejad was one person in the Iranian leadership structure through whom Satan was implementing his plans. Like a Hitler, he was the strategic gateway for high level evil spirits to work on earth.

I sent out a prayer notice to some other intercessors in our cohort and told them about the significance of August 22. We prayed in the name of Jesus Christ that these demons working in Ahmadinejad would be bound and unable to carry out their terrible plans of destruction. As the date of August 22 drew closer, the battle in the heavenlies intensified.

On Monday, November 14, 2016 the 21st I prayed with my prayer partner Richard White at the Community of the Cross, and we bound these spirits of death and destruction working through Ahmadinejad. We also prayed that the Father would intervene and prevent Ahmadinejad from taking any actions that would set in motion an attack against Israel. The rest of the day on Monday, which would be the 22nd in Iran, I just welcomed the Holy Spirit to pray through me. I did not experience any counter attacks, but was aware that in the spiritual realm something was happening. I was not sure exactly what, but the date came and went and nothing terrible happened.

I continued, however, with a sharp and persistent intercessory prayer focus on President Ahmadinejad, in whom I believed we were fighting the Devil. I followed Rees Howells's example and persistently prayed for the Holy Spirit to "prevail" against Satan in Ahmadinejad. The one other time Jesus commanded me up the mountain in an intense engagement to bind the evil spirits working in him was when he spoke at the United Nations in September 2012. At that speech before the world body, on the soil of the United States of the America—which the Iranians call the Great Satan— Ahmadinejad stepped into the role of a prophet speaking Satan's plans. From the *Christian Post News* Bulletin:

> Iranian President Mahmoud Ahmadinejad delivered his address before the United Nations General Assembly on Wednesday, saying that the return of Jesus Christ was soon to come, along with the Islamic end-time figure the 12th Imam.

> "God Almighty has promised us a man of kindness, a man who loves people and loves absolute justice, a man who is a perfect human being and is named Imam Al-Mahdi, a man who will come in the company of Jesus Christ (peace be upon him) and the righteous," Ahmadinejad said, according to a transcript by PolicyMic.[20]

This sounds comforting and hopeful until we consider that this is not the Jesus Christ of the Jewish and Christian scripture and messianic expectation, but an Islamic version who will come and "break the cross," kill all Christians and Jews, and bring the worldwide hegemony of Islam.[21] Indeed, this is the embodiment of the archon, the Man of Lawlessness and the Anti-Christ. (2 Thessalonians 2:1-12, 1 John 2:18)

At the United Nations, Satan had spoken a prophetic word-curse through his servant Iranian President Mahmoud Ahmadinejad intended to set in motion the fulfillment of the Islamic vision of the end of the world. Satan can use such prophetic word curses to create the reality.

I have already demonstrated in Book I how Satan prepared the soil of the minds, hearts and culture of the German people to participate in the Holocaust through Hitler's public proclamations to annihilate the Jews. [22] Satan was doing the same thing in Ahmadinejad on the soil of the United States at the United Nations. This prophetic word did not reach the level of the curse that Hitler spoke to al-Husseini and his demonized inner circle of the "final solution of the Jewish Problem," which did set in motion the events leading to the murder of millions of people.

The word curses setting in motion the actual sequence of events to launch attacks against Israel or the United States would most likely be spoken within the chains of command starting from the core of the stronghold rather than in the public forum. It was, nonetheless, a part of Satan's plans toward that terrible end as revealed in Shia Islamic apocalyptic teaching.

To move against these word curses, the Holy Spirit fell upon our intercessory cohort calling us into the gap. He specifically told us to speak in the name of Jesus Christ against these words of President Ahmadinejad.

Our prayer was to break, in the name of Jesus Christ, the power of the Islamic anti-Christ and the Man of Lawlessness, and then to announce that Jesus Christ is Lord and that his kingdom will come.

We also, in prayer, in the name of Jesus Christ, commanded that the archons influencing President Ahmadinejad be disconnected from him. We were not very sure how this would happen, but we prayed that he would be discredited by other leaders, fall out of favor with the Islamic establishment, or in some way compromise his ability to provide leadership and implement his apocalyptic expectations.

In the following months of 2013, his term as President ended, and he seems to have diminished in influence.[23] Since then, the intercessory prayer burden lifted and we were called to focus in other directions.

However, throughout this engagement to bind the demonic powers working through Ahmadinejad, we were aware that behind him was another figure strategic to Satan's work. We suspected that it was Iran's Supreme Leader Ayatollah Ali Khameini. Later the Holy Spirit did lead us into preemptive warfare prayer to bind the curses spoken through Khameini. (We report on that engagement in the next chapter.)

Much of this battle with the Anti-Christ or the Spirit of Lawlessness took place in the heavenly sphere where we were reaching the limits of our authority. It was clear, however, that Jesus was asking us to do our part in the work of prayer. These battle plans following the script of Islamic Apocalyptic expectation continue to pose a terrible threat from the demonic stronghold of the Islamic Republic of Iran. Until the true believers in the 12th Imam are removed from leadership, we as intercessors must continue to be ready at Jesus' command to join him in binding both the human leaders and the Devil.

Adding to the great danger posed by the Shia stronghold is the rise of the Sunni Apocalyptic cult of the Islamic Caliphate and the Islamic State. The Islamic Anti-Christ, the Spirit of Lawlessness, Gog, Moloch, and the Spirit of Amalek have formed a new and terrible way of implementing Satan's end-times battle plan. Unless they are destroyed, these two Shia and Sunni demonic strongholds will provide Satan with the means of accomplishing his four terrible schemes to fulfill Islamic end-time prophecy. As we move on to look at the leaders of ISIS and what they are doing under demonic influence, I need to prepare you for what is to follow.

The Dilemma of Confronting Evil

Before going any further in reading this book, I need to explain something about my decision to open up for you the abyss of evil that we are marching to confront. Most of us do not want to believe that such evil exists. Our response is to avoid the battle because we do not want to look upon unpleasant things that could cause nightmares. One of my editors after reading the next section, in which I present the evil of ISIS in pictures, wrote this,

> Dear Brad,
> I was working on Chapter 11 yesterday, making good progress until I came to the pictures. You have added in at least one more, and it was too awful. It seared my soul. I have been haunted by it since. I don't think I can look at it again. It is too much for this woman who lost her own child. The horror and grief is overwhelming. So, I am weeping as I write this. I want you to reconsider putting the pictures of the beheaded children in. At the very least, you must give warning about them. If I were just a reader of the published book, I would have a hard time finishing the book after this point. I know I am quite sensitive to this stuff, but I am probably not the only one.

Despite this warning, I decided at the time to include the

picture of the little Christian girl in the cute blue dress who had been beheaded, and was now held in the arms of her grieving father. I know it is terrible, and I know it will be very difficult for many readers to keep going. Nonetheless, it shows the true heart of darkness in Radical Islam. I know that many will recoil in horror when they see the graphic evidence of ISIS following the commands of their prophet Muhammad. However, it is the revelation of just such horrors today that is causing many thousands of Muslims to renounce Islam and follow Jesus, just as many in ancient Rome, seeing the witness of Christians horribly killed led them to embrace Jesus Christ. "The blood of the martyrs is the seed of the Church" still today. Such pictures have the power of truth in them. Also, in pictures such as these we see past all the trivial gibberish of political correctness into the war that is being waged between good and evil.

I have chosen only three of the least gruesome pictures I might have included. Google "Christian Persecution by Muslims" and the results *will* sear your soul! As we ponder this great evil, I see these pictures as prophetic warnings of what Satan is planning on a vast and terrible scale. They are call to become true soldiers for the Kingdom. They are a trumpet call to get into this battle and fight the good fight as God's royal priesthood.

I know that we all respond to these horrors in different ways. I am called to hate this evil with a "perfect hatred." The root and core of this evil is Satan's deceptions in Muhammad that form the basis of the religion, culture, and political system of Islam. This is what is driving me to write this book and take part in forming an army of intercessors through whom Jesus will work to defeat Radical Islam and advance the Gospel into the Muslim world.

Let your response to the horrors of the beheading of little Christian girls be the call from Jesus Christ to join the great army of intercessors who will prevent the further growth of this evil. For some it may be the call to join the military. For others, at least in America, to exercise our second amendment rights and be armed.

For others, it will be a call to pray for the victims of the evil. For others, it will be a great compassion and a call to evangelism for those Muslims who are in the grip of Satan in this religion that condones such evil. Let the Holy Spirit guide you as you deal with the monstrous evil of Radical Islam.

Binding the Demons
in the Leaders of the Islamic State

The Holy Spirit called me to bind the evil spirits in ISIS even before their outbreak of terror in the early summer of 2014. I also prayed for Jesus to pour out the Holy Spirit upon the Christians and Christian communities coming under attack, empowering them for martyrdom. I was also praying for the Lord to open the eyes of our government and military leaders to comprehend what those with prophetic vision had already seen—that ISIS, driven by apocalyptic Islamic ideology, would become a virulent and deadly demonic stronghold. However, we did not have clear guidance about how to pray, except for this threat to be stopped.

Then I read the following report by Catholic Online (NEWS CONSORTIUM) on August 8, 2014 and was appalled at the gruesome pictures. The Holy Spirit fell upon me and called me into urgent intercession.

Islamic State terrorists have begun their promised killing of Christians in Mosul [Iraq], and they have started with the children. According to a report via CNN, a Chaldean-American businessman has said that killings have started

in Mosul and children's heads are being erected on poles in a city park. The terrorists who have invaded Mosul and other ancient Christian communities in Syria and Iraq have made music videos of themselves murdering civilians and captured soldiers. They are literally enjoying the act of killing and the fear and suffering experienced by others. This sadism may be the purest manifestation of evil witnessed since the Rape of Nanking during WWII. According to Arabo, women are being raped, then murdered, and men are being hanged. [Others are crucified.] These are the people who were warned—convert to Islam or be put to the sword...[24]

The picture of a little Christian girl dressed in a sweet blue dress who was beheaded has been removed at request of readers who found it too terrible to look at.

A distraught father in Syria holds the lifeless body of his decapitated daughter, executed by militants because she was of a Christian family. Allegedly, Christian children in Mosul are being systematically beheaded and their little heads placed on poles in a park as a warning to others who love their children.
http://www.catholic.org/news/international/middle_east/story.php?id=56481&wf=rsscol

I made myself look at the awful pictures and asked, "Whose work is that?" Of course, this is the work of the hands of human beings, but who is working through them? The Lord said to me, "This is the work of Moloch who delights in the death of the innocents." The Holy Spirit then said, "Under Moloch is a host of other demons who have possessed and demonized these deceived men of Satan's stronghold of Radical Islam." These lesser demons' names were given in graphic mental images in my mind as: "murder," "blood lust," "sexual lust," and others too terrible to name in print. Then I asked, "Who are they working through?" In this case, it was difficult to get the names of those involved. The Holy Spirit then led me into a time of prayer to bind these demonic powers in the name of Jesus Christ. As I prayed, I saw images of what was happening in the spiritual realm: of angels being unleashed to destroy the hosts of wickedness that were working on earth.

A terrible struggle in the heavenlies took place. For my role in the battle, I had to depend entirely upon the guidance of the Holy Spirit instead of any objective evidence. From the pushback of spiritual warfare and the awareness of evil lashing back at me, I knew I was touching something deadly and satanic. I am ashamed to admit it, but I found within my own fallen nature the powerful draw of such evil. I realized as a fallen human being like those Islamic fanatics that, "There but for the grace of God go I!"[25]

When I read the report, and saw the picture of a little Christian girl (who could have been the age of my granddaughter) dressed in a sweet blue dress and beheaded, there arose in me a great anger. I think this anger was not just me, but the wrath of God. This was anger so intense it felt supernatural; it was against Satan and those who had yielded themselves to his plans. These verses of the Psalm came to me in the King James Version.

> [19]Surely thou wilt slay the wicked, O God: depart from me therefore, ye bloody men. [20]For they speak against thee wickedly, and thine enemies take thy name in vain. [21]Do not I hate them, O LORD, that hate thee? And am not I grieved with those that rise up against thee? [22]I hate them with perfect hatred: I count them mine enemies. (Psalm 139:19-22 KJV)

I found that I did hate these Radical Islamists beheading

Christian children in obedience to their deceived prophet Muhammad with that "perfect hatred." I was discovering why God had created human beings with the capacity for hatred. It was to share in his wrath against the Devil and the evil he has wrought on earth. [26] With this anger, this absolute hatred of evil, the Holy Spirit was calling me not to yield to evil at all, but to yield to the Father. I am to offer myself as the means through whom the Holy Spirit may fight and defeat the demons working on earth, using all the weapons of our warfare. This requires a willingness to throw ourselves into the battle to the utmost, joyfully willing to sacrifice even our own lives.

Satan's plans for the replacement of God's way of life with eternal death, the genocide of God's chosen and redeemed people, and the subjugation of millions is so colossally evil that it must be totally redeemed by the blood of Jesus Christ or absolutely destroyed by the authority of Jesus Christ. There can be no compromise and no middle way.

As I was churning with all of this, feeling the intensity of the hatred and about to slip into wanting to get revenge for the deaths of those Christian children, the Lord spoke again, [19]*Do not avenge yourselves, dear friends, but give place to God's wrath, for it is written, "Vengeance is mine, I will repay," says the Lord.* (Romans 12:19) I replied, "Yes, Lord, but those are innocent children they murdered." I believe that the Lord will indeed avenge this great and terrible evil. Yahweh will do it through us, by our stepping into the gap as intercessors and spiritual warriors, "giving place to God's wrath." In the spiritual realm, this means praying at the prompting of the Holy Spirit and in the authority of Jesus that the Father will destroy both the demons and their human slaves.

As we pray, it is possible that we may be the means through whom God unleashes his wrath. Many intercessors have had this experience that takes place almost like a vision or a dream. Each time I am called into such a battle, it is as if Jesus is directing me in what to say and do. Sometimes I speak words such as "I break the power of murder and blood lust." Sometimes I prophetically act out swinging the sword of the Spirit, which I imagine as a sword of light cutting howling demons to pieces. While we often do not understand what all these prophetic actions accomplish, they are common in the Bible, helpful to us to throw our whole selves— body, mind, and spirit—into the prayer, and when directed by the Holy Spirit these images are no longer just my imagination, but Jesus doing the fighting through me. It is really happening in the realm of the spirit.

Our capacity for imagination when joined with faith becomes an open door into the spiritual realm where all this is happening. For those who have not experienced this, I know it sounds fantastic or delusional. However, this experience is no different than what we experience when the shift takes place in our cooperating with Jesus Christ: it is no longer us speaking, preaching, ministering, or fighting, but the Holy Spirit. Still, it is nonetheless us acting as fully aware, fully free, fully volitional, fully human, and fully engaged servants of the Most High.

After this battle against demons committing atrocities half a world away, I was exhausted. Touching such evil, binding and fighting with powerful demons, sent me into confession. I had to rest in Jesus Christ who is the only one who can cleanse our sinful hearts and liberate us from Satan's power. I also needed prayer and restoration from the prayer team.

Does This Binding of Demons have any Effect in the Human Realm?

What was the effect of this prayer engagement during ISIS's massacre of the Christians of Mosul [Iraq]? Did it stop jihadists from killing? Did any Christian girls and women escape being raped or sold as sex slaves? We may never know. The story is yet unfinished. But we must proceed in faith and in obedience to the guidance of the Holy Spirit. We trust that he is the director of a vast, complex, spiritual and earthly assault against the forces of evil. I do know that this binding of evil spirits in the name of Jesus is part of his work of binding the strongman, who is Satan.[26] The work of binding Satan does not begin on earth but in the spiritual realm, which is often beyond our awareness. Often after battles like this, I have found news reports confirming that these actions in the spiritual realm have had empirical results.

From my own experience with this type of prayer engagement, I have found that having a picture of the people involved is most helpful, even if I do not know their names. I suggest that as the Lord calls you into this battle, ask him to give you a photo of radical Islamists carrying out atrocities. You may find such photos on www.jihadwatch.org and other news media that have not censored or denied this persecution of Christians by Muslims. Then we can pray specifically for the individuals pictured there.

We must also pray for the top leaders of ISIS, through whom the archons are exerting their control. In the name of Jesus Christ, bind these demons and cut them off from their human operatives. Make sure you are being led by the Holy Spirit in this type of specific binding work. Otherwise, it can open you up to demonic counter-attacks.

As a model prayer for binding and breaking the powers of demons in Islam, here is a prayer by an Anglican priest, The Rev. Benjamin McIntyre, who is also engaged in this prayer work of binding evil spirits related to Islam. When prayed in faith, at the direction of Jesus Christ, and in agreement with others, this prayer may be anointed by the Holy Spirit to bind high level demons.

A Model Prayer against the Demons of Islam

Almighty and most merciful Father in Heaven, Your Son our Savior said we were blessed when others hated and persecuted us for His name's sake. Today, Lord, many of our brothers and sisters of every age and in countries all over the world are slaughtered, imprisoned, and oppressed for Your name by others who act in the name of Islam. Lord, we thank you so much for their faith, commitment, and perseverance, and pray that You would make Your presence known to them in the midst of their plight. Comfort and encourage them. Grant them the wisdom, discernment, and gifts they need to minister in Your name to their persecutors and to others oppressed in the false name of Allah.

Lord, we ask that You would send Your holy angels, armed and empowered, to wage war against the powers, principalities, and rulers of darkness active in Islam and the Islamic world.

We pray for the lifting of the oppression clouding the countries controlled by the false god who denies You as the Risen Lord and Creator. The spirits acting through Islam have blinded the eyes, clouded the minds, and hardened the hearts of Muslims and non-Muslims the world over. They have hindered the proclamation of the Gospel. From Mohammed of old to ISIS, Al-Qaida, the Taliban, and the rulers of Iran today, these fallen spirits have instigated those made in Your image to undertake horrific acts of violence and warfare against others in the name of Allah and his prophet. In the name of Jesus Christ, the Ruler and Victor, Your Church says No More.

You, Savior Jesus, stripped these fallen beings of their authority, and You disarmed them through Your blood. Your victory was so decisive that You triumphed over them, humiliating them as a spectacle and leaving them as nothing. Destroy entirely their evil works in the world today. You said that even the gates of Hell would not stand against Your Church, so we ask now for freedom and liberation for all those who are held captive by the deception of Islam. Let their eyes, hearts, and minds be opened to the liberating light of Truth. Bombard them with dreams, visions, and conviction of the Truth of Jesus Christ until they know You and You know them. Equip Your people the world over to proclaim Your truth in the power of the Holy Spirit, through the signs and wonders You perform, especially those of healing the hurting and the casting out of demons from those they have bound. We pray this especially for our brothers and sisters suffering under the plight of Islam. Grant them courage and the gift of prayer. Raise up intercessors who will stand with them in prayer and help turn back the tide of this false god.

Let those engaged in violence for the sake of Islam be overwhelmed by love, charity, and mercy toward those they seek to harm, so that they will abandon the path of jihad and turn their swords into plowshares. Bring to justice those whose hearts are so hardened and minds so closed that they will not repent. Prevent them from doing any more harm to others in the name of their faith.

Let Your name be glorified and Your Spirit poured out upon the Mid-East, Africa, Indonesia, and every place affected by spirits associated with Islam, all the way down to individual apartments and households. Let all affected by this religion come to know the true God, Who revealed Himself in the Incarnation, life, death, Resurrection, and Ascension of Jesus Christ, and let the stronghold of Islam be forever powerless in the world. Heal those hurt by this faith. We pray this for the glory of Your Name, and for the sake of Your love for the world. In the name of Jesus Christ the Victor, Who lives and reigns with You and the Holy Spirit, One God, now and forever, Amen.

You may find this prayer effective as a corporate prayer spoken in unison during Sunday morning worship. In addition, be led by the Holy Spirit in the powerful name of Jesus Christ to use your own prayers to break the power of the demonic spirits at work in Islam and in the strongholds built on the deceptions of Islam.

Breaking Satan's Curses

God works in the human/material world through speaking His word. In this chapter, we show how Satan has corrupted this dynamic for his own evil purposes. In summary, God gives his Word to us as the sword of the Spirit to defeat Satan and build the Kingdom of God. Satan gives his slave armies his lies planted in the Quran and Hadith as curses to destroy the loving Kingdom of God and to enslave hearts and minds in Satan's empire of Radical Islam.

The Dynamic of "Word and the Holy Spirit" and "Curses and Evil Spirits"

The dynamics of Satan working in the world are like God working in the world. The similarity arises from the fact that Satan is not a creator. He can only copy, twist and subvert what God has created.

Below is a summary chart of this dynamic embedded in God's Word, which includes our speaking and acting in faithful obedience to the guidance of the Holy Spirit during a kairos moment. This cooperation enables the Holy Spirit to advance the Kingdom of God in cooperation with us. For a more complete description of this dynamic, what I call the "Dance of Cooperation," please see my book, *Growing the Church in the Power of the Holy Spirit: The Seven Dynamics of Cooperation* co-authored with Cindy Strickler and Paul Stokes. [1]

Kairos moments in *chronos* time

These spiritual principles of God working in the world are perverted by Satan to accomplish his work in the world. So, Satan's working on earth through human beings follows the pattern below. Each component of this divine and human cooperation is replaced by the conditions for Satan enslaving and using human beings. God's pattern is on the left; Satan's copy is on the right.

Divine/Human Cooperation Jesus sets human free to be his friends and coworkers	Satan enslaving and using human beings
Kairos Moments in Chronos Time	Hours of the Power of Darkness
Love is the context for the working of the Holy Spirit–for God is Love.	Hatred, unforgiveness, seeking revenge, deception and sin is the context for the working of Satan
Human beings discern the kairos moment and prepare to cooperate	Satan deceives human beings into being his agents in the Hour of the Power of Darkness.
God's friend and coworker—the visionary, prophet, anointed leader or intercessor—receives the word of God, vision or plans (guidance) for what God wants to accomplish in the kairos moment.	Satan's deceived human agents are given Satan's lies and plans for the Hour of the Power of Darkness.
Human faith is then clothed with actions of speaking, writing or acting the intent of the guidance from God.	Human faith is then clothed with actions of speaking out, writing or acting the intent of the commands of Satan.
These words—acted or spoken or written—function as blessings that when received in faith by human beings welcome the Holy Spirit to work within human hearts and	These words—acted or spoken or written— function as curses that when received in faith by human beings welcome Satan and demons to work within human hearts and

human events.	human events.
God–The Father, Jesus Christ and the Holy Spirit—manifests His presence in the world and accomplishes his purposes. These purposes will be in accord with the nature of God as revealed in Jesus Christ.	Satan and his kingdom of evil spirits manifest their presence in the world and accomplish Satan's purposes. These purposes will be in accord with the nature of Satan as revealed in the Bible and in his works.
When God's power and presence is manifested in the world through objectively verifiable works, human faith is built in God and his Word and revealed plans. The calling, anointing and authority of God's coworkers are confirmed. All of which then opens the doors for the dynamic of God and his coworkers working in the world to continue.	When Satan's power and presence is manifested in the world through objectively verifiable works, human faith is built in Satan's lies and revealed plans. The calling, empowerment and authority of Satan's slaves are confirmed. All of which then opens the doors for the dynamic of Satan and his demonic and human agents working in the world to continue.

Let's begin by showing how the Lord works, as described in the column on the left. The Apostle John gives us a glimpse of this dynamic in his vision of the throne room in heaven:

> [6]Then I saw standing in the middle of the throne and of the four living creatures, and in the middle of the elders, a Lamb that appeared to have been killed. He had seven

horns and seven eyes, which are the seven spirits of God sent out into all the earth. (Revelation 5:6)

Through the Holy Spirit who is sent out into all the earth, both the Father and the Son are present and at work. While the Spirit of God is everywhere, whenever he is manifestly present to work within the time/space sphere, a Kairos moment occurs. Kairos time is the Greek understanding of time that is fulfilled or ripe, the time ready for God's activity. This type of time contrasts with "chronos" time which is sequential time, such as seconds, minutes, hours, or years. This is time shown on a "chronograph," or a clock. Kairos time is discerned by the inner witness of the Holy Spirit and corroborated by the Bible and by objective observations. A biblical example of kairos time is indicated by these words of Jesus Christ: "*The time is fulfilled and the kingdom of God is near. Repent and believe the gospel!*" (Mark 1:15)

The "time is fulfilled" is the Greek word kairos, meaning that the Holy Spirit is working on earth amongst human beings and that our actions are required. In the above case, the action is repentance and believing the Gospel. When these actions are taken in a time of the moving of the Holy Spirit, there will be an amplifying and multiplying effect because the people will be participating in the Father's actions, which will bring his intended results. In this case, those who repent and believe will be born again into the Kingdom of God and will begin to participate in the new life brought by Jesus Christ.

There are many examples of "kairos moments" in the Bible when the Holy Spirit is moving and ready to work to fulfill the Father's intentions. If you review every story of God mightily at work in the Old or New Testament, you will find that they all take place within the context of the moving of the Spirit of Yahweh. You will also find within the pattern that such moments require human faith and obedience for God's intended actions to take place. For instance, when Moses and the liberated people of Israel are being pursued by Pharaoh's six hundred chariots, Yahweh reveals to Moses each of their roles. [16]*"And as for you [Moses] lift up your staff and extend your hand toward the sea and divide it...[17]And as for me [Yahweh], I am going to harden the hearts of the Egyptians so that they will come after them..."* (Exodus 14:16-17) Moses in faith obeys, [21]Moses stretched out his hand toward the sea, and the LORD drove the sea apart by a strong east wind all that night, and he made the sea into dry land, and the water was divided. (Exodus 14:21)

Another example is Mary the mother of Jesus responding with a word of faith to the visitation of the angel announcing that she will conceive a child by the power of Holy Spirit. [38]*"Yes, I am a servant of the Lord; let this happen to me according to your word."* (Luke 1:38) There are many more examples in the Bible as well as in church history of this dynamic of the Holy Spirit moving in kairos moments and God's people speaking or acting in faith. The result is manifestations of the reality of Jesus Christ and the advancement of the Kingdom of God on earth.

Satan's Actions
in the "Hour of the Power of Darkness"

Satan also moves in the demonic equivalent of kairos moments when similar conditions of human faith and obedience are present. Jesus identifies what we may call demonic kairos moments while he is being arrested. "Day after day when I was with you in the temple courts, you did not arrest me. But this is your hour, and that of the power of darkness!" (Luke 22:53) "Hour" here is a different word from "kairos." Only our Father, the Creator, is Lord over time; whereas Satan works within the same constraints of chronological time that we do. The hour of the power of darkness is a time when the words and actions of Satan's human agents will be demonically empowered, resulting in the furthering of Satan's plans on earth (in this case, the crucifixion of Jesus Christ). In history, there are many examples of the *hour of the power of darkness* when actions by Satan's human agents connect with the working of demons and human cooperation to accomplish Satan's purposes. When the right conditions are aligned for Satan to empower his demonized human agents, these actions amplify and multiply satanic darkness.

Kristallnacht, the night of broken glass, is an example of this dynamic. On November 9-10, 1938, the Nazis in many German and Austrian cities went on a coordinated rampage attacking and killing Jews, destroying their shops and business, and burning synagogues. This took place in an *hour of the power of darkness*. These horrific actions were empowered by demons working in the hearts of those human beings forming the stronghold of Nazism to set in motion an escalating cycle of evil culminating in the extermination of over six million men, woman, and children. The history of Satan's fourteen-hundred-year campaign through Islam of replacing Judaism and Christianity through extermination and subjugation provides countless examples of Satan forming the hour of the power of darkness and calling his slave agents into them to accomplish his diabolical purposes.

In this period of the gathering storm, when Satan is busy building the strongholds of Radical Islam, there have been and will be occasions when the conditions are in right alignment for an *hour of the power of darkness*. These have often, like the Kristallnacht, been initiated by major outbreaks of evil by radical Islamic terrorists; for instance:

- the attack by the al Qaeda terror network flying airplanes into the World Trade Towers and the Pentagon, killing over three thousand people on September 11, 2001,

- the 2014 conquest of the Iraqi city of Mosul by ISIS, who committed atrocities against the Christians there,
- the terrorist attack by ISIS in Paris, France in 2015, when 130 people were murdered.

These evil actions function as curses that demonic spirits use to connect with the lies already sown in human hearts, inspiring human actions which set in motion further chains of events that Satan then uses to bring about even greater evil. These curses are the practical ways that Satan uses to extend the power of Radical Islam. When people act upon these curses, they fulfill Satan's four schemes: the replacement of God's salvation with the deception of Islam; the genocide of Jews and Christians; quenching the wind of the Holy Spirit in the House of Islam; and implementing the Islamic Caliphate to bring the world under Islamic tyranny.

Word Curses that Take the Form of Fatwas

In Satan's construct of Radical Islam, he has built the near perfect mechanism of speaking curses. These are called fatwas. A summary definition of a fatwa is as follows: "In Islam, there are four sources from which Muslim scholars extract religious law or rulings, and upon which they base their fatwa. The first is the Quran, which is the holy book of Islam, and which Muslims believe is the direct and literal word of God, revealed to Prophet Muhammad."[2] Most fatwas offered by the religious leaders based on Islamic jurisprudence are matters that pertain to Islamic dietary or social behavior.

Satan uses these rulings from religious authorities to weave Islam's culture of deception. Thus, a fatwa may become a curse against God's chosen and redeemed people when it contains Allah's authorization for Muslims to kill or subjugate Jews and Christians and put in place other aspects of Satan's program. When these fatwas are received in faith by Muslims as the infallible word of Allah that must be obeyed without question, Satan uses them as curses to implement his purposes. For instance, Satan used the fatwa of the last Caliph of the Ottoman Caliphate to launch the genocide against Armenian, Greek, and Assyrian Christians during World War I. Today Satan regularly uses fatwas delivered by the leaders embodying the radical Islamic strongholds in Iran, al-Qaeda, and ISIS, to advance his agenda.

Iran's Supreme Leader Ayatollah Ali Khamenei Used by Satan to Speak the Curse "Kill All Jews, Annihilate Israel"

A fatwa or decree by Iran's supreme leader Ayatollah Ali Khamenei was reported in an article entitled: "Ayatollah: Kill All Jews, Annihilate Israel": Iran lays out legal case for genocidal attack against 'cancerous tumor.' Published: 02/05/2012 at 9:30 PM[3]

> The Iranian government, through a website proxy, has laid out the legal and religious justification for the destruction of Israel and the slaughter of its people. The doctrine includes wiping out Israeli assets and Jewish people worldwide. Calling Israel a danger to Islam, the conservative website Alef, with ties to Iran's supreme leader, Ayatollah Ali Khamenei, said the opportunity must not be lost to remove "this corrupting material. It is a 'jurisprudential justification' to kill all the Jews and annihilate Israel, and in that, the Islamic government of Iran must take the helm."[4]

Notice the role of demonic cloaking in having this come from "a website proxy" with ties to the supreme leader. Regardless of whether the words are spoken directly by the Supreme leader or released by a proxy, they are coming with the imprimatur of the Supreme leader and will be used by Satan to mobilize those Muslims in whom he has already planted the lies and the faith to act upon them. In this case, the call is to the entire nation of Iran. This scenario fits with the lies planted by Satan in the apocalyptic vision of the coming of the 12th Imam that may be hastened by Iran launching genocidal attacks against Israel and the United States.

Visions of the worldwide hegemony of Islam and genocidal attacks against Israel and the nations of the West were given to me

while praying at the Community of the Cross in March of 2010. The revelation of this fatwa and the exposure of the delusions of the 12th Imam provide the objective verification of the guidance I received in prayer. Also, the objective verification that these are the actual beliefs and plans of the religious leaders of Iran is the fact that Iranians are making the preparations for implementing them. This has all been exposed as actionable intelligence by many who have pierced

Ayatollah Seyed Ali Khamenei (http://www.iranchamber.com/history/akhamenei/ali_khamenei.php)

Satan's cloaking. Here is one example.

In the book *A Time to Betray*,[5] the CIA spy in the revolutionary guards reveals the mindset of the Shi'ite clerics and how they aspire for the destruction of the world. They truly believe the end of time is here. As revealed last year, the Iranian secret documentary "The

Coming is Upon Us" clearly indicates that the radicals ruling Iran believe the destruction of Israel will trigger the coming of last Islamic Messiah.[6]

This fatwa based on the supposed infallible word of Allah and the apocalyptic end-times deception has already been used by Satan to create the conditions as well as the military means for an "hour of the power of darkness." A moment will come when, both in the spiritual and in the human realms, these conditions will come into alignment. Then Satan will use these word curses to unleash genocide against Israel, the Jewish people worldwide, and the United States of America. In the spiritual realm, these words of the supreme leader Ayatollah Ali Khamenei are equivalent to the word curse of the final solution that Hitler spoke to his demonized core of Nazis, including Satan's primary gateway into Radical Islam, the Grand Mufti of Jerusalem al-Husseini. Unless decisively overturned in both the spiritual and human realms, this curse spoken by Ayatollah Ali Khamenei to "Kill All Jews, Annihilate Israel" will have even more catastrophic results.

The Role of the Intercessor to Wage Preemptive Spiritual Warfare

How can this word curse that Satan has spoken through his human agents be broken? It is easy to look back, after the fact, when these terrible predictions have come to pass, and deduce what should have been done to prevent them from happening. We must remember that Hitler's curse of the "final solution to the Jewish problem" was not publicly known until after it had had its terrible effect.[7] So the challenge is to wage *preemptive* spiritual warfare to prevent terrible things from happening. In the current situation, we have been given the intelligence needed to cooperate with Jesus Christ in doing just that.

The best-case scenario would be for a high level Islamic cleric or leader to become a convert to Jesus Christ—a modern day follower of Islam meeting the resurrected Jesus Christ and becoming a Muslim Saint Paul. Such a person could then speak the words of Jesus in the New Testament clothed in the language and words of the Quran to break these death fatwas with Jesus' words of life and blessing. I believe the Lord is calling us to focus our intercessions on converting to biblical faith a high profile Islamic religious leader—like the Grand Mufti of Saudi Arabia or the Supreme Leader of Iran. Let us pray that Muslims themselves will turn from Satan's way of death to Jesus' way of life.

Intercessors Breaking these Curses
in the Name of Jesus Christ

The Holy Spirit is calling us to take part in this process of bringing Muslims to faith in Christ, and to prevent Satan's curses from having their terrible effect by stepping into the gap. Here are some of the specific ways that we have been led to pray by the Holy Spirit:

- In the authority of the mighty Name of Jesus Christ, we break the power of this fatwa spoken by Iran's supreme leader Ayatollah Ali Khamenei calling for the destruction of the State of Israel and the extermination of all Jews worldwide.

- In the Name of Jesus Christ, we confuse and negate the schemes of Satan to use these words for his evil purposes, namely, to destroy the Jewish people.

- In the Name of Jesus Christ, we command the following archon (name them and other high level evil spirits as led by the Holy

Spirit) to be separated from the mind and heart of Iran's supreme leader Ayatollah Ali Khamenei and to no longer be able to express their infernal will through him.

- By the power of the One who has all authority in heaven and on earth, Jesus Christ, who gave us the command to "Make disciples of all nations," we break the strongholds of Satan's deception that would block the fulfillment of this command in nations under the bondage of Islam.

- We pray, Lord, that you will bring Iran's supreme leader Ayatollah Ali Khamenei to a saving knowledge of Jesus Christ. Lord Jesus, have mercy on his soul, and on the souls of all those over whom he has authority. Speak to him in a vision or through the means of your choosing, as you spoke to Saul, the Jewish persecutor of the Church, on the road to Damascus.

- Lord, for the sake of your chosen people the Jews and the Church of Jesus Christ, silence this man whose words are being used by Satan against your Kingdom. Silence him until the day his words become words of witness for Jesus!

We have had many intense engagements where we have been led to speak out these commands both in the public context and in prayer engagements in the heavenlies.

This prayer battle has continued to the time of this writing in September of 2016. From the time these deep plans and methods of Satan were revealed in the Shia stronghold, there has been an extended prayer battle. So far there has not been a final decisive prayer engagement, but many. Over the years, the Holy Spirit has repeatedly called intercessors into the gap to break the power of this curse.

These engagements have taken place, for instance, when Iran's proxies Hezbollah and Hamas attacked Israel, and when Iran's President Mahmoud Ahmadinejad announced the coming of the 12th Imam and Jesus Christ at the UN, and in the 2015 nuclear talks with Iran led by the Obama administration. In addition, actions taken in the human sphere especially by Israel, the United States, Great Britain, France, and Russia, have all been a part of this preemptive war.

So far these dire events called forth in the fatwa against the Jewish people have not come to pass. I am convinced that—for now—God in his love and mercy is using all these efforts in the spiritual and human realm to constrain the fulfillment of Satan's plans for genocide of Jews, Christians, and "apostate" Muslims. His continued protection, however, depends on both the intercessors' and on our political and military leaders' constant vigilance and faithfulness to the task.

Other Forms of Curses Used by Satan

We have focused on this curse calling for the death to the Jewish people delivered by the Supreme Leader of Iran, but Satan has used the leaders of other demonic strongholds of Radical Islam to deliver many curses in the form of religious edicts that have great power over Muslim hearts and minds. To seek guidance as to which fatwas we as intercessors are called to break, pay close attention to the news, especially news from Robert Spencer of "Jihad Watch" and Raymond Ibrahim. Their worldview, deep knowledge of Islam, and fluency in Arabic alerts them to the significance of the statements being made. It is also revealing to pay attention to the religious and secular Jewish News services. Jews have learned to pay attention to what their enemies are saying. In any event, ask the Holy Spirit for revelation about which of these many fatwas Satan is using to bring us to the next *hour of the power of darkness.*

There are other forms of curses that do not reach the level of a religious fatwa, but are nonetheless potent tools for Satan. One notable aspect of the leaders of Radical Islam has been their constant declarations of the fulfillment of their plans before they have in fact been fulfilled. These are declarations of the ultimate victory of Islam. Here are two examples:

> I say to America that the Islamic Caliphate has been established. Don't be cowards and attack us with drones. Instead send your soldiers, the ones we humiliated in Iraq. We will humiliate them everywhere, God willing, and we will raise the flag of Allah in the White House. (Vice News)[8]
>
> ISIS today sent out a "coming soon" documentary titled "Warning: Message Signed With Blood Coming Soon To 'Nation Of The Cross.'" It will be as ISIS promised, showing a wave of Christian blood which it has spilt. It is quite horrifying.[9]

These forms of curses taking place in the context of Islam attain their power by connected with specific words of the Quran or by citing examples and words of Muhammad as given in the Hadith. As explained earlier, Satan has carefully built a framework to ensure that these words from the Koran and examples of Muhammad give him power over the hearts and minds of Muslims. First, this binding framework of deception has made the Quran the direct, literal, infallible word of Allah which is beyond analysis and must be unquestionably obeyed. Second, Muhammad must be emulated by Muslims in every way because he is portrayed as the embodiment of the perfect man submitted to Allah.

Actions Demonstrating Faithfulness to the Words of Allah are Curses

Many have been perplexed that ISIS has videotaped their terrible atrocities and then posted them on the internet for the entire world to see. These are terrible acts of violence and hatred—Christians crucified, infidels being burned to death, mass killings, and women raped or sold as sex slaves. Usually what we in the West see in the news media is a news clip of the Christians in orange suits being lined up to be beheaded. Followed by a quick glimpse of the next gruesome pictures of the results or a hint of the result as the ocean water was dyed blood red. But as I have made myself look at the actual videos released by ISIS, the Holy Spirit has revealed the true nature and reason for both the atrocities and their publication. In the ISIS video, the full gory killing takes place to the

chanted or written verses from the Quran and the Hadith, punctuated with the repeated refrain of "Allah Akbar, Allah is Greater." When these actions are coupled with the words of the sacred texts of Islam condoning them, they function as curses that unleash the Devil's power.

Go back to our diagram of how God works with his

coworkers. There we find that one's faith or trust in God must be "clothed with action," otherwise the faith does not open the door for the Holy Spirit's work on earth.

This same dynamic is taking place in ISIS proudly presenting to the whole world their atrocities, coupled with the verses from the Quran and Hadith.

> "Kill the unbelievers wherever you find them." (Koran 2:191) "Make war on the infidels living in your neighborhood." (Koran 9:123) "When opportunity arises, kill the infidels wherever you catch them." (Koran 9:5) "Any religion other than Islam is not acceptable." (Koran 3:85) "The Jews and the Christians are perverts fight them..." (Koran 9:30) "Maim and crucify the infidels if they criticize Islam." (Koran 5:33) "Punish the unbelievers with garments of fire, hooked iron rods, boiling water melt their skin and bellies." (Koran 22:19) "The unbelievers are silly, urge the Muslims to fight them." (Koran 8:65) "Muslims must not take the infidels as friends." (Koran 3:28) "Terrorize and behead those who believe in scriptures other than the Qur'an." (Koran 8:12) "Muslims must muster all weapons to terrorize the infidels." (Koran 8:60)[10]

Satan is now using the combination of the words of the Quran with images and videos of the "true Muslim" carrying out that word as a curse to build faith in Islam and release even more evil. By their acts of violence and hatred, they prove they are following the example of Mohammed in obedience to the Quran.

These curses and the faith they generate are then used by Satan to draw other Muslims with the seeds of deception already sown in their hearts into the demonic strongholds. The result is that both the individuals and the organization are given demonic and earthly power to carry out Satan's purposes. Like a raging forest fire, it forms a maelstrom of evil which grows larger and larger by sucking more and more fuel into itself.

This enables ISIS to recruit fighters from all over the world; it is Satan working through their words and actions drawing them into the stronghold.

The greatest danger is to dismiss these curses as the words and actions of mad men and psychopaths, or to dismiss their statements of ultimate victory as the fantasies of deluded people. To do this is to miss the dynamic of how reality is shaped and how Satan accomplishes his purposes in the world. To do this is to ensure that their prophecies of victory will indeed come true.

Publicly Spoken Curses Must Be Broken Publicly

When Islamists make these statements publicly, quoting the Hadith that predicts the real holocaust or stating that the Quran is calling on Muslims to kill Jews and Christians, our role is to publicly expose and denounce these statements as not coming from God, but from Satan. Christians in the anointing of the Holy Spirit and in the authority of Jesus must replace those words of death with Jesus' words of life and freedom.

This must be done publicly and in the public arena. If their word curses are spoken, in writing or over the internet on YouTube videos, then we must break the curses over the same medium. Sometimes Islamists may speak their curses in our hearing. Then we must challenge them directly face to face and in the power of Jesus Christ speak the word given by the Holy Spirit to us.

Cursing us directly may happen in subtle ways. For instance, once while in Jerusalem I was on my way to visit the Western Wall. I knew that I would need to wear some type of head cover, and, as I had left my Tilley hat at the hotel, I stepped into what I thought was a Christian shop to buy a Jewish skullcap. In Hebrew, this is called a "kippah" or "yarmulke." I could pick up a free one at the Western Wall, but they are so light they often blow off. This shop had lots of them. I picked a blue one with silver embroidery and a Star of David. Immediately the old shopkeeper and his son surrounded me and pointed out the other lovely Jewish and Christian items they had for sale. I said, "No I just want this Kippah!" But my eye had strayed to a lovely necklace I knew my wife would love. That was my fatal mistake, and they seized the opportunity.

They pressed in upon me and asked how many wives I had. "Just one, thank God!"

"How many daughters?" I stumbled again and fell deeper into their trap by answering "Two!" During this conversation, I asked, "Are you Christian or Muslim?" The old shopkeeper hesitated and said, "I cannot lie to you, Sir, Muslim." I looked right at him and said, "I am a Christian, a follower of Jesus Christ." Then I pulled my wooden cross out from under my jacket. That provoked a power encounter that at the time so befuddled me that I was not aware of what was happening. The shopkeeper said, "Well, here we all live together in peace—Jews, Muslims and Christians."

After that, in looking back many times over the half-hour engagement that followed, I realize he wove into our conversation the words "God is Great," and each time a wave of confusion went over me. After spending much more money than I intended to spend, I finally broke away and made it back to where we were staying.

That night was terrible! Wave upon wave of thoughts of violent revenge swept over me. I found myself fighting against speaking curses against that shop keeper and against all Muslims. It was as if a door to hell had opened and Satan was trying to lure me into his schemes of death and destruction. The next morning, I had to confess to the whole prayer team what had happened. They had to pray for cleansing and to break the curses put upon me. I had to renounce my thoughts of revenge. After my spiritual eyes were cleared through confession and prayer, I realized that when the shopkeeper said, "God is Great," what I should have done is to counter it with the Christian proclamation that "God is Love!" I should have blessed him and his shop right when I was there with him face to face.

After this episode, I felt like a complete failure as a Christian, an intercessor, and a warrior in the service of Jesus Christ. I am highly embarrassed to confess this in print, but I must to expose the subtle ways that the Devil will lead us unsuspectingly into his snares.

Breaking the Curses by Muslims
Spoken in Christian Churches

Sometimes this breaking of curses spoken by Muslims may take place directly face to face as they have invoked the name of Allah in Islamic prayer in Christian churches. An instructive example of this occurred in Germany when the church leaders were foolish enough to invite an Imam to give the Islamic Call to prayer at the Memorial Church of the Reformation in the Rhineland city of Speyer, built to honor Martin Luther. [11] This has happened in several locations in the name of interfaith dialogue, including at the National Cathedral in Washington DC.[12]

No doubt this is done with the best of intentions of fostering understanding and relationships between Muslims and Christians. However, the invocation of Allah, who is not the one true God revealed in the Old and New Testaments, is an invitation for demonic spirits to invade the Church. It is also part of Satan's plans through Islam to replace the truth of Christianity with the deception of Islam, and to turn churches focused on Jesus Christ as revealed in the Old and New Testament into mosques focused on the false Jesus of the Quran, on Allah and the prophet Muhammad. Unless opposed in the name of Jesus Christ, these invocations serve as curses that give grounds for evil spirits to remain in the Church and work out Satan's purposes of opposing the Kingdom of God.

When this took place at the Memorial Church of the Reformation in Speyer Germany, a Christian woman provided a model for how the Lord may call us to engage in breaking such curses. This was reported in CBN News with a video and the following report:

> "The Armed Man: A Mass for Peace" by Welsh composer Karl Jenkins was supposed to be an interfaith event to bring Christianity and Islam together. But when the Muslim imam began his call to prayer during the concert, he was interrupted by a small woman in the balcony proclaiming that "Jesus Christ alone is Lord of Germany," and shouting, "I break this curse."[13]

She was later thrown out of the church. But in the power of the Holy Spirit, she accomplished the mission Jesus Christ gave her.

Our words must be spoken forth to human beings as well as to the demonic powers in the spiritual realm. These may be our own Holy Spirit directed words and Holy Spirit led quotes from God's Word. When Jesus was being tempted by Satan in the wilderness, He repeatedly responded to Satan's deceptions with "It is written...." In our battles with Satan's word curses, we would do well to follow Jesus' example. For some who know the Quran or the Hadith, the Holy Spirit may even use the words of the texts of Islam as a witness against itself.

Breaking Word and Action Curses from Satan
Spoken by Islamists

When Jesus calls us to break the power of Satan's curses, He expects us to follow His guidelines for empowered prayer:

- In relationship with Jesus Christ (John 15:4-5, 7-8, I John 5:14-15)
- in the name of Jesus (John 14:12-14, Acts 3:1-10)
- in agreement with one another (Matthew 18:19-20)
- asking and receiving in faith (Mark 11:22-24, Matthew 17:20-21)
- and led by the Holy Spirit. (Romans 8:26-27)

When we speak these words aloud, whether publicly over the internet, in a private prayer gathering, or alone with Father, we are providing the Holy Spirit what he needs from us to defeat these curses. (See the diagram of this dynamic presented earlier in this chapter.)

Remember, do not curse back! As you say yes to Jesus' call to break Satan's curses, seal upon your heart the warnings of Jesus and St. Paul:

- *27"But I say to you who are listening: Love your enemies, do good to those who hate you, 28bless those who curse you, pray for those who mistreat you."* (Luke 6:27-28)

- *14Bless those who persecute you, bless and do not curse.* (Romans 12:14)

- *19Do not avenge yourselves, dear friends, but give place to God's wrath, for it is written, "Vengeance is mine, I will repay," says the Lord.* (Romans 12:19)

When we are faced with an evil as terrible as ISIS or Boko Haram, the great danger is to fall into hatred ourselves by cursing them back or seeking vengeance. The moment we do this, we fall prey to one of Satan's snares. When demonic counter-attacks come against intercessors, I suggest a hard look at ourselves to see if we have violated any of these biblical guidelines.

As we seek, by prayer, to "return evil with good, I suggest the following:

- When they curse us with death, we must denounce these words as from the devil and not God, and declare firmly what Jesus Christ says of himself: *"I am the way, and the truth, and the life. No one comes to the Father except through me".* (John 14:6)

- When they announce that Islam will rule the world, we must denounce that as a lie from Satan, and instead proclaim the good news of the Gospel.

  We announce the Father's inevitable victory of Jesus: *9As a result God exalted him and gave him the name that is above every name, 10so that at the name of Jesus every knee will bow—in heaven and on earth and under the earth—11and every tongue confess that Jesus Christ is Lord to the glory of God the Father."* (Philippians 2:9-11)

- When they validate their atrocities as the will of Allah, and speak to us words from the Quran or the Hadith, we reject it all as lies from Satan. We break their power by declaring that the truth, salvation and the destiny of humanity is found only in Jesus Christ.

- When Muhammad is announced as the final prophet and the fulfillment of the promise of Abraham, we decree: for *"salvation is from the Jews,"* (John 4:22) and we boldly proclaim of Jesus: [12]*"...there is salvation in no one else, for there is no other name under heaven given among people by which we must be saved."* (Acts 4:12)

- When Muslims announce the coming of the Islamic Jesus who will break the cross, and the Mahdi who will establish the Islamic Caliphate and worldwide Islamic hegemony, we must declare that these are the plans of Satan and not God.

- We proclaim that Jesus Christ who died on the cross, was resurrected from the dead, ascended to the right hand of the Father will come again in glory, that he has poured out his Holy Spirit, and through his redeemed people is building the Kingdom of life and grace that brings justice and peace.

Who is Called to Break Satan's Curses and to Speak the Vision of God's Kingdom?

In another great contest with the Devil which took earthly political and military form in Nazism, God especially called and, I believe, anointed Sir Winston Churchill. Churchill did not flinch from naming the Nazis a "monstrous tyranny, never surpassed in the dark and lamentable catalogue of human crime."[14] He called for total war and total victory over this great evil, and he called forth the vision of freedom. "If we can stand up to him (Hitler), all Europe may be free and the life of the world may move forward into broad, sunlit uplands. But if we fail, then the whole world, including the United States, including all that we have known and cared for, will sink into the abyss of a new Dark Age, made more sinister, and perhaps more protracted, by the lights of perverted science."[15]

Again, Rees Howells was called and empowered by God to break the power of Nazism and to counter their curses of a Nazi-dominated Europe. Howells was called to pray this out alone in his prayer closet and with a small circle of high-level intercessors doing battle in the heavenlies. Howells also lived it out as he worked to save orphaned Jewish children. He also spoke God's word of hope to the British public. Most notable was his book, "*God Challenges the Dictators: The doom of the Nazis predicted.*"[16] This booklet was published in 1939 when the dictators were moving from one victory after another, and their doom was anything but certain. In the middle of impending military disaster at Dunkirk, on May 20, 1940, Rees Howells notes in his prayer journal, "Today I have sent the book to Mr. Chamberlain, Lord Halifax, and Mr. Churchill—in the darkest hour."[17]

When such words are spoken, written or acted out in the anointing of the Holy Spirit, they no longer represent fine political rhetoric or great oratory. The Holy Spirit uses them as part of his overall strategy to defeat the lies of Satan and advance the Kingdom of God.

So now, whom is God raising up for just such a time as this? On whom has the mantle of anointing come to speak God's word against the lies of Satan embodied in Radical Islam? Let us rise to the calling to be God's royal priesthood, so that it will not be just one or two lonely figures who dare to speak the truth against the lies of the enemy.

Already at this juncture in the battle against Radical Islam are Benjamin Netanyahu, Prime minister of Israel, and Abdel Fattah el-Sisi, President of Egypt, both naming the evil of Radical Islam and calling for victory over it. They are joined by a number of American political leaders as well, most notably former senator Joseph Lieberman and Senator John McCain. The Rev. Franklin Graham has spoken forth God's Word on this subject. Baptist minister and former Arkansas Governor Mike Huckabee has not held back. Let us pray for the Holy Spirit to anoint many other Christian leaders to speak forth God's Word with clarity and power to overcome the lies of Satan.

Be open to hearing God calling you to speak his Truth within your own sphere of authority. You do not have to have name recognition to exercise the authority of Jesus Christ to do this speaking as led by the Holy Spirit. You must recognize Jesus' name and be a citizen of his Kingdom!

Many times, I have been led to break the death curses spoken by Satan's deceived servants over the internet and on video. This is also the reason why I am writing this book. This is in obedience to the guidance of the Holy Spirit to mobilize, equip, and deploy an army of intercessors. While most of us are without reputation in the eyes of the world, such actions, undertaken with the guidance of the Holy Spirit, do have power in the spiritual realm to destroy the strongholds of Satan and advance God's Kingdom.

Dividing Satan's Kingdom

In this chapter, we offer what could be called the "nuclear option" of spiritual warfare. Jesus Christ may call us to join him in the tactic of dividing the Kingdom of Satan. This is based on our Commander's own words, [17]"Every kingdom divided against itself is destroyed, and a divided household falls." (Lk. 11:17)

The Strongholds of Radical Islam Replicate Satan's Slave Empire

To understand this strategy of dividing Satan's kingdom, we must refer to the way Satan forms strongholds at the human level. For a stronghold to be formed there must be an intense unity among the leader and the creative minority, a unity of vision and purpose that radiates down from the demonic through the human organization of the stronghold.

Satan's empire is one of fear, torment, and slavery. The more one studies Islamic culture, the more one realizes that it mirrors in the human realm Satan's slave empire. This bondage is most clearly revealed in the command that anyone who leaves Islam is to be killed.[1] This is the same reprehensible bondage that we see in satanic cults. Satan's slave state and slave armies present a formidable challenge to free democratic societies based on a Judeo-Christian worldview and reflecting the influence of the book of Galatians. During fourteen hundred years of jihad against the West, Islam has boasted many victories. But it is not invincible.

The point of weakness in this entire totalitarian system is that Islam itself is riven by two major divisions—the Sunni and the Shia—with countless other divisions among them. Satan's strategy, which is a very risky one, is to use the cohesion provided by the common deceptions and hatreds within each of these divisions. ISIS is Sunni, while the Islamic Republic of Iran is Shia. Both Sunni and Shia expressions are committed to destroying Israel, exterminating the Jewish people, destroying America, killing Christians and subjugating the entire world under Islam and Islamic law. But they hate each other, consider each other apostates from the true faith; and if the vise of Satan's control is loosened, they readily disintegrate into warring factions. These inherent divisions are their Achilles' heel.

In the Authority of Jesus Christ, Declare, "Satan's Kingdom is Divided and Fallen"

As intercessors, Jesus may call us to join him in dividing the kingdom of Satan at the source of the stronghold's power and coherence. The biblical basis in this tactic is well described by Asher Intrater in his book *From Iraq to Armageddon: The Final Showdown Approaches*.[2]

Jesus Christ teaches that a basic rule of spiritual warfare is dividing the forces of the enemy. If Satan can divide the body of Christ, then he will get the victory over us. But if Satan's kingdom is divided, then Christ gets the victory over Satan's work on earth. One of the first rules of spiritual warfare, taught by Yeshua, is dividing the forces of the enemy. [17]"Every kingdom divided against itself is brought to desolation, and a house divided against a house falls. [18]If Satan also is divided against himself, how will his kingdom stand?" (Lk. 11:17b-18)

One day, as I was meditating on this passage, I realized that it also could be used as a weapon against the devil. If Satan's[3] kingdom is divided, it will not be able to stand. We have authority to bind demons. Why could we not use that authority to pray division into Satan's kingdom?

I decided to try it. I began to pray by faith and declare, "Satan's kingdom is divided and fallen." As I said that, I had a vision in my heart. The ground beneath me turned to glass. And I could see down into the kingdom of Satan. My words were being broadcast on a loud speaker throughout the corridors of hell. Satan and all of his forces were paralyzed and forced to listen.

Although demonic ranks have a hierarchy under Satan, their unity is only held together by fear and hatred. There is no essential unity or loyalty among them. They would be more than willing to destroy one another. Our prayers to bring division into the ranks of Satan's forces can have tremendous power and effectiveness. Casting out a demon brings deliverance to one person. Praying for division among Satan's forces can cause them to fight among themselves. It can bring destruction and confusion on multitudes of demons. The effect is exponential.[4]

I believe this guidance is right from the Holy Spirit. Often I have tended to pray that Jesus' human adversaries will be divided and will destroy themselves. There is certainly a biblical basis for this approach. However, this guidance given through Asher is an offensive attack going for the very heart of the human/demonic organization of the stronghold of Islam by directly attacking the kingdom of Satan. Using our authority in Jesus Christ to divide Satan's kingdom will have the result on the physical battlefield of the armies of Islam being divided and turning their weapons upon one another.

Tactics in Applying this Strategy

Ask the Holy Spirit to give you guidance as to when there is an opening in the demonic cloaking to—in faith and in the name of Jesus—speak this word of division into Satan's kingdom. If this prayer is to be effective, it must be done at the leading of the Holy Spirit and into this opening. Notice in the report given by Asher that he not only received the guidance, but also had the vision of the earth turning to glass enabling him to see into the demonic realm. This was the sign that the cloaking had been pierced and his Holy Spirit led prayers would be effective.

Likewise, when we pray for the piercing of the demonic cloaking, we may expect God to show us when these prayers are effective by seeing with the eyes of the Spirit. We may also use our gifts of analysis of events on earth that may be windows into the spiritual realm. Because Satan's kingdom is mediated on earth through human structures and events, we may see glimpses of the potential weaknesses in Satan's defenses from news reports. Perhaps this will be when the enemies of Christ and humanity have just suffered a major battlefield defeat and there are doubts about their invincibility. Another time of opportunity is during outbreaks of protest or violence revealing the hatred between the different divisions of Islam. These events in the human time/space realm may be hints of potential divisions and vulnerabilities within Satan's Kingdom in the heavenlies.

These observations of events on earth, however, must be confirmed as we are "sitting with Jesus in the heavenly places" and can see with Jesus' eyes into the spiritual realm. When that affirmation comes, Jesus may well call us to join His battle by speaking in His name the proclamation, "Satan's kingdom is divided and fallen."

The Command, "Satan's Kingdom is Divided and Fallen" Applied to a Specific Location or Situation

There have been many times when we have been called to apply this tactic when fighting Satan's aggression in local arenas. God led me into an almost daily prayer battle from July 8 to August 25, 2014, when Hamas fired 3,852 rockets into Israel. In that battle, I was led to focus on the demons embedded in the human Islamic terrorists launching the rockets. The Holy Spirit told me to cut these demons off from the demonic hierarchy serving as Satan's administrative and spiritual link between demons on the ground and their commanders in the heavenlies. I used the following commands that I adapted from the rites of exorcism and the process of deliverance.

- I announce that by the blood of Jesus Christ on the Cross, Satan is defeated. In the name of Jesus Christ, I sever you demons of murder and blood lust in the local fighters from your higher authorities.

- In the name of Jesus, I speak confusion in your communications with your higher authorities.

- In the mighty name of Jesus who defeated your dictator Satan on the Cross, I rescind the orders of Satan that compel you to stay in your unity of command, purpose and actions. I also cut you off from other demons with the same assignment that you have."

In giving these commands for Satan's kingdom to be divided, we are not being led to cast the demons out of the individuals. The reason is that to remove demons from the individual fighters would require that the ground of entry be removed. This ground of entry may be the false beliefs of Islam or deep wounding that has taken place in the person's life. To remove this ground would require both the person to come to faith in Jesus Christ, to renounce the lies of Satan in Islam, and to receive deep inner healing.

What we can do, however, and what is very much in our sphere of authority, is dividing Satan's kingdom at those points where it extends beyond the individuals and connects with the higher demonic powers. Recall that we, as created in the image of God, provide the nexus between the spiritual and human realms. It is in this location between the human realm and the third heaven (the Father's center of operations) that Jesus has granted us vast authority in this war. There, in the power of his name, we can disrupt the unity of Satan's kingdom.

Results of Applying the Tactic

When we give this command to divide Satan's kingdom in the authority of Jesus Christ, demons are released from the unity of command under Satan and high level demons. With their vicious, hateful nature unconstrained, they will destroy one another as well as their human hosts. Demons warring against one another now make the transition to human beings killing each other.

Because sin taints every human heart, this can happen in any gathering of human beings including Christians. But those in bondage to Islam are especially vulnerable to this tactic of dividing Satan's Kingdom. Islam, unlike Christianity, is not a religion of love, forgiveness, and grace.[5] Lacking these Christian graces, those in bondage to Islam are often filled with unhealed hurts, ancient hatreds, and unforgiveness of wrongs—all of which give ground to demons. So when the coercive power of centralized demonic and human authority is lifted, Muslims turn from hating and killing Jews and Christians to hating and killing one another.

This tactic, like all the tactics of engaging Satan's army, requires a high level of unity in the Body of Christ. Christians whose lives are riven with unexamined hurts, resentments, bitter roots and divisiveness are in no condition to do this kind of warfare. Without Christian unity, Satan will turn our attempts to divide his kingdom against us. He will divide the body of Christ so he can destroy us. Therefore, let us turn to the issue of Christian unity which is essential in overcoming the kingdom of Satan.

Unity in Biblical, Trinitarian Faith

For the Church to be the means through which Jesus Christ divides Satan's kingdom, we must be in unity. As Asher Intrater said recently "Luke 11:17,[1] the 'division prayer' is the flip side of John 17:21[2] the 'unity prayer.'"[3] That is, Jesus bringing disunity in Satan's kingdom depends on unity in the Body of Christ. Our authority as intercessors rests upon the unity of the Church.

We must face the reality that much of Satan's success in advancing his empire of evil is due to divisions in the body of Christ. Satan knows the power of the unity of the Body of Jesus Christ, and over the centuries has developed many strategies for destroying this unity. Three major divisions within the Church are highly relevant to Jesus' war with Radical Islam.

The first is the great divide within the Roman Empire between the Latin-speaking Western Church and the Greek-speaking Eastern Church. This has often left the Greek-speaking Church unsupported in its 1400-year frontline battle with Islam. Another major division was brought by the Reformation. The victorious battles at Lepanto in 1571 and at Vienna in 1683 that halted Islam's jihad into Europe were won by Catholic fleets and armies. To this day, the immense sacrifices and strategic accomplishments of these Catholic leaders and soldiers seem either unknown or unappreciated. As in those days, this jihad is against all believers in Jesus Christ, regardless of our different traditions and divisions. To defeat this jihad, we must unite under the banner of the cross of Jesus Christ.

The second division forms around the Trinity which provides the basis for the existence of the Church in the world. The result is that the Church does not experience the full work of each person of the Trinity, nor the means of transforming all dimensions of human life.[4]

The third division separates Jewish believers and Gentile believers in Jesus Christ. This results in a Christianity severed from her Jewish roots and the Jewish people being unable to receive Yeshua as their Messiah. Satan's success in this dividing strategy has paved the way for his greatest victories over the Church through Islam. The Church has been powerless to resist Satan's strongholds of Islam and has, until recently, been powerless to take the Gospel to Muslims.

In this chapter, we address the issue of our biblical Trinitarian faith. In the next chapter, we will deal with Jewish-Gentile unity. I am not called to be a link between the Eastern and Western Church, so I will leave that breach in our defenses against Islam to be addressed by those who are.[5]

Biblical Trinitarian Faith

Ever since Pentecost, in wave upon wave, the Holy Spirit has been moving on earth to advance the Kingdom of God. Each generation in each location is given a unique mission, but all have the same strategic goal of making disciples of Jesus Christ for the building and extending of the Kingdom of God. The Holy Spirit is doing this in three ways, often veering from one neglected area to the next, but always working to keep Jesus' disciples in a dynamic balance among the three. The elements of this balance are (1) the authority of the Word of God (the Bible) and our obedience to it, (2) our full cooperation with the Holy Spirit's equipping work, and (3) the experience of the saving work of Jesus Christ and submission to His Lordship.

This perpetual work of the Holy Spirit is holding in dynamic balance these three foundations for the Kingdom of God on earth. This is what makes real the Body of Christ, in which there is achieved not just in theory or doctrine, but in fact the multifaceted nature of the Church described in Galatians 3:26-29.

26For in Christ Jesus you are all sons of God through faith. 27For all of you who were baptized into Christ have clothed yourselves with Christ. 28There is neither Jew nor Greek, there is neither slave nor free, there is neither male nor female—for all of you are one in Christ Jesus. 29And if you belong to Christ, then you are Abraham's descendants, heirs according to the promise.

This is the army that has the full power and authority of Jesus Christ to defeat Satan's strongholds and to advance the Kingdom of God. The Church, when unified in her Trinitarian faith, is the great bulwark and final line of defense against Islamic jihad. There is no

other force on earth that can defeat the demonic stronghold of Radical Islam except the Christian faith embodied in the Church.

Historically, When Christians Lose their Biblical Trinitarian Faith, Satan Prevails

When Christians have been divided at the foundation of biblical Trinitarian faith, then Satan has prevailed. This biblical faith is the core and the deep spring of our Western culture, providing the spiritual core, worldview, and moral structures of our democratic institutions and liberal pluralistic culture. When this faith foundation is lost, then Satan prevails through Islam and other totalitarian ideologies and movements. Geert Wilders, in an analysis of why Islam could so quickly conquer large portions of the Christian world, provides the following summary that I take as a prophetic warning today:

By then, [the beginning of Islamic conquest after the death of Muhammad in 632 AD] Christianity had been weakened by 300 years of theological disputes that had led to the emergence of strong heretical churches rejecting the divine nature of Christ and the existence of the Holy Trinity. The heresies of Arianism [6], Nestoriansm [7], Monphysitism[8], Ebionism[9], and the Nazarene sect[10] became dominant forms of Christianity in many regions—though not in Rome, Constantinople, or the Greek heartland of the Byzantine Empire.

Many of these heretical movements felt attracted to the simplicity of Islam, which adhered to similar beliefs that there was no Trinity and that Jesus was not divine but merely a prophet of God. Consequently, Monophysite Syria and Arian North Africa and Spain could not muster the resistance to oppose Islam. By 700, Christianity had lost more than half its territory.

In contrast, Trinitarian Christianity—whether Greek Orthodox or Roman Catholic—resisted Islamic encroachments. Constantinople, the Byzantine capital, was besieged twice by Arabs, in 674-78 and in 717. The Byzantines held Islam at bay for 800 years, twenty-five generations long, before finally succumbing to the Turks in 1453. The valiance of the Greeks, the tenacity of Byzantine culture, and the strength of Constantinople's walls saved the rest of Europe from the Islamic invasion from the East. In 1683, the Turks pressed into the heartland of Europe, but were defeated at Vienna by John III Sobienski, the King of Poland.

Islam's western assault on Europe had already been stopped at Tours 950 years earlier, in 732, by Charles Martel and his ferocious Franks. The Franks had converted from Germanic paganism to Trinitarian Christianity around 500 AD. If they had become Arians like the Goths and the Vandals, history might have taken a far different course.[11]

There is much more complexity in this history and the causes that Geert Wilders does not cover in this summary statement. He omits entirely the biblical understanding of the Kingdom of God which has profound implications for economies and unjust systems of land ownership which made these areas vulnerable to Islam.[12] These kingdom issues of land and economics may have been just as decisive as the alleged lack of Trinitarian faith in creating this vulnerability to Islam.[13] He does, however, discern the core spiritual foundation of the Church for all times and places—biblical Trinitarian faith. Where it is lacking, the Church is weakened. So it would be in the doctrine of the Trinity that Satan is probing for chinks in the armor of faith, however slight.

We must take a lesson from history and observe that Satan's master plan has always been to defeat the Kingdom of God, not in frontal assaults against the advancing unified army of Christ, where he always loses, but by bringing divisions within. In our present period of the gathering storm, Satan is using the stronghold of Liberal Progressivism to divide the Church at the heart of her biblical Trinitarian faith.[14] Satan's work of dividing the Body of Christ is intensifying at this very time in history when this unity is most urgently needed to engage the war against Radical Islam.

My Struggle to Find this Unity

For those of us called as intercessors, the unity of biblical Trinitarian faith must be the foundation upon which we stand to do battle against the onslaught of the powers of darkness in Islam. The challenge for many of us is how do we find that unity of faith in the present situation when major mainline denominations in the United States, Canada, The United Kingdom and Europe have rejected or abandoned their foundations in biblical Trinitarian faith? We are faced with a question, "Must we have complete unity in the whole body of Christ before we can move into spiritual warfare at all?"

The ideal would be yes. But the practical reality is that until Christ returns in glory, our unity will only be partial. So it becomes a matter of the unity within portions of the body of Christ, within the specific units in the army of Jesus Christ that the Holy Spirit is mobilizing to advance his Kingdom over a particular demonic stronghold in a particular location.

My own story as a spiritual warrior may be helpful to demonstrate how to work out enough unity within a fallen world to be covered for these high-level engagements.

First, I am associated with a strong local evangelical congregation. Second, I am the executive director of an international ministry in which there are lines of accountability, first to the board of directors, and then within a ministry team. In addition to these formal lines of accountability, I belong to an extended international network of believers called the Dunamis Fellowship International.[15] While our unity is not perfect, we are all connected by the same commitment to Jesus Christ and to a common vision to be led by the Holy Spirit to advance the Kingdom of God. This gives us the foundation from which to engage in this prayer work.

For myself, when I have been called to engage in such prayer battles, I have submitted these calls to my accountability partners. For instance, in writing book I and II on the prayer strategy, I presented the project to the leadership team, gained permission from the PRMI Board, and requested intercessors in our global network to pray for this prayer work. This has provided the covering to do this dangerous work of naming the evil and helping equip and deploy this army of intercessors.

The implications of this for all of us called into this battle are that we need to seek the prayer support and spiritual covering of our accountability partners. For some, the unity that will support us in these battles will be no more than two or three strong believers who are "subject one to another out of reverence for Christ." This is Jesus' most basic requirement for using power keys of prayer. In Matthew 18:19-20, Jesus gives the following instructions:

> [19]Again, I tell you the truth, if two of you on earth agree about whatever you ask, my Father in heaven will do it for you. [20]For where two or three are assembled in my name, I am there among them.

For many of us, this unity within a small group may be

sufficient, but I have found for myself that the more the Holy Spirit expanded my role in this war, the more critical it became for me to be associated with a larger unit of the Body of Christ with whom I was in essential theological and spiritual unity.

There is No Perfect Unity

The lesson for all of us living in this fallen world where perfect unity in the Body of Christ is an impossibility is to seek to be in unity with those with whom we are called to be in fellowship. There may be differences of opinion on many issues of doctrine and practice. However, the one area where that unity is essential is in the profession of our faith in Jesus Christ as revealed in the Bible and in the basic creeds that affirm the Trinitarian nature of our faith. Without that basic unity, we cannot effectively wage spiritual warfare against Satan's stronghold of Radical Islam.

We must do whatever it takes to put ourselves in the context where that essential unity in Jesus Christ is present. For some of us it may require us leaving some beloved denomination rich in history and memory because it departed from the essential profession that Jesus Christ is Lord and Savior; a sad step I had to take. So, I am now a teaching elder in the Evangelical Presbyterian Church.

Before returning to the tactic of dividing Satan's Kingdom, we must address another place where Satan has divided the body of Jesus Christ. This is the division between Jews and Christians. In this battle with Satan, who through the stronghold of Radical Islam is scheming to murder Jews and Christians in a new holocaust, our unity in Jesus Christ will lead to victory. Our continued division will lead to certain defeat. In this next chapter I address what could be a fatal weakness in the prayer army of Jesus Christ.

The Authority of Born Again Jews and Gentiles in Unity

I deal here with the most basic division within the body of Christ which is of immense strategic importance to our present war with Radical Islam. This is the division between Jewish and Gentile believers. In the beginning, the Church was entirely Jewish. Then, with the outpouring of the Holy Spirit on the household of Cornelius in Acts 10, the Church began to add non-Jewish believers. For a short season, both Jews and Gentiles who came to faith in Jesus Christ integrated in worship and practice.

In Acts chapter 15, the issue to be dealt with by the Jerusalem Council is concisely stated in verse 1. *"Unless you are circumcised according to the custom of Moses, you cannot be saved."* Further, there were those in the religious party of the Pharisees who had believed in Yeshua who pushed the issue with the contention, [5]*"It is necessary to circumcise the Gentiles and to order them to observe the Law of Moses."* (Acts 15:5) The conclusion of their discernment process was written in a letter carried by Judas and Silas:

> [28]For it seemed best to the Holy Spirit and to us not to place any greater burden on you than these necessary rules: [29]that you abstain from meat that has been sacrificed to idols and from blood and from what has been strangled and from sexual immorality. If you keep yourselves from doing these things, you will do well. Farewell. (Acts 15:28-29)

In essence, the Council decided that Jewish believers in Jesus would remain Jewish, keeping the Jewish rituals including circumcision. Gentiles who believed in Jesus Christ, on the other hand, did not have to receive circumcision, but were required to follow the Noahic and Abrahamic Covenants in those areas needed to set them apart from the demonized pagan culture.[1] In summary, "The verdict of the first Jerusalem Council then is that the Church is to consist of two segments, [Jewish and Gentile], united by their faith in Jesus."[2] This is the true nature of the Body of Christ: a fusion of born-again Jewish believers who are the root, and born-again Gentile believers engrafted into the Jewish root.[3]

Satan's long term strategic plan is to destroy the unity of Jew and Gentile in the Body of Christ. This is a long and terrible history which we need not review here. Just two key turning points: first, Satan used the Edict of Milan in 313 under Constantine, which granted tolerance to Christians, to plant a seed of division by not granting similar tolerance to Jews.[4]

Second, Satan's triumph came nearly 350 years later in the Second Council of Nicaea in 787 which banned from Church membership the Jews who had accepted Jesus Christ as the Messiah while remaining Jewish in culture, rites and customs.[5] They even banned remnants of any Jewishness whatever anywhere in the Church, thus effectively burning the bridge with Jews permanently, and blaming the Jews for the death of Jesus. This shrewd tactic divided the body of Christ at its core and cut off the Gentile Church from its Jewish root. This has provided Satan with the building blocks for powerful demonic strongholds of anti-Semitism as well as Jewish rejection of Yeshua as the Messiah. The result has been great suffering for the Jewish people, and compromised power and authority to fulfill the Great Commission in the Gentile Church.

Satan's master strategy for destroying the Kingdom of God on earth includes concentrating his attacks through the strongholds of Radical Islam on this point of fatal weakness—the body of Christ divided between Jewish and Gentile believers. Satan's strategic battle plans for genocide for both Jews and Christians is revealed in the Quran![6]

Fight those who believe not in Allah nor the Last Day, nor hold that forbidden which hath been forbidden by Allah and His Messenger, nor acknowledge the religion of Truth, (even if they are) of the People of the Book, until they pay the Jizya with willing submission, and feel themselves subdued. Quran (9:29)

The "People of the Book" is us! —Jews and Christians. These plans are proven to be active today when Muslims chant, "Death to Israel and death to America," or in fatwas that call for Muslims to kill Jews and Christians or Crusaders.

The reason? Together we are God's way of salvation offered to all humanity and the last bulwark against global Islamic tyranny and the genocide of billions.

Needing a Jewish Believer with me to Bind the Demons in Radical Islam

The Lord started showing me the role of born-again Jews in this battle with Radical Islam while I was teaching at the Evangelism Dunamis event at a conference center on Lake Michigan. During a short break, the Holy Spirit led me to go outside to pray. As I did, I felt a brooding evil, like a tornado forming, about to bring destruction on America. The Holy Spirit said, "These are curses that are being spoken against my people and my Kingdom by radical Imams. You must break these curses or they will continue to gather power for destruction."

This guidance was completely unexpected and out of the flow of the teaching. Nevertheless, I went back into the teaching room, told the group what had happened, and asked what is located in the direction from which I had felt the brooding evil coming. They all answered, "Dearborn! The largest concentration of Muslims in America." As I started to lead the group of over 100 to pray about this, the Holy Spirit clearly said, "Stop! You will not have the full authority in the Name of Jesus Christ to break the power of the deception of Islam unless you are joined by Jews, my chosen people who know me as the Messiah." I was stunned at this guidance! It took me totally by surprise.

I said "Ok, Lord, what do I do?" Just silence back from the Holy Spirit, so I knew the ball was in my court. Feeling rather foolish, I asked, "Is there anyone here in the group who is Jewish?" Immediately a man who had been very obnoxious with relentless and challenging questions about my teaching stepped forward and said, "Yes, I am Jewish!" He went on to say, "I believe that Jesus is the Messiah, my Savior and Lord, but I have not stopped being a Jew, which has been the source of great conflict for me!"

After a short time of mutual confession, we grasped one

another's arms and joined in prayer. The Holy Spirit fell upon us. In the name of Jesus Christ, we broke the curses of Islamists who were proclaiming, "Death to America and Death to Israel." There was power and unity in our prayers that I had not experienced before. The rest of the group joined us in a period of prayer for the Gospel of Jesus Christ to enter the hearts of those in captivity to the demonic stronghold of Radical Islam. After a while, the awareness of brooding evil about to break loose diminished and finally lifted completely. So we moved into a time of praise and worship exalting Messiah Jesus.

Often when I have had such encounters in the heavenlies in which there is the awareness of Jesus' victory, there is some corresponding event on earth. In this case, we never heard anything in the news that served as confirmation that this had been a real engagement with the demonic powers. Sometimes we must keep going forward in obedience, trusting that the Lord is working in ways that cannot be detected in the human realm.

After this prayer engagement, the Jewish brother said, "You're the first Christian who has ever invited me into unity of prayer in the name of Jesus just because I am Jewish! Thank you!" Then he had a deeply troubled look and said, "What if Christians and Jews had been united in such prayer in the 1930s? Would the evil of the Holocaust have been avoided?" That question has haunted me and motivated me to explore the role of the Jewish people and The Land of Israel in the Father's plans for salvation.

I have concluded that the answer is "Yes!" A second Holocaust of Jews and Christians can be and must be avoided. This is why I believe the Holy Spirit is calling us to implement this prayer strategy for the victory of Jesus Christ over the demonic strongholds of Radical Islam.

Understanding the Role of the Jewish People in Defeating Islam

This experience left me deeply struggling to understand the role of Israel and the Jewish people in God's redemptive purposes and in advancing the Kingdom of God on earth. Were the Jews no longer God's chosen people? Had the Old Testament promises of the Land and the role of the Jewish people been replaced by the Christian Church as "spiritual Israel"? Does that mean that for Jews to be saved through Jesus Christ they must stop being Jews and become Christians? On the other hand, were the Jews saved and brought into the Kingdom based on the Old Covenant alone which meant that they did not have to come to salvation through Jesus Christ? However, Jesus (who never stopped being Jewish!) said, "*I am the way, and the truth, and the life: no one cometh unto the Father, but by me.*" (John 14:6 ASV) So that does not work either!

Ben Juster praying for me at the PRMI Community of the Cross in North Carolina

On October 1, 2014, the lights went on for me! Two leaders of the Messianic Jewish movement who are part of Tikkun Ministries International presented a program at the Community of the Cross. [7] Ben Juster and Rabbi David Rudolf explained, in ways that I had never fully grasped before, how God is fulfilling Romans 11, which speaks of the Jewish people coming to salvation through Jesus Christ and yet remaining Jewish. We joined in prayer together—they as born again Jews and I as a born again Gentile. I was overwhelmed with emotion as I realized that I was experiencing the fulfillment of what Paul had presented in Ephesians 2:14-16.

[14]For he is our peace, the one who made both groups into one and who destroyed the middle wall of partition, the hostility, [15]when he nullified in his flesh the law of commandments in decrees. [16]He did this to create in himself one new man out of two,[8] thus making peace, and to reconcile them both in one body to God through the cross, by which the hostility has been killed.

Together we are the *"One New Man out of Two!"* I do not become Jewish, and they do not become Gentile Christians. Together by Jesus Christ, we are the long hoped for new reality of all people joined together in the Kingdom of God by faith in Jesus Christ.

Further, I realized that Tikkun embodies the same movement of the Holy Spirit that PRMI embodies. As we were praying together in the Holy Spirit, with a jolt of joy like recognizing long separated blood brothers, I realized that they and we are part of the same great wave of the Holy Spirit.[9] This was the beginning of my discovering the importance of *"the One New Man out of the Two"* in defeating the demonic strongholds of Radical Islam. How does this unity of Jews and non-Jews all work out in practice? What are the strategic and tactical implications in our war with Satan in Islam?

The Unified Army of the "One New Humanity"

Why do Islamic fanatics the world over chant "Death to Israel" and "Death to America"? Why does their Allah in the Quran (9:29) contain the specific inclusion of Jews and Christians as the People of the Book to be fought against with the sword until we convert to Islam or pay the tax and submit to Islamic hegemony over us?

Satan knows that only Jews and Gentiles who know the

Messiah, in praying together in the power of the Holy Spirit, can defeat the demonic stronghold of Radical Islam that he has raised up to destroy the Kingdom of Jesus Christ. Further, it is only in this unity that the world would know that the Father truly sent his Son Jesus. [10] Satan knows all this. This is why, in the Nazi holocaust of the Jewish people, he nearly succeeded in eliminating God's Kingdom witness on earth. Satan's plans went beyond the genocide of the Jewish people. Through Nazism he planned to quench the witness of the Christian Church.[11]

Now Satan is plotting again in Radical Islam to accomplish his purposes that failed in Nazism. He is so desperate to keep Christians and Jews separated and at odds that he is taking the extreme measures through the new demonic strongholds of Radical Islam, of forcing us all to be converted to Islam, or to be so subjugated that we have no public witness to challenge his hegemony in Islam. Satan's "final solution" to the challenge of Jews and Christians coming together in Jesus Christ is genocide of both who refuse conversion or subjugation.

Blocks to Unity Within Ourselves

How do we practically work out being Jesus' army of the "One New Humanity"? Most of us are not called or able to visit Israel, much less move there. Many of us have no contact at all with Messianic Jews. Once again, I am very much in the learning mode, seeking guidance from the Holy Spirit as to how practically to join in the Father's redemptive plans. I recommend the following:

First, for those of us who are non-Jewish Christians, we need to gain a clear understanding of the Old Testament Jewish roots of our Christian faith. Furthermore, many of us must get past some streams of theology that are contrary to the Bible's view of the role of the Jews in the history of salvation. Especially, we must understand what the Holy Spirit is telling us through Paul in Romans 9, 10, and 11 concerning the final restoration of the Jewish people through coming to faith in Jesus Christ.

For me to wrestle with this, I have had to listen intently to the teaching of two Jewish Messianic scholars, Dr. Dan Juster and Asher Intrater. Through them the Holy Spirit started to open my eyes. However, I still did not get it until I went to Israel and joined them in prayer and worship. Then I started to understand more fully the role of the Jewish people in God's overall redemptive purposes. Frankly, I had to see with my own eyes Satan's intentional attempts through Islam to replace Jewish and Christian holy places before I understood. Throughout Jerusalem, and including the Temple Mount, virtually every place revered by Jews or Christians has a Muslim Mosque built *directly on top of it.* Not down the street, in peaceful harmony and mutual respect. No, ON TOP, so as to obliterate and replace all things Jewish and all things Christian. Seeing is believing. Without this visual evidence, we want to believe that Muslims really, at heart, would like to co-exist peacefully with us. Not so. This expressed desire, at most, is a temporary strategy on the way to replacing the Kingdom of God with the kingdom of Satan.

Second, we must also overcome Satan's strategy to keep Jews and Christians antagonistic to one another. One of the most pernicious over the centuries has been anti-Semitism. This hatred of the Jewish people by Christians has been one of Satan's most effective means of keeping Jews from knowing Jesus as the Messiah. Satan has also used this hatred as the cement to construct demonic strongholds to bring death to the Jewish people and deception and bondage to Christians. We must face this terrible history.

We must ask the Holy Spirit to examine us and bring into the light any seeds of hated that may be hidden within us. In myself, I did not find anything. But upon further examination, there came to my memory remarks made by my parents that now, looking back years later, I realize were anti-Semitic. I have had to repent of all those remarks and cut them off from me just to make sure there is no ground in me for the enemy.

As I was asking the light of Jesus to probe the deep recesses of my heart, a memory came back to me with horror. While growing up we had some wonderful next-door neighbors—an elderly Jewish couple. He worked at the same bank as my father, and they were friends. We knew they were Jewish because along with a Christmas wreath on their front door, in their window was a menorah for Hanukkah. They spoke English with a heavy German accent.

The memory that horrified me was of a group of us boys including my little brother wearing plastic Nazi German style helmets, playing army along the street in front of our houses. The Jewish lady with lovely white hair looked out the window, and I saw the disturbed look on her face. This was long before I was aware of the horrors of the Holocaust, so our game was all in compete innocence. But her look troubled my young soul. She must have talked to my parents. The next day my mother threw away our army helmets and said some things that I did not understand about the terrible suffering the Jews had been through during the war. She also said that they were God's chosen people and that Jesus himself is Jewish. When this memory came back, I was overwhelmed with grief and shame. I needed to confess it to Jesus. How I wish I could have gone back to that lovely couple and asked forgiveness for what I unknowingly did to them as a child.

I urge all of us who are Christians to ask Jesus to search our hearts and reveal anything in us that may be used by Satan to continue this tragic division.

I am personally still working out how this unity in Christ and the army of the "One New Humanity" is to be strategically and tactically deployed. I do, however, trust that as we get past the barriers that divide us, the Holy Spirit will guide us to support each other and work together in the battle.

In Part V, I will return to this topic of the strategic role of Jews who are coming to faith in Messiah Jesus and returning to The Land of Israel. There we describe the waves of the Holy Spirit converging in Jerusalem that are part of God's strategy to bring Muslims to faith in Jesus Christ.

Conclusion to Part II
Engaging the Demonic Powers

It would be wonderful if Jesus would use the unity of the Church and our prayers to force Satan's evil empire just to crumble. Or that suddenly all those in thrall to Islam would just be released from this bondage and turn to faith in Jesus. This is what I saw in my vision of the angelic forces defeating the demonic powers holding human beings in captivity, with those being liberated running and leaping with joy in Jesus Christ. That is a prophetic glimpse of this war's final outcome, to be expected when Satan is utterly defeated and all the nations of the world come streaming into the Holy City. (Revelation 21:23-27)

Another good outcome would be to see Satan's kingdom divided, causing the warriors of Allah to be splintered into warring factions destroying one another. At present, there are hopeful signs that our prayers and the unity of the body of Christ are in some areas dividing Satan's kingdom and Islamists are fighting and killing each other. These are the beginnings of what will be universal at the Last Battle when "every man's sword will be against his brother." (Ezekiel 38:21)

If this time of the "gathering storm" is the final gathering of the armies of Armageddon and the Beast—the Islamic Antichrist—is already appearing, then we can expect this division in the kingdom of Satan to result in the complete defeat of Islam by Jesus Christ. However, we do not know exactly where we are in the end time's countdown. We do not know for sure if these are the final stages of preparation for the last battle.

I personally believe that while that hope is ever before us, we must not expect that God will relieve us from the duty and tribulations of this warfare. It would be a disaster for the advance of the Kingdom of God if we were to take a rest from this prayer and spiritual combat and passively wait for Satan's armies to destroy themselves by their own hands.

Further, in this phase of our warfare I doubt that, short of the return of Jesus, these engagements in the spiritual realm will decisively defeat Satan's strongholds. My doubts are based first on a realistic assessment of the effectiveness of the demonic cloaking protecting the unity of Satan's command. Secondly, an insidious disunity still exists within the body of Christ.

In a time of partial victories on the spiritual front, we must face the grim reality that Jesus calls us to another front in this war. Every battle in the war must be partly military, partly spiritual. Only when we do both the "Joshua" part and the "Moses" part together can we hope to defeat these evil strongholds. As a sober reminder of the task before us, ponder the history of Rees Howells and the students at the Bible College of Wales. They fought and won decisive battles against the demonic powers behind the stronghold of Nazism, but it still required human armies to destroy the human structures of Satan's war machine at the cost of millions of lives. It is to this human front in the war that now we must turn.

Part III
The Second Battlespace

Engaging the Demonized Leaders and Creative Minority
of the Strongholds of Radical Islam

God Removes the Leaders Through Conversion to Christ

Defeating Satan and his organization of evil spirits in the spiritual realm is our priority as intercessors as described in Part II. In Part III we turn our attention to a secondary but necessary part of this war. The human dimension—the individuals, organizations, armies, and human cultures Satan has used to construct the stronghold of Radical Islam. In the actual prayer engagements with the stronghold, our battle will include both spiritual and human dimensions. The human dimension we are about to address includes the entire cultural, ideological, totalitarian, political and legal system that is Islam.

The Root Evil is the Totalitarian, Political Ideology of Islam

What must be defeated to prevail over the stronghold of Islam? It is people, but also an ideology. In this regard, we must be careful to affirm that not all Muslims are terrorists, nor are all Muslims our enemies. While many Muslims, perhaps the vast majority, are peace-loving people, the ideology of Islam, at least in the form embodied by Muhammad and enshrined in the Quran and the Hadith, is not peaceful, loving, or moderate. If we are to win the victory, we must recognize that we are engaged in a war with a political ideology that in its foundation is committed to the destruction of all other political systems and ideologies. Islam is especially hostile to and, as already demonstrated, designed to destroy cultures of human freedom and equality that have arisen out of the Judeo-Christian worldview.

Dr. Sebastian Gorka, whose Hungarian family suffered the totalitarian oppression of Communism, names our enemy for what it really is:

Today, as a nation we face a new totalitarianism, one that is potentially even more dangerous than fascism or communism. Today's threat is *hybrid totalitarianism* that goes beyond man-made justifications for perfecting society along politically defined lines and instead uses the religion of Islam and Allah to justify mass murder.

Our enemy today is again a totalitarian. I call it the global jihadist movement. The members of this movement, be they Al Qaeda, ISIS, or Hezbollah, have a vision of the future world that is exclusive and absolutist. Either the whole planet is under their control or they have lost. There is no middle ground. No peaceful coexistence is possible. Ever.

The infidel must submit or be killed.[1]

The totalitarian visions of jihadism as well as of Communism and Fascism are contrary to our Judeo-Christian worldview. Those who have grown up in Western culture, whether they believe in God or not, have a view of reality with a separation between the sacred and the secular. Americans express this as the "separation between church and state." The basis for this distinction lies within our Judeo-Christian tradition. It is summarized by Jesus when asked if it was right to pay taxes to Caesar or not. When shown a denarius, the coin used for the tax, Jesus said, "'whose image is this, and whose inscription?' They replied, "Caesar's." He said to them, "Then give to Caesar the things that are Caesar's, and to God the things that are God's."' (Matthew 22:17-21) In whose image are we created? God's image. (Genesis 1:26-27) In Jesus' words, humanity is acknowledged to have our own sphere in which we may act with freedom, creativity, and responsibility, but within the framework of relationship with God. This concept is rooted in God's action at creation of giving our first parents Adam and Eve freedom and dominion with the wide parameters access to eat of all the fruit of the garden—including the tree of life—except for the tree of the knowledge of good and evil. This human freedom and responsibility is designed to take place under the sovereignty of God and the Lordship of Jesus Christ. There are, within this framework of human freedom under the Lordship of Jesus Christ, checks against absolute expressions of evil.

Islam allows no space for human freedom; it is of one fabric with all other totalitarian ideologies like Nazism and Communism that have motivated humanity to destroy freedom, creativity, and life itself. Geert Wilders in *Marked for Death*, in his chapter entitled "Islamofascism", points out the basis for this in the Quran as well as in Islamic history. He compares Islam to Nazism:

Usurping the powers of religion, Nazi rulers substituted a political ideology for the conscience of the free individual. Ideocratic states like Nazi Germany are ruled by governments whose legitimacy is grounded in claims to be the guardian of morality and truth. Anyone who opposes such a state is considered to be an enemy of the truth, a vessel of immorality and falsehood who deserves to be silenced. This explains why such states—whether revolutionary France, the Soviet Union, or Nazi Germany—exterminated their perceived enemies with guillotines, gulags, and gas chambers.

There is no fundamental difference between ideocratic states and theocratic states, because the totalitarian impulse erases the difference between state and religion. A state can use religion to enforce draconian social control, such as in Iran or Saudi Arabia today, or it can be totalitarian absent a religious framework, such as the Soviet Union and Nazi Germany. A state can also be rooted in religious principles without being theocratic, such as the United States—a strongly religious country that proudly proclaims itself "one nation under God," as the U.S. Pledge of Allegiance says. This God is the Judeo-Christian God.

"Our Saviour...has taught us to judge the tree by its fruit," Thomas Jefferson, America's third president, wrote to Martin Van Buren, America's eighth president. That is precisely what we should do with regard to Islam, which constitutes the greatest political threat facing the West today. Many people underestimate this threat. Some do not see it at all, believing Islam is merely a religion like any other. The threat, however, is political, because Islam seeks to exert totalitarian control over every aspect of life. Islam claims it all: God's part and also Caesar's.[2]

The fact that Islam's god Allah, working through the messenger Muhammad, imposes on humanity a totalitarian theocracy is final proof that Muhammad's Allah is not the same spiritual being revealed in the Jewish Torah and the Bible. Islam and Christianity are alike in claiming the allegiance of all humankind. However, the different spiritual beings at their root produces entirely different trees which yield different fruit. One of tyranny and death the other of freedom and life. Contrast Jesus with Muhammad and the difference is stark.

Philippines 2:9-11 affirms   the universal Lordship of Jesus Christ:

> [9]As a result God exalted him
>   and gave him the name
>   that is above every name,
> [10]so that at the name of Jesus
>   every knee will bow
>   — in heaven and on earth and under the earth —
> [11]and every tongue confess
>   that Jesus Christ is Lord
>   to the glory of God the Father.

However, his kingship is "not of this world," that is, not a "power and might" kingship because he is "gentle and lowly of heart," and his leadership does not work by force. He writes his laws on hearts by the Spirit. He has received this "name that is above every name" not by the "sword" which he certainly had the power and authority to do because he is the Second Person of the Godhead, but instead:

> [7]Emptied himself
>   by taking on the form of a slave,
>   by looking like other men,

> [8]and by sharing in human nature. He humbled himself,
> by becoming obedient to the point of death
> — even death on a cross! (Philippians 2:7-8)

Allah and his messenger are diametrically opposite to this. Their rule is all by power and might, by the law and by force. Indeed, this spiritual entity demanding it all is the same power who tempted Jesus with the words, [6]"To you I will grant this whole realm—and the glory that goes along with it, for it has been relinquished to me, and I can give it to anyone I wish. [7]So then, if you will worship me, all this will be yours." (Luke 4:6-7) If Jesus had not resisted and had bowed down to the Devil, the result would not have been freedom for humanity, but slavery.

Unlike Jesus and the values embodied in our Judeo-Christian heritage, Hitler, Stalin, Mao Tse Tung, today's Islamic jihadists, and countless other tyrants have all accepted Satan's offer to seize both Caesar's share and God's. The result is always the same—tyrannical, totalitarian forms of human government.

For Islam, this choice was made by its founding prophet who was deceived into taking the Devil's offer. Sam Harris, in a book with whose premise I totally disagree, entitled *The End of Faith: Religion, Terror, and the Future of Reason*, does get it right in confirming that Islam is at war with the West and is an enemy of humanity.

> We are at war with Islam. It may not serve our immediate foreign policy objectives for our political leaders to openly acknowledge this fact, but it is unambiguously so. It is not merely that we are at war with an otherwise peaceful religion that has been "hijacked" by extremists. We are at war with precisely the vision of life that is prescribed for all Muslims in the Koran, and further elaborated in the Hadith, which recounts the sayings and actions of the Prophet. A future in which Islam and the West do not stand

on the brink of mutual annihilation is a future in which most Muslims have learned to ignore most of their canon, just as most Christians have learned to do. Such a transformation is by no means guaranteed to occur, however, given the tenets of Islam.[3]

The rest of Harris' chapter is a devastating critique of Islam as a totalitarian system of oppression. However, he believes that the root problem is faith itself—Christianity, Judaism, Islam, Buddhism—any faith. His theory reflects the liberal progressive worldview, with which, of course, I do not agree. This rejection of all faith because he sees it as the root problem also renders all those who hold this worldview helpless in the fight to overcome the Islamic faith.

Only faith in the true God (Yahweh) revealed in the Jewish Torah and in the New Testament, can defeat this faith in a false god (Allah) embodied in Muhammad (as false prophet) which brings such catastrophic results for humanity. Let us not jettison the truth just because Satan has come up with a counterfeit.

De-Islamization Is the Only Way to Fight ISIS

All who form the core of the stronghold of Radical Islam, whether it is ISIS or Iran or any other expression, are self-proclaimed adherents of Islam. The problem is not that they are extremists or terrorists, but that they are captivated by Islam and are committed to following the commands of Allah given in the Quran and the Hadith and embodied in Muhammad.

In *Front Page Magazine* of the David Horowitz foundation, I found the following article that traces the core of the problem of ISIS to Islam itself: "De-Islamization Is the Only Way to Fight ISIS", by Daniel Greenfield:

It's hard to destroy something if you don't know what it is. And it's hard to know what a thing is if you won't even call it by its name or name its ideology. The left loves root causes, but the root cause of ISIS isn't poverty, unemployment or a lack of democracy...

It's Islam. ISIS is not a reaction. It's the underlying pathology in the Muslim world. Everything planted on top of that, from democracy to dictatorships, from smart phones to soft drinks, suppresses the disease. But the disease is always there. The left insists that Western colonialism is the problem. But the true regional alternative to Western colonialism is slavery, genocide, and the tyranny of jihadist bandit armies...

As long as the Middle East is defined in terms of Islam, some variation of the Islamic State or the Muslim Brotherhood bent on recreating the Caliphate will continue reemerging. We can accept that and give up, but the growing number of Muslim migrants and settlers mean that it will emerge in our country as well.

. . . .

We have a choice between Islamization and de-Islamization...We don't only need to defeat ISIS. We must defeat the culture that makes ISIS inevitable.[4]

This Jewish writer has boldly named the problem and what needs to be done about it. In doing research for this prayer strategy, I have found that it is often those with a Jewish background who are doing the strategic thinking about the threat of Islam. They have learned through terrible experience to take seriously those who say they intend to kill you. The rest of us, if we expect to avert the holocaust promised us by Islamists, must listen to them.

While there are many political approaches that may be taken and indeed must be taken to insure Western culture prevails over the culture of Islam, that is not the solution to the root cause of Islam. The only way that Islamists can be de-Islamized is by being set free from the spiritual bondage of Islam through faith in Jesus Christ. Without this conversion, de-Islamization will lead to some other new deception and new tyranny and the formation of some new stronghold of oppression, very possibly those that afflict Westerners—greed, materialism, shallowness, addictions, brokenness. The only way to de-Islamize the culture created by the deception of Islam is by embedding within the hearts of Muslims the Judeo-Christian and enlightenment cultural values that served as the roots of our democratic, pluralistic, Western society where liberty and opportunity ideally exist for all. While socialization into Western values may result, and must be part of Western society's strategy for defeating the jihad, intercessors must go to the root and source of those values. This is our biblical faith. We must pray that the Church will be empowered by the Holy Spirit and driven by the love of Father to share the biblical Jesus with Muslims everywhere as Son of God, Savior and Lord.

Some may ask why not focus just on evangelism and not worry about the struggles of praying for the advance of Western cultural values? Why do we need to bother with the clash of civilizations at all? This is not arrogance on the part of Westerners. Rather, five thousand years of human history have shown that this particular culture is the best option for taming chaos and restraining tyranny.[5] So the advancement of this particular culture over Islamic culture, must be our goal. While Western culture is not perfect, and must constantly be called back to its own biblical roots, in a fallen world it is the best option for humanity.

The Tactic of Praying for Islamic Leaders to Come to Faith in Jesus Christ

The Holy Spirit is calling us to deploy the tactic of praying that the Father will convert the leaders, around whom the strongholds are forming, to faith in Jesus Christ. The goal is twofold: First, they must be removed from the bondage of Islam where they are so useful to Satan. Second, they may become the means of bringing the Gospel to other Muslims. Jesus converted Saul to become the Apostle Paul. Pray for him to do the same with these Muslim zealots.

Ask our Father to convert the leader of ISIS, Abu Bakr al-Baghdadi, and other key leaders in the world of Radical Islam. By the time you are reading this prayer strategy and are called to apply it, the people through whom Satan is working may well have been removed or the leadership morphed into a different configuration of personalities. So, you must be constantly paying attention to the news as well as listening to the Holy Spirit.

Let us bid our Father to use visions, dreams, signs and wonders, and the testimony of the Christians they are murdering to overwhelm them, whoever they are, with the love and truth of Jesus as the only way to truth and life.

Each time I see a picture of a member of ISIS waving a black  flag or chanting Allah Akbar, or committing an atrocity, I take this as an invitation to bind the evil spirits controlling him in the name of Jesus. I ask the Holy Spirit to move aggressively into the person's mind and heart, showing him the person of Jesus Christ. I ask the Father in the name of Jesus to raise up an army of modern day Islamic Pauls, all converted from persecutors of the Church, to become Jesus' Holy Spirit-empowered witnesses.

In the picture shown, while we do not know their names, you may be led to pray that each of the masked men behind the Christians they are about to behead will come to faith in Jesus Christ. The Lord knows their names and can break into their hearts. I am being led to pray that each of them will become a powerful witness to Jesus Christ and help win over millions of Muslims to saving faith in the Lord.

We may undertake the same prayer when we see pictures of the Mullahs of Iran, or the leaders of Islamic terrorist groups. Whenever we see groups of Muslims chanting death to America or death to Israel, it is an opportunity to pray for a mass outpouring of the Holy Spirit to fall upon them all. In ways beyond our grasp, the Holy Spirit may well use our words of prayer to impact first the spiritual realm, and then the human realm.

I know that for me to pray effectively for these leaders' salvation, I need to ask Jesus to give me the miracle of loving my enemies. You may need to do the same. The other guidelines that Jesus gives us for effective prayer, such as asking in faith, in agreement, and in his name also apply.

Lee Grady's Guidelines for How to Pray When Terrorists Are Beheading Christians

Lee Grady's article in *Charisma Magazine* entitled How to Pray When Terrorists Are Beheading Christians (10:00AM EST 2/18/2015[6]) was most helpful for me. It may be an encouragement for you too if, like me, you are more prone toward vengeance than love.

He expresses this much better than I can. From what I know of him, he truly practices what he recommends. He has, for a number of years, served for me as an example of Christian love to Muslims, which I pray by God's grace to emulate.

After laying out the unthinkable phenomenon of Radical Islamists beheading Christians in the name of Allah, he provides the following excellent guidelines to accomplish this prayer strategy:

> So, what can we do? Military action will likely become necessary, especially if the terror hits our shores. But before suicide bombers attack Dallas or people are beheaded in the streets of Pittsburgh, the Christian community must wake up to the need for emergency prayer. Here are six biblical ways you can pray:
>
> 1. **Pray for a bold witness of the Gospel in the midst of persecution**. Persecution was a reality for the New Testament Church, but it did not stop the early disciples from spreading the gospel. After Peter and John were arrested and told to stop preaching, they announced: "We cannot stop speaking about what we have seen and heard" (Acts 4:20). Pray that persecuted Christians will not be intimidated or silenced by acts of terror.
>
> 2. **Pray for supernatural miracles to confirm the gospel**. When the early Church faced opposition, they prayed not only for boldness but also for a display of God's power. They prayed in unity in Acts 4:29-30: "And now, Lord, take note of their threats, and grant that your bond-servants may speak your word with all confidence, while You extend Your hand to heal, and signs and wonders take place through the name of Your holy servant Jesus." Pray that God will bare His arm and show the world that He is

real, especially to militant Muslims who don't know the Savior.

3. Pray that the seed of the martyrs will produce a harvest of converts. When an angry crowd stoned Stephen, the first martyr of the early Church, he cried out on his knees: "Lord, do not hold this sin against them!" (Acts 7:60) His death was tragic, but it was not in vain. A great outpouring of the Holy Spirit followed his martyrdom. When a born-again Christian gives his or her life for Jesus, God takes note and responds. This could be the greatest hour of spiritual awakening in the Middle East.

4. Pray for heavy conviction to fall on those who persecute the Church. Saul was bent on arresting and killing the early disciples, and he watched as Stephen was martyred. Yet shortly after Saul launched his terror campaign, he fell on his face on the Damascus road and was dramatically converted. (Acts 9:3-4) This same miracle can happen today to leaders of ISIS. Don't limit God's power— and don't pray vindictive prayers of judgment on these people. Pray that the most militant persecutors of the Church will have a head-on collision with the Son of God.

5. Pray for angelic protection and intervention. During one wave of persecution against the New Testament Church, an angel appeared in Peter's prison cell, woke him up, and caused his chains to fall off (see Acts 12:7). Later, after King Herod refused to stop his rule of terror, an angel struck him dead (see 12:23). The Bible does not say the Church prayed for Herod's death; we should never pray with a vengeful spirit, but we should leave room for the wrath of God when mercy runs out.

6. **Pray that the global Christian community will work for peace and justice in the Middle East.** We cannot just sit back and watch our brothers and sisters being beheaded for their faith while we enjoy our First World comforts. We must be in solidarity with them, not only in prayer but also in action. We should actively support government and church leaders who are working behind the scenes for reconciliation, humanitarian aid, and protection for the victims of injustice.

Our response to this wave of terror cannot be fear—or hatred. Don't just curse the darkness. Be proactive by praying fervently. Ask God to unleash in the Middle East a great outpouring of the Holy Spirit that will not only bring peace-loving Muslims to Christ, but also bloodthirsty Islamic militants who are sharpening their knives for the next attack. [7]

This is really good! In my own prayer battle with al-Qaeda over Osama bin Laden, there was about a year when I (with others) were led to pray for his salvation. The battle for me was "Lord, am I willing to let you give me your love for this man to truly pray for his salvation?" As we do this work of prayer for those committing such atrocities, we must be governed by love. But such love as this comes only from the Holy Spirit dwelling within us, who connects our hearts with Jesus' heart.

Martyrdom to Seed the Church Must be Coupled with Prayers and Empowered Witness to Muslims

As I was revising this prayer strategy, I read the following headline in the *Christian Post*. "ISIS Fighter Who 'Enjoyed' Killing Christians Wants to Follow Jesus After Dreaming of Man in White Who Told Him 'You Are Killing My People.' Is God Using 'Jesus Dreams' to Reach Islamic State Militants and Convince Them to Follow Christ?"[8]

Fadely, who appeared on the VOM radio program along with Kevin Sutter, another YWAM leader, went on to share that this Islamic State jihadi confessed not only to killing Christians, but "that he had actually enjoyed doing so.
"He told this YWAM leader that he had begun having dreams of this man in white who came to him and said, 'You are killing my people.' And he started to feel really sick and uneasy about what he was doing," Fadely continued. "The fighter said just before he killed one Christian, the man said, 'I know you will kill me, but I give to you my Bible.' The Christian was killed and this ISIS fighter actually took the Bible and began to read it. In another dream, Jesus asked him to follow him and he was now asking to become a follower of Christ and to be discipled.
"So who knows? Perhaps this man will be like Saul in the Bible that persecuted Christians and be turned from that persecution of the early church to become the Apostle Paul who led it," Fadely added. "God can turn it around." [9]
Note: Gina Fadely is the Director of Youth With A Mission Frontier Mission Inc. (YWAM).

This full article offers the strong confirmation of what we have already known and celebrate: God is sending waves of the Holy Spirit to Muslims, often reaching them through visions, dreams, signs and wonders. Now God is adding the martyrdom of Christians as a further means of conversion.

This testimony confirms the maxim of the 2nd-century Church Father Tertullian who wrote "the blood of martyrs is the seed of the Church." [10] However, martyrdom seeding the Church is not automatic nor the guaranteed outcome. Satan's plan in killing Christians is simply annihilation of the Church. In many locations of Islamic hegemony, the result of Muhammad's campaign of the sword and subjugation of Christians has been that the Christian community has ceased to exist in that place. Much of what is now the heartland of Islam were once flourishing centers of the Christian faith. In many places, the blood of the martyrs is buried by the deceptions of Islam, and while remembered in heaven, on earth they have been forgotten and silenced.

The blood of the martyrs is the seed of the Church, yes—but only if the soil is prepared and the seeds are nurtured and protected with the prayers, spiritual warfare engagement, missionary outreach with the presentation of the gospel. Therefore:

1. Pray that the seed of the martyrs will produce a harvest of converts.

2. Pray for heavy conviction to fall on those who persecute the Church.

I believe that we have a vision of the end times in the book of Revelation of all those who have been martyred for their faith. Among them will be a vast number who have died and will die at the hands of those in the satanic bondage to Islam.

⁴Then I saw thrones and seated on them were those who had been given authority to judge. I also saw the souls of those who had been beheaded because of the testimony

about Jesus and because of the word of God. These had not worshiped the beast or his image and had refused to receive his mark on their forehead or hand. They came to life and reigned with Christ for a thousand years. (Revelation 20:4)

9Now when the Lamb opened the fifth seal, I saw under the altar the souls of those who had been violently killed because of the word of God and because of the testimony they had given. 10 They cried out with a loud voice, "How long, Sovereign Master, holy and true, before you judge those who live on the earth and avenge our blood?" 11Each of them was given a long white robe and they were told to rest for a little longer, until the full number was reached of both their fellow servants and their brothers who were going to be killed just as they had been. (Revelation 6:9-11)

King Jesus—Yeshua—is calling us to join our earnest prayers with the prayers of the vast number of Jews and Christians martyred at the bloody hands of Muslims. These prayers may bring down mercy and grace from the Father upon all in Satan's bondage through Islam. Our prayer and our hope is that these zealots for Allah, imposing Satan's plans for death and bondage will, like St. Paul, be liberated from Satan's deception of Islam. We pray that Jesus will baptize them with the Holy Spirit to be his empowered witnesses. We urgently need these Muslim brothers and sisters as Jesus' friends and co-workers leading the vanguard of the Father's counter-offensive of life by taking the Gospel to the Muslim world. That is our hope and the best option both for the Kingdom of God and for the eternal salvation of those in Islamic bondage.

God Removes the Leaders of Radical Islam by Death

What if the leaders forming the core of these strongholds reject God's gracious outreach to them? The Holy Spirit may well lead us to cooperate with Jesus by praying for their removal from leadership. In certain circumstances, the Holy Spirit may lead us to pray that they will be removed through death.

A storm of protest from faithful Christians may greet this proposal. They may feel that praying for someone to be killed is an unacceptable idea. Let us deal with this difficult subject, and do so in such a way that we do not become as evil as our enemies while not missing the opportunity to cooperate with the Holy Spirit in fulfilling the Father's purposes.

How to Remove Leaders Who Have Built
Fortresses of Death

How God may call us to pray for the removal of a person Satan is using to build a stronghold depends on the system the person is in or has created. In America, Canada, the United Kingdom, or Israel, if a politician is being used to promote evil, we may work through democratic processes to remove him. Christians in these situations need to pray, vote, and engage in the political process.

In situations where a leader or an entire governing system uses death to implement their vision, these options are not available. God may supernaturally intervene with a vision, dream or angelic visitation to get past all these human defenses. But if, by a leader's willful choice, demonic spirits have taken such control that there is no longer room to welcome God's supernatural intervention for grace, what then? There comes a time when the Holy Spirit no longer strives with such a person. As in the example of Hitler or Stalin, the inward deception is upheld by an outward fortress to silence, through imprisonment, torture, and execution, anyone who dares challenge the leader's evil authority. I suspect that with ISIS and other demonic strongholds of Radical Islam, the situation may have reached this level of inward and outward bondage.

The implication is that the more oppressive and dictatorial the system, the more violent the options for their removal become: betrayed and killed in a coup, struck down in a military attack, or killed suddenly by a divinely sent heart attack. Our sovereign King is in charge; however things transpire.

The political, cultural system of Islam and the demonic strongholds built on Islam have chosen the means of death to accomplish their purposes. What is more, through Sharia law, Radical Islam has built an entire system of total control. All those tyrants who choose death and subjugation as the means of imposing their will give their intended victims no choice but to use the same means to resist their plans of death and subjugation. I know all this raises many questions. Is it right for those who follow Jesus Christ to pray for the removal of leaders of a stronghold of death—by means of the death of the leader? Many Christians back off at this point and become squeamish.

Can We Not Just Pray, "Father, Thy Kingdom Come, Thy Will Be Done?"

A brother in Christ while editing this book asked this very good question:

> Brother Brad, this is interesting. But since we are not the Almighty, it is up to him how he'll remove the leaders of the stronghold in response to his children's prayers in Jesus' name.
> I think we need to express our desire first for a Damascus Road experience for the whole lot of them as a way for us to reject our natural response of hatred. You've done that well. How about we call Christians throughout the process simply to leave it in the Lord's hands—that is, "Father, thy kingdom come, thy will be done," as preface to our honest feelings for the Radical Islamist to be killed, shared before the Lord, and then again as our concluding prayer?

Good question. I think that may well be the approach the Holy Spirit will call many intercessors to take. However, there is a major check that I have. What if it is indeed God's will to remove a leader who is working to build a stronghold of death to slaughter others; in this case, potentially millions of people, by killing him or her?

The dilemma is that God has made the decision to give us dominion on earth and to work through us, the body of Christ, in the spiritual realm as intercessors, or to work in the earthly sphere through those common grace structures of governments and military that he established for the welfare of humanity.

This implies that just as the Holy Spirit may work through our intercessions to remove these leaders through converting them to faith in Jesus Christ, he may also work through our intercessions to remove them by killing them. God may answer our prayers for their conversion by direct supernatural intervention of a dream or vision, but he may also answer our prayers by sending someone as Jesus' witness through the preached Word or martyrdom or both. However it works out, our Father invites our involvement. Either way it requires our human participation and faithful obedience.

Likewise, Father may choose to answer our prayers to remove a leader through death, either by direct supernatural intervention or by giving them a heart attack, a debilitating stroke, or a providential accident of friendly fire. He may also turn leaders against one another so that they kill one another. As noted before, that may be the result of our prayers to divide Satan's kingdom. The Father may also choose to answer our prayers through a special operations team or a remote piloted drone sent to kill the leader. For those in the military, it may be through their own hands that the vengeance of the Lord is brought upon those who have chosen death.

The Father Invites our Cooperation with him in Carrying out his Will on Earth

The key in all of this is getting guidance from the Lord as to how to pray and then, when the guidance is hard, not to shrink back with, "let's just pray that God's will may be done." I am convinced that as God's friends and coworkers, he brings us into his plans and expects us to participate with him as he calls. We see this dynamic in the story of Abraham negotiating with Yahweh to preserve the city of Sodom for the sake of a few righteous in Genesis 18. At Abraham's persistence, the Lord agreed to spare the city if only ten were found to be righteous. Not even that many were found. Only Abraham's brother Lot with his with his wife and two daughters were led out of the city before it was consumed in God's wrath. Important for us as intercessors in cooperating the Holy Spirit in dealing those who have chosen the means of death is Abrahams' attitude. He sought mercy for all the inhabitants for the sake of the few righteous even through most were incorrigibly wicked. In the Holy Spirit praying through us which may at times be to bring God's wrath, we must have the heart of Jesus longing for their redemption.

Another example is in Acts chapter 12 when the Church is coming under persecution.

> [1]About that time King Herod laid hands on some from the church to harm them. [2]He had James, the brother of John, executed with a sword. [3]When he saw that this pleased the Jews, he proceeded to arrest Peter too. (This took place during the feast of Unleavened Bread.) (Acts 12:1-3)

It is clear from these actions that King Herod Antipas was continuing the policy of his father Herod the Great of choosing the means of death to destroy the leadership of the nascent church. Satan, having failed to kill the baby Jesus, now was working through Herod to take out the young leadership. At these very beginnings of the Church, the loss of Peter could have been fatal to the movement. The response to this persecution and to Peter being kept in prison guarded by four squads of soldiers is that those in the church were earnestly praying to God for him. (Acts 12:5) We do not know the exact contents of the prayer that the Holy Spirit was leading the members of the early Church to pray. It was no doubt for the release of Peter. I suspect that it was also for God to intervene and to save not just Peter, but the Church from the crushing hand of Herod.

God answered their prayers by miraculous intervention, sending an angel to set Peter free from prison and certain death. Note too that as part of God's answer to their prayers, he also killed King Herod.

> [21]On a day determined in advance, Herod put on his royal robes, sat down on the judgment seat, and made a speech to them. [22]But the crowd began to shout, "The voice of a god, and not of a man!" [23]Immediately an angel of the Lord struck Herod down because he did not give the glory to God, and he was eaten by worms and died. [24]But the word of God kept on increasing and multiplying. (Acts 12:21-24)

The point here is that they were allowing the Holy Spirit to pray through them. They were providing the means by which God was to accomplish his will and intentions on earth. In this case, these means included not just getting Peter out of prison, but also by death removing King Herod through whom Satan was trying to destroy the Church.

God Works through Earnest Prayer

Before applying these lessons learned, we must note the nature of the prayer that the Christians were praying for Peter, which provided the means of God's intervention on earth. It was *earnest* prayer. R.A. Torrey gives a clear explanation:

In the Revised Version, "without ceasing" is rendered

"earnestly." Neither rendering gives the full force of the Greek. The word means literally "stretched-out-ed-ly." It is a pictorial word, and wonderfully expressive. It represents the soul on a stretch of earnest and intense desire. "Intensely" would perhaps come as near translating it as any English word. It is the word used of our Lord in Luke 22:44 where it is said, "He prayed more earnestly: and His sweat was as it were great drops of blood falling down to the ground."

We read in Heb. 5:7 that "in the days of His flesh" Christ "offered up prayers and supplications with strong crying and tears." In Rom. 15:30, Paul beseeches the saints in Rome to STRIVE together with him in their prayers. The word translated "strive" means primarily to contend as in athletic games or in a fight. In other words, the prayer that prevails with God is the prayer into which we put our whole soul, stretching out toward God in intense and agonizing desire. Much of our modern prayer has no power in it because there is no heart in it. We rush into God's presence, run through a string of petitions, jump up and go out. If someone should ask us an hour afterward for what we prayed, oftentimes we could not tell. If we put so little heart into our prayers, we cannot expect God to put much heart into answering them.

We hear much in our day of the rest of faith, but there is such a thing as the fight of faith in prayer as well as in effort. Those who would have us think that they have attained to some sublime height of faith and trust because they never know any agony of conflict or of prayer, have surely gotten beyond their Lord, and beyond the mightiest victors for God, both in effort and prayer, that the ages of Christian history have known. When we learn to come to God with an intensity of desire that wrings the soul, then shall we know a power in prayer that most of us do not know now.

But how shall we attain to this earnestness in prayer? Not by trying to work ourselves up into it. The true method is explained in Rom. 8:26, "And in like manner the Spirit also helpeth our infirmity: for we know not how to pray as we ought; but the Spirit Himself maketh intercession for us with groanings which cannot be uttered." (R.V.) The earnestness that we work up in the energy of the flesh is a repulsive thing. The earnestness wrought in us by the power of the Holy Spirit is pleasing to God. Here again, if we would pray aright, we must look to the Spirit of God to teach us to pray.[1]

God calls us to earnest, Holy Spirit-led prayer in this war with the demonic stronghold of Radical Islam. During this Holy Spirit led and empowered "earnest prayer," we may be specifically told by God what to pray for. At other times, we may not know precisely how to pray, but will welcome the Holy Spirit to pray through us. The secret is to be empowered and led by the Holy Spirit.

So, we must seek Father's guidance in how we are to take part in removing those in leadership who have chosen the means of death. As I have read and studied Dietrich Bonhoeffer, I have come to realize that times may come when we are in prayer communion with our Father when it is fitting to bid him remove tyrants by killing them. In Bonhoeffer's situation, the final decision to join the plot to kill Hitler came only after a long struggle and the realization that the demonic stronghold of Nazism had reached such a level of total control that killing Hitler was the only way to start to unravel the monstrous system he had built.

In all this I know that Yahweh says "Thou shall not murder." But murder is the taking of innocent life. In no place, does Yahweh prohibit capital punishment or killing for defense or even aggressive war when he calls for it. Killing Hitler certainly falls into the category of killing for self-defense. Jesus tells us to "turn the other cheek." But Jesus is talking about personal offenses. He does not tell us to turn the other cheek when a terrorist chops a child's head off and then reaches for the next child if it is within our power to stop the murder. We tend to avoid such calls for violent retribution in the Psalms, but there they are. David declares, *"Let death take my enemies by surprise; let them go down alive to the grave, for evil finds lodging among them."*   (Psalm 55: 15)

Earnest Prayer that the Father would bring Osama bin Laden to Faith in Jesus Christ

For a long time after 9/11, a cohort of intercessors was engaged with breaking the curses spoken by demons through Osama bin Laden and other leaders of al-Qaeda. These were intense engagements in the spiritual realm.

Then the Holy Spirit said to me leading the cohort, "Now pray for his conversion to faith in Jesus Christ." That was a real struggle for me! The Lord said, "Will you let me give you my love for Osama bin Laden so you can pray for his salvation?" After a struggle, I said yes and found that I could love with Jesus' love this man who had brought such death and evil into the world. I found a part of that was forgiving him for the 9/11 terrorist attacks. Others on the cohort did better with this genuine desire to see him converted then I did. So, they took the lead in these prayers.

There was one period of several weeks when the Holy Spirit called and anointed us for earnest intercessory prayer for Osama bin Laden's salvation. We prayed for God to break past the walls of deception and let bin Laden know Jesus Christ. As we were praying, the Lord gave one of the intercessors a clear vision of bin Laden in his place of hiding. In the vision was a young man with access to him who could be a witness to the Gospel. With this vision came the invitation to pray for this young man to be bold and empowered by the Holy Spirit. We were also led to pray that the Holy Spirit would give bin Laden dreams of Jesus to prepare his heart to receive this young man's testimony. In earnest prayer we struggled for bin Laden's soul. The intensity was there only for a few days, during which we suspected that the Holy Spirit was working on him. We, however, continued to pray for bin Laden to know Jesus for many months. We had no way of knowing if any of this was connecting with reality, but we did have much agreement in our spirits that this was the direction to pray.

The Call to Pray for Osama bin Laden's Removal

Then suddenly the guidance clearly and unmistakably came, "Now stop praying for his conversion. I am going to remove him." The other intercessors confirmed this guidance. Then, months later, the Lord said, "Pray now that the demonic cloaking will be pierced and his hiding place will be exposed." In the name of Jesus, we also bound the demonic powers giving him power and authority. We prayed this for months and months. Then the Lord led me to pray for his removal which could take place any way the Lord wanted, like a stroke or heart attack or being betrayed by one of his bodyguards or an accident, or whatever. I felt like the means were God's business. My role was to keep praying.

Then one day, while I was out on a bike ride, the Holy Spirit very clearly said, "Now pray for the protection, guidance and empowerment of the military unit who are going to carry out my plans to remove Osama bin Laden." As I prayed in tongues I was aware of a rushing movement and clashes in the heavenly realms and knew my prayers, in ways I may never understand, were supporting and enabling some sort of military operation that was underway. This clash in the heavenly realms reached a climax and subsided. Then Holy Spirit lifted from me. Not long afterwards, I heard the news and realized that the time of being caught up in the Spirit had coincided with the raid into Pakistan by Seal Team Six. They had killed Osama bin Laden.

I am sure that I was not the only intercessor called into the gap during this battle. I look forward someday to comparing notes with unknown brothers and sisters in Christ who were also moved by the Holy Spirit into this prayer assault at the same time as I! I would also like to have conversations with those involved in the operation to do the same regarding when the breakthrough came.

What I learned from this is that the Father was calling me as his coworker. I also learned that I was not the one making these changes in the focus of the prayer. It was the Holy Spirit. I knew that we make these transitions only at the guidance of the Holy Spirit, and not out of hatred, revenge, or anger. In ways I do not fully understand, but must affirm, our Father depends on us as his friends and coworkers to do his work on earth. We truly have a role in shaping history.

Praying for the Removal of the Leaders Who Have Chosen the Means of Death

This area is so sensitive and so dependent on the guidance of the Holy Spirit that I do not think it is wise to name specific people to pray for. I think we should ask the Holy Spirit to reveal those around whom the demonic stronghold of Radical Islam is coalescing, and then ask the Holy Spirit to guide as to how to pray.

I have personally found it very helpful to have a picture before me as I am seeking this guidance. For instance, I found a picture on the internet of ISIS leader Abu Bakr al-Baghdad. It is clear that he is person around whom Satan is building the demonic stronghiold of ISIS. When I look at his picture I truly do not know how to pray. So, I just pray in the Spirit and am committed to pray according to the guidance the Lord should give. At this writing in 2016 the focus is on Abu Bakr al-Baghdadi but the leaders and those forming the creative minority are constantly changing. Thus to pray according to the guidance of the Holy Spirit requires constant discernment along with prayers to pierce the demonic cloaking.

You will need to pray as led by the Holy Spirit. Please weigh what has been presented here and ask the Holy Spirit to guide you! Let's entrust our thoughts and prayers to our Father, openly and honestly, and then agree with him, "Father, thy kingdom come, thy will be done, on earth as it is in heaven." And Lord, show me how you want me to cooperate with you in praying, "Thy Kingdom come!"

Part IV
The Third Battlespace

Defeating the Jihadist Armies of Radical Islam

Military Force Destroying Jihadist Armies

We can hope that by removing the leaders around whom a stronghold is coalescing, the stronghold itself will come unraveled and lose its power. But whether this happens or not depends on the level of maturity the stronghold has reached when its leaders are removed. At the beginning stages of the stronghold's formation, the removal of key leaders would be a fatal blow. Later, however, when the DNA of the leader and the creative minority has been embedded in an entire organization, the loss of the key leader or visionary has minimal impact on the overall structure. When a stronghold reaches this tipping point, it requires even greater levels of spiritual and human power for it to be destroyed. Then it must be destroyed by opposing human organizations endowed with superior cultural, political and military power.

The Stronger the Stronghold,
the More Force Required to Destroy It

This is the lesson of the growth of Nazism. If, in the early stages of the movement, Hitler had been neutralized, the demonic stronghold of Nazism would not have achieved its enormous power. Even after Hitler gained control of the government and military, Churchill notes in his memoir *The Gathering Storm* the occasions when decisive actions by Britain and France could have stopped the development of the Nazi death machine. For instance, if France and Britain had responded to Hitler's audacious invasion of the Rhineland in violation of the Locarno Treaty with the massive military force they had available to them, there would have been some loss of life, but Hitler's spell of omnipotence would have been broken. There is a very good chance that the military itself would have risen up and removed Adolph Hitler. Even Hitler admitted that, "If France had then marched into the Rhineland, we would have had to withdraw with our tails between our legs."[1] But the Allies, blinded to Satan's true purposes in Nazism, did nothing. Opportunity after opportunity was missed; the demonic fortress of Nazism grew in lethal power until it took the combined forces of Great Britain, the United States and the Soviet Union to destroy it. Then it cost the world millions of deaths and whole nations demolished.

In dealing with the rise of ISIS, opportunities to stop the stronghold when it was just forming were repeatedly missed. At present, removal of a few leaders would make little difference. The death and conquest machine of the Islamic Caliphate has been put in place and is gaining power daily—though at the time of this writing, the American military has managed to take out many key leaders. Now, the effort requires a good deal more than just this one tactic. ISIS must now be stopped by more massive efforts to retake cities and defeat armies. We see the same process in the growing political and military power of the Islamic Republic of Iran. Opposing them will become infinitely more complex and costly if they are allowed to add a nuclear arsenal to their military weapons.

Note too that in this war with Radical Islam, it is not just about military power. We must mobilize and deploy the more intangible sources of power that arise from our culture of freedom and limited government, our Judeo-Christian values and our living faith in the one true God revealed in the Old and New Testament. It is these that give the will and the wisdom to utilize military power. Clausewitz calls these "moral factors," and uses this powerful image:

> Hence most of the matters dealt with in this book [On War] are composed in equal parts of physical and of moral causes and effects. One might say that the physical seem little more than the wooden hilt, while the moral factors are the precious metal, the real weapon, the finely-honed blade.[2]

From the perspective of us as intercessors, the moral and spiritual factors are the most important. However, without the "wooden hilt," the instruments of military force, the spiritual and moral factors will lack the means to defeat Radical Islam. It is to this aspect of physical and military force in combination with the spiritual power and authority that we must focus on in this section.

The Human Organization and War-Making Ability Must Be Destroyed

When any stronghold reaches this level of maturity, it functions like a vortex that accumulates more and more power by drawing more demons, more people, more organization, and more power into itself. When it reaches this stage of development, Satan has acquired the political, economic, cultural, and military means to implement his plans, and these will be carried out until the stronghold itself is destroyed. It will not stop by itself.

This is the situation with Radical Islam in its present and growing forms in ISIS and the Islamic Republic of Iran, as well as with other Radical Islamist movements like Boko Haram. The war we are called to fight and to win against Radical Islam has escalated to the two following objectives:

Self-defense against Satan's Spiritual, Cultural and Military Offensive

In 2016 those Muslims who reject the ideology of Radical Islam must defend against conquest by Radical Islamic forces. Israel too must defend its borders and its right to exist against Radical Islamic movements that have sworn its destruction. And the West must defend against the Islamists' assault against free democratic pluralistic societies based on Judeo-Christian values. Radical Islam is the point of the spear of a whole movement of Islamification of the West which includes destruction of free speech and the takeover of Western culture by imposing Sharia law. Increasingly the West must defend against jihadist military attacks both from within and from without. Jews and Christians must also defend themselves against hatred and violence perpetrated by Radical Islam.

Offensive Operations to Destroy both the Demonic and Human Structures of the Stronghold

The campaign to destroy the destroyer before he destroys us must be indomitably aggressive and unrelenting if we are to take part in the Father's strategies to prevent Satan from carrying out his full plans.

Let us take a moment to consider the issues from the standpoint of Christian ethics, as debated down through the ages. The phase of defensive and offensive warfare against the stronghold of Radical Islam is part of the spiritual warfare dimension part of praying, "Father, thy Kingdom come." (Matthew 6:10) According to the Heidelberg Catechism, this comes under the heading of destroying the works of the Devil. The other part of praying Thy Kingdom come is advancing the Gospel. The Heidelberg Catechism, in explaining the meaning of the Lord's Prayer, reads as follows. (Q & A 123[3])

> Q. What does the second petition mean?
> A. "Your kingdom come" means: Rule us by your Word and Spirit in such a way that more and more we submit to you. Preserve your church and make it grow. Destroy the devil's work; destroy every force which revolts against you and every conspiracy against your holy Word. Do this until your kingdom fully comes, when you will be all in all.

This gives the big picture of our prayer and spiritual warfare into which Lord Jesus has called us in order to advance the Kingdom of God. The Catechism summarizes the teaching of John Calvin which is based on the Bible, that there are two separate operations in the Father's victory strategy.

The first focus is building up the Kingdom of God. The second is defeating the works of the Devil so that God's Kingdom may prevail. Defeating the jihadist armies of Radical Islam on the battlefield, however, is not evangelism by the Christian sword. It is defending ourselves from their assault and liberating those enslaved by Islam so that there will be the freedom for the Gospel to be presented and received.

The unity of these two aspects of praying Father, thy Kingdom Come is necessitated by the spiritual, political, cultural and military unity of both the religion of Islam as well as the demonic stronghold of Radical Islam.

These concepts are often difficult for Westerners, especially American Christians, to grasp. We have been profoundly influenced by the concept of the separation of church and State. Also, there is within Christianity (from St. Augustine and later Martin Luther as well as from the Enlightenment) the understanding of the two related but distinct spheres—the sacred and the secular. There are no such concepts in Islam. They are one![4] And their defeat must include both the spiritual and what we would consider the secular.

Working with Jesus Christ to advance the Kingdom of God to resist and destroy this human and demonic system requires the following additional tactics.

Praying for the Deployment of Military Power

Our call as intercessors is to pray for the deployment of the military power needed to destroy Radical Islam's soldiers, organization, and war-making capabilities. The tragic and terrible reality is that these structures consist of human beings, enslaved and incorporated into a war machine to carry out Satan's designs.

Many of those involved are not themselves demonized or are even evil people. Nevertheless, they are part of a machine that is evil and does have evil intentions. Think back to the Nazi death machine built of millions of human beings—some directly enslaved by the Nazi system, others captivated by Nazi ideology, others coerced to comply with Hitler's orders. Stopping the Nazi conquest and death juggernaut required making total war against this entire system until either it was destroyed or it surrendered. This history of the terrible cost to destroy Nazism does not bode well for defeating Radical Islam which has chosen the same means and is growing in similar totalitarian power.

Our hope is that the wave of the Holy Spirit that is already moving in the Muslim world will dissolve the army and organizations of Radical Islam by bringing them to saving faith in Jesus Christ. The best scenario is that the wave of the Holy Spirit will convert the leaders, unraveling the stronghold from the inside and converting millions of human beings so that the whole tyrannical structure disintegrates.

That is our ardent prayer and also the intention of our work of fulfilling the Great Commission in evangelism and mission. We shall return to this in the last section of the book where I lay out our participation in the four great waves of the Holy Spirit. However, for now we must deal with the military option.

Islam's Bloody Past Points to the Need for Military Force in the Future

Why do we have to move to this level of military engagement? Cannot the forces of moderation and peace prevail against the mature strongholds of Radical Islam? Can the goodness of human nature, or better communication, or even the Gospel of Jesus Christ overcome this evil and subvert Satan's plans of genocide, replacement of God's way of salvation in Christ, and subjugation of the world to Sharia law? We can hope that this will be the case!

However, history does not give us much hope of resisting or pushing back Radical Islam without the use of military force when it has reached the level of a Caliphate and is committed to Muhammad's commands to spread the Islamic deception by means of jihad.

Some Muslim apologists point to the fact that jihad is an inward spiritual conflict. However, the sacred text of Islam that Satan has used to form the demonic stronghold of radical Islam, fourteen hundred years of history, and present genocide against Jews and Christians, belies this definition of jihad.

To the contrary, all the history and present facts show that the stream of Islam going back to Muhammad has chosen and continues to choose physical force—the sword, killing people who do not submit to the creed of Allah or allow themselves to be subjugated and humiliated as second-class citizens under Sharia law. In the past and the present, this choice of these violent means has rendered Jewish and Christian minorities silent and powerless either because they are dead or subjugated.

The jihadists declared war on us; and so we have no choice, unless we want to be exterminated or subjugated, but to fight back with superior force.

The long terrible history of Islam's conquests by the sword and subjugation has largely been obscured from the modern mind and memory by Satan's cloaking. So too, do we tend to forget that the West has succeeded now and then to push back against Islam by military force and often decisive, bloody battles. There is no room here to bring all this to light freshly. Others have done that historical work as well as analysis of the present threats of Radical Islam. I recommend a review of this history from the following:

Hanson, Victor Davis. *Carnage and Culture.* New York: Anchor Books, Random House, Inc., 2001.

Moczar, Diane. *Islam at the Gates: How Christendom Defeated the Ottoman Turks.* Manchester, NH: Sophia Institute Press, 2008.

Spencer, Robert. *The Politically Incorrect Guide to Islam (And the Crusades).* Washington, DC: Regnery Publishing, Inc., 2005.

Spencer, Robert. *Not Peace but a Sword: The Great Chasm Between Christianity and Islam.* San Diego: Catholic Answers, Inc., 2013.

Stark, Rodney. *God's Battalions: The Case for the Crusades.* New York: HarperCollins Publishers, 2009.

When we have gained at least an overview of this history, the conclusion that it will take military force to defeat Radical Islam's war-making abilities no longer seems so outlandish. Instead, this conclusion becomes an urgent necessity if we are to prevent our own extinction.

This fact that military force must be part of the response to Radical Islam is not just my conclusion, but the conclusion of many who have discerned the true nature of Islam in the past. In his book, *Marked for Death: Islam's War Against the West and Me*, Geert Wilders presents the following discernment made by the American founding fathers. This section of the book is a devastating exposé of the many untruths that President Obama told at his famous speech on June 4, 2009 at al-Azhar University in Cairo. Obama made some statements about how Islam is part of America, and that America and Islam "overlap and share common principles." He referred to the founding fathers. A careful reading of Obama's speech reveals a set of interwoven deceptions that are part of Satan's cloaking to keep the world blinded to Islam's true nature and purpose. [5] There is no space to address these many inaccuracies and deceptions, but let me identify the basic ones concerning the war Islam has declared on the West.

First, "There is also no proof that John Adams, America's second president, was convinced of the "tranquility of Muslims," since Adams did not write the lines Obama attributed to him. But John Adams' son, John Quincy Adams, America's sixth president, wrote several essays on the threat that Islam posed throughout world history. Muhammad, Adams argued, "poisoned the sources of human felicity at the fountain, by degrading the condition of the female sex, and the allowance of polygamy; and he declared undistinguishing and exterminating war, as a part of his religion, against all the rest of mankind. THE ESSENCE OF HIS DOCTRINE WAS VIOLENCE AND LUST; TO EXALT THE BRUTAL OVER THE SPIRITUAL PART OF HUMAN NATURE" [emphasis in the original]. Further contradicting Obama's innocent view of Islamic history, John Quincy Adams wrote that war had been raging between Islam and Christianity for twelve hundred years. This conflict he argued, "**cannot cease but by the extinction of that imposture [Islam]**, which has been permitted by Providence to prolong the degeneracy of man." He posited that as long as "the merciless and dissolute dogmas of the false prophet shall furnish motives to human action, there can never be peace upon earth."[6]

Many may dismiss Adams' discernment as extreme and certainly a distortion of the true nature of Islam. Nevertheless, beheaded and crucified Christians, women sold as sex slaves and the mass killings of fellow Muslims all proudly presented to us by ISIS as proof that they are following their prophet Muhammad and obeying the will of Allah, make for ample objective evidence to the contrary.

John Quincy Adams got it right, pointing to the fact that the military option will be the necessary option whenever and wherever Islam gains enough earthy power to implement its goals. John Quincy Adams takes us beyond the military option by noting that this war will not cease except with the "extinction of that imposture [Islam]." From the context of his comments, which I found when I read the original, I am convinced that this "extinction" could only come by Muslims gaining freedom from the deception of Islam by the truth of Jesus Christ. Until then, their defeat on the battlefield is necessary.

One more conclusion drawn from history that displays the necessity of military force comes from Geert Wilders. He quotes Teddy Roosevelt who understood the importance of the victories at Tours and Vienna for the survival of Christian civilization.

> Wherever Mohammedans have had a complete sway, wherever the Christians have been unable to resist them by the sword, Christianity has ultimately disappeared. From the hammer of Charles Martel to the sword of Sobieski, Christianity owed its safety in Europe to the fact that it was able to show that it could and would fight as well as the Mohammedan aggressor.[7]

After about a century pause in Islam's overt war against the West, a pause in which Satan was using the strongholds of Nationalism, Nazism, Fascism and Communism for Westerners to kill and enslave each other, Radical Islam is returning to its traditional role as Satan's tool of death and subjugation of humanity. I am convinced that if Radical Islam is allowed to continue at its present rate and trajectory, both the Christian Church and Western culture will again require the "hammer of

Charles Martel and the sword of Sobieski." [8]

Where does this study of history of Islam's war against the rest of humanity take us? Does it mean that we should stop our work of prayer or give up doing evangelism in order to take up arms? Of course not. We must, however, expand our vision and understanding of all the different assets the Holy Spirit will be mobilizing to ensure Jesus' victory over Satan's plans in Islam. Yes, we continue to pray that Jesus will appear in dreams and visions to Radical Islamists so they may repent and becomes followers of Jesus Christ. In addition, we need to pray ardently for the success of soldiers taking up arms against the entire war-making system, organization and ideology of Radical Islam.

The Responsibility of Government to Wage War

If Satan has used strongholds of Radical Islam to declare not just a spiritual war but actual physical war of extermination against God's chosen and redeemed people—Jews and Christians, and all who refuse to submit to Islam's tyranny, who then is responsible for waging defensive and offensive war to protect them? Is it consistent with the teachings of Jesus for Jews and Christians to take up arms and defend themselves, their families and cultures? Would the Holy Spirit truly lead us as intercessors to pray for military leaders like Charles Martel, Don Juan de Austria, and John III Sobieski to raise up armies who can defeat and kill the jihadists attacking us under the green, yellow and black flags of Islam?

To answer the above questions, we must shift our thinking from the individual and the prohibition against murder to the role of governments established by God for the protection of those in their domains.

For help in these dilemmas I go to John Calvin. He was dealing with the Anabaptists who were advocating not only personal pacifism, but also a pacifist government. Some believed that because the Kingdom of Jesus Christ had come, there was no longer any need for governments or armies.

Their understanding seems similar to that of some today in dealing with the deadly evil of Radical Islam. The argument against killing those who have declared a war of extermination on races and whole cultures seems to come from a lack of understanding that while the Kingdom of Jesus is present and will triumph, we still live in a fallen world. In a fallen world, non-violent resistance and diplomatic initiatives to determined enemies like Nazis, Ottoman Turks and today's Radical Islamists only enables the fulfillment of their genocidal objectives. Therefore, governments, criminal justice systems, and armies are necessary. According to John Calvin, God established these institutions with the responsibility to protect citizens under their sphere of governance from evil people within and from enemies attacking from without.

John Calvin on Just War

In the sections in the *Institutes* concerning Civil Government, the role of the magistrate, and the role of Just War, John Calvin offers the following guidance:

But here a seemingly hard and difficult question arises: for the law of God forbids all Christians to kill [Ex 20:1513; Deut. 5:17; Matt. 5:21], and the prophet prophesies concerning God's holy mountain (the church) that in it men shall not afflict or hurt [Isa. 11:9; 65:25]—how can magistrates be pious men and shedders of blood at the same time?

Yet if we understand that the magistrate in administering punishments does nothing by himself, but carries out the very judgments of God, we shall not be hampered by this scruple. The law of God forbids killing; but that murders may not go unpunished, the Lawgiver himself puts into the hand of his ministers a sword to be drawn against all murderers (Institutes, Book IV, Ch. XX, Sec. 10). [1]

Apply Calvin's principle to the present situation: The demonic stronghold of radical/militant Islam, which includes ISIS and their ilk, are not only committing murder on a grand scale, but have also made genocide and subjugation of others their objective and method, and have further justified it with lies from Satan found in the Quran and Hadith. Further, the demonic stronghold of the Islamic Republic of Iran and their proxy terrorist organizations have publicly declared "Death to America and Death to Israel," and are working tirelessly to obtain the military means of fulfilling their slogans.

In light of these very real threats, Calvin continues to affirm the role of "just war" that those given authority must wage.

Therefore, both natural equity and the nature of the office dictate that princes must be armed not only to restrain the misdeeds of private individuals by judicial punishment, but also to defend by war the dominions entrusted to their safekeeping, if at any time they are under enemy attack. And the Holy Spirit declares such wars to be lawful by many testimonies of Scriptures. (Book IV, Ch. XX. Sec. 12)[2]

Our role as intercessors when we are called into engagements to defeat those strongholds will be to pray for those in governmental authority who have been given a "sword to be drawn against all murderers."

If those given such authority in the face of such a deadly threat do not draw the sword and defend against these murderers, they dishonor Christ by shirking divinely given responsibility while abandoning the people within their sphere of authority to grave dangers of capture, torture, subjugation, or annihilation. When this happens, then we must pray and work for the removal of such leaders and their replacement by those who can provide the leadership needed to discern the threats and mobilize to defeat them. In our democratic nations, this means intercessors are called to discern who has the needed leadership qualities and take part in their election. (We cover more of this complicated political role that we as intercessors fill in the upcoming chapters.)

The Scope of the War Declared on Cultures Based on Judeo-Christian Values

Muhammad and those who take up his jihadist mantle have declared war upon Jews and Christians, and have pursued this war of subjugation and extermination for 1400 years whenever they have had the means to do so.

This war started by Satan through Muhammad is total. Therefore, our prayer response must be total as well. Our ministry of prayer and spiritual warfare must be all-out, so that the Church can fulfill the Great Commission unimpeded, including sharing it with the entire Muslim world. Wherever Satan erects demonic strongholds based on Islam, the way of death chosen and the sword lifted against us, we must also respond not just defensively, but offensively with all the weapons our western culture, science and technology. We must destroy those who have declared total war against us. Until Muslims in word and deed renounce the means of the sword and subjugation chosen by their prophet Mohammed to impose their vision upon us, there will be no lasting peace. Winston

Churchill, who defeated Nazi tyranny by mobilizing the spiritual, moral, cultural and military strengths of "Christian civilization",[3] provided this astute analysis of the need to fight Islam with all the weapons of our Judo-Christian culture. He gives a non-politically correct assessment of the true results of bondage to Satan's deceptions in Islam on humanity. His words are just as relevant today in fighting ISIS as they were in 1899 in Sudan when fighting that era's manifestation of the Islamic anti-Christ, the Mahdi.

How dreadful are the curses which Mohammedanism lays on its votaries! Besides the fanatical frenzy, which is as dangerous in a man as hydrophobia in a dog, there is this fearful fatalistic apathy. The effects are apparent in many countries. Improvident habits, slovenly systems of agriculture, sluggish methods of commerce, and insecurity of property exist wherever the followers of the Prophet rule or live.

A degraded sensualism deprives this life of its grace and refinement; the next of its dignity and sanctity. The fact that in Mohammedan law every woman must belong to some man as his absolute property, either as a child, a wife, or a concubine, must delay the final extinction of slavery until the faith of Islam has ceased to be a great power among men.

Individual Moslems may show splendid qualities, but the influence of the religion paralyzes the social development of those who follow it.

No stronger retrograde force exists in the world. Far from being moribund, Mohammedanism is a militant and proselytizing faith. It has already spread throughout Central Africa, raising fearless warriors at every step; and were it not that Christianity is sheltered in the strong arms of science, the science against which it had vainly struggled, the civilization of modern Europe might fall, as fell the civilization of ancient Rome.[4]

In the 21st century this threat of Islamic jihad to "Christian civilization" is immensely more dangerous than when Churchill provided the unflinching analysis above. The danger is not just jihadist access to modern weapons, but also Western culture's diminishing will to fight back or even to acknowledge the threat.

Since the 1920s, the stronghold of liberal progressivism has been destroying our Judeo-Christian values and worldview within church, synagogue, volunteer organizations, and government institutions. We are losing the moral, spiritual and cultural resources to defend ourselves and defeat the jihad at its spiritual, cultural and religious roots.

This impending disaster unfolding before us is well documented in a prescient book by Mark Steyn, *America Alone: The End of the World as we Know it.*[5] A result of losing our Judeo-Christian values and worldview is "Exhaustion of Civilization." The consequences are summarized as follows:

> Steyn argues that Western nations are so focused on moral and cultural relativism—with "diversity" and "racism" as their new favorite words—that they are unable to see that their existence is threatened. Specifically, he argues that European nations have given up defending themselves and rely on America for their defense. He views anti-Americanism as a symptom of civilizational exhaustion, whether manifested by Muslims (to whom America symbolizes gay porn, children born out of wedlock, immodest women, and immorality) or by Europeans (to whom America symbolizes a crude and radical Christianity, fat rednecks and uncontrolled firearms). However, in his view America is the most benign

hegemonic power the world has ever seen. According to Steyn, America will be the last and only country—as all others will be taken over by Muslims—that will retain its sense of self-preservation, but this is not a given, as America's enemies know that it ran from Vietnam and they hope that America will continue to flee when faced with a challenge.

Steyn's final argument is that the Muslim world will not need to carry out an outright attack. Instead, Europe will collapse from "wimpiness" or "multicultural 'sensitivity,'" leading to betrayal of the state's core values. Thus, during the Danish 'cartoon jihad' of 2006, Jack Straw, then British foreign secretary, hailed the 'sensitivity' of Fleet Street in not reprinting the offending representations of the Prophet."[3]6

This has progressed much further in Western Europe than in America and Canada. The present vulnerability of Europe to jihadist attacks and large antagonistic Muslim communities within them are but harbingers of what will come to the rest of us in the West if not resisted by our first line of defense, which is spiritual and moral.

This clear and present danger from radical Islamists who have declared war against Judeo-Christian culture calls for defensive and offensive war in which all expressions of our culture must take up responsibility. We must defend against those who would rob us of our bulwark against tyranny—free speech. Our judicial system and culture must emphatically resist any encroachments by Sharia law, however subtle or seemingly benign.

Western governments, militaries and cultural institutions must fulfill their God-given responsibilities of defending us by aggressively destroying this enemy with all the weapons and means given them by our Western Culture. For the sake of our Judeo-

Christian faith foundations and all future generations, we must engage in the total war against those who have declared total war against us. This is the responsibility of all nations and all peoples under threat from the nemesis of Radical Islam.

For the Church of Jesus Christ, this is the work of evangelism and missions to all those including Muslims who are not in the Kingdom of God. Also on the spiritual front, we must tirelessly work with the Holy Spirit to mobilize, equip and deploy a global army of intercessors and spiritual warriors who can work with Jesus Christ to defeat the demonic powers behind Islamic strongholds and support those in the cultural and military battlespaces.

The Role of Joshua the Warrior

Praying for the political, military and religious leaders who can lead this multifaceted war to defeat the demonic strongholds of Radical Islam is urgent. Beyond the few key leaders are many others who are called onto the front lines—the warriors actually doing the fighting who also must be backed up and sustained in the spiritual realm by the intercessors. In numerous battlespaces, their task will be to thwart Satan's plans for genocide and Islamic tyranny and to create the conditions where a free, pluralistic and democratic culture may prevail and flourish.

The grave danger in any counterattack against despotic cultural and political systems is that Satan may turn victories won into new means for accomplishing his plans of death and tyranny. After the stronghold of Nazism was defeated, Satan replaced it with the totalitarian oppression and mass death of strongholds of Communism in the Soviet Union and China. Stalin and Mao Zedong (毛泽东) exterminated and subjugated millions more people than Nazism did.[1] So whoever is in leadership and on the frontlines in defeating Radical Islam must possess the leadership gifts and vision to build the foundations for the complete transformation of the spiritual and cultural roots of Radical Islam so that this ideology is no longer fertile soil for Satan's plans of genocide and tyranny.

They must also be wise enough in such a war not to fall into hatred, revenge, and all the other human sins that give Satan ground to build new strongholds of tyranny and death.

What kinds of leaders do we need to pray and work for to be in positions of leadership to lead the United States, Great Britain, Canada, and Israel? Who can face down and prevail over the threat of Islamic jihad? This same question needs to be asked of other nations under threat in Europe, Russia, China, and India.

We can learn much from a review of great battles in the past when the West defeated Islam

A review of the past battles in the centuries-old war with Islam provides us with some guidance as to the qualities of the leaders who defeated Islam in the past. They are models of what is needed in the present and future to gain victory. For nearly 1400 years we have been in a clash of civilizations in which the West has, on several occasions, nearly been overrun by Islamic jihad. The West was saved through decisive military victories as well as the long campaign of the "Reconquista" by Catholic Spain. The West must now triumph again.

To understand this long war, I have found Victor David Hanson, the classical and military historian, helpful in providing profound insights. Dr. Hanson clearly defines the unique strengths and weaknesses that derive from our Western culture with its roots in classical Greek and Roman history, literature and philosophy as well as in the Judeo-Christian faith, history and worldview. His book *Carnage and Culture: Landmark Battles in the Rise of Western Power*, has given me great hope for victory in the war before us. He also warns of the great perils we face. Victory is by no means certain. He reviews two great battles—the battle of Tours in 732[2] and the great naval battle of Lepanto in 1571.[3] These battles decisively pushed back Islamic advance. These are forgotten today, but at the time, the names of the heroes who led these victorious campaigns were on the lips of all Christians in thanks to God for his salvation from the scourge of Islam.

It has been an awakening for me to review this military and cultural history in preparing the prayer strategy for our present battle with Islam. However, I am seeking to push past the cultural, political, and military dimensions of these battles that Dr. Hanson and others have described so brilliantly, to the spiritual dimensions.[4] My intention is to provide a biblical paradigm for how God calls human beings to cooperate with him in defeating his enemies that are both spiritual and human. This will enable us to know better what types of leaders and combinations of leadership the Holy Spirit will call us to pray for.

Two Motifs
Moses the Intercessor and Joshua the Warrior

In Chapter 3, I introduced the roles of Moses, Aaron and Hur as the model roles in an intercessory prayer cohort. We return to the battle against the Amalekites to draw another lesson by adding the role of Joshua, the motif of warrior to the motif of intercessor. They had to work together to defeat those blocking the advance of the Kingdom of God in the Old Testament battle against Amalek in Exodus 17:8-16. This battle provides a paradigm of the interrelationship between the work of prayer in the spiritual realm and the means of how God is working in the material and human realm to answer those prayers. Review the story again from this perspective.

Exodus 17:8-16

[8]Amalek came and attacked Israel in Rephidim. [9]So Moses said to Joshua, "Choose some of our men and go out, fight against Amalek. Tomorrow I will stand on top of the hill with the staff of God in my hand." [10]So Joshua fought against Amalek just as Moses had instructed him; and Moses and Aaron and Hur went up to the top of the hill. [11]Whenever Moses would raise his hands, then Israel prevailed, but whenever he would rest his hands, then Amalek prevailed. [12]When the hands of Moses became heavy, they took a stone and put it under him, and Aaron and Hur held up his hands, one on one side and one on the other, and so his hands were steady until the sun went down. [13]So Joshua destroyed Amalek and his army with the sword. [14]The LORD said to Moses, "Write this as a memorial in the book, and rehearse it in Joshua's hearing; for I will surely wipe out the remembrance of Amalek from under heaven." [15]Moses built an altar, and he called it "The LORD is my Banner," [16]for he said, "For a hand was lifted up to the throne of the LORD--that the LORD will have war with Amalek from generation to generation."

In this battle between the Israelites and the Amalekites, we find a complex interrelationship between the Holy Spirit working in the intercessor in the spiritual realm, and the Holy Spirit working in armies on earth. Through this complex relationship, we see God's Kingdom work taking place. Both Moses and Joshua are warriors, Moses in the spiritual realm with spiritual weapons, and Joshua in the human realm with human weapons. Each had weapons suitable for that realm needed to defeat those similarly armed. Together they defeated those who blocked the fulfillment of God's redemptive plans for humanity.

Moses was up on the hill interceding; Joshua was down in the valley leading the military battle. However, notice the connection between prayer and physical action. Moses was obedient in prayer and Joshua was obedient as he led the army into battle. If either had stopped doing what they were called to do, the battle would have been lost. This is the key lesson here: victory is a *both-and* proposition.

It is important to note that neither Moses nor Joshua worked alone. Aaron and Hur held up Moses' arms and his staff. An army of fellow warriors accompanied Joshua. This teaches us that while there may be prominent leaders, their roles usually incorporate other supporting roles. All through history, we find the Lord working through his anointed and gifted servants in these two roles of Moses and Joshua to defeat Satan's strongholds.

This dynamic is so essential for victory over strongholds that are both demonic and human, that intercessors and military warriors must understand it. Once grasped, this interpretive framework helps us understand the historical data. We see these roles showing up repeatedly wherever there are victories over tyranny.

For instance, in the colossal battle to defeat Nazism, we find the Moses role modeled in the intercessor Rees Howells, who was joined by the students and staff of the Bible College of Wales and countless others on the home front praying for their loved ones on the frontlines. The Joshua role was embodied in the commanders and armies that fought on the battlefield. The Joshua role is especially evident in great wartime leaders such as Prime Minister Sir Winston Churchill and President Roosevelt and in such British and American generals as Bernard Montgomery and Dwight D. Eisenhower. Just as Joshua at the battle against Amalek was joined by an army, so too were these great wartime leaders joined by vast armies implementing their strategies for victory. Let us apply this motif to a decisive battle where Islam was defeated and pushed back: The Siege of Vienna on September 11, 1683.

The Motifs of Moses and Joshua
at the Battle of Vienna on September 11-12, 1683

The date was September 11, 1683. A massive army of 250,000-300,000 Muslims had gathered at the walls of Vienna, ready to take over the rest of Western Christendom. Their months-long siege had reduced the remaining 5000 defenders of the city to starvation and a plague of dysentery.

The Muslims were tunneling under the walls and placing massive explosive charges. The Christian relief army had just arrived with only about 70,000 soldiers, far fewer than the besieged had hoped for. The situation looked bleak, as if the city would fall and Islam, in short order, would be marching on to Rome. Then, on September 12th the Muslim army was so completely defeated that the tide was turned. Islam was repelled and the Islamic Caliphate started its long retreat from Western Europe. What happened?

This amazing victory, a miracle, I believe, took place because of two great men of Christian faith. Marco d'Aviano, a Capuchin friar, took on the Moses role of intercessor and spiritual warrior, while the King of Poland, Jan III Sobieski, assumed the warrior role of Joshua with an army and the right strategy to win the earthly victory. This great battle and the spiritual dynamics of these two great men of God, is depicted in a recent movie entitled, "Day of the Siege." Be assured this will not go down in history as a great movie! However, they did an amazing job of depicting Marco the friar as a man of great Christian faith.[5]

The leader who embodied the prayer work as well as bringing unity to the Christian factions was Marco d'Aviano, the Capuchin friar, who was committed to bringing Muslims to salvation in Jesus

Christ even if he was martyred in his efforts. The Holy Spirit anointed him to move in signs and wonders. He was a man of prayer. While Marco d'Aviano had a passion to bring Muslims to faith in Jesus Christ, he also saw the need for the military to defeat the armies of Islam, and he worked among the Christian armies to prepare them for battle. "He always maintained a strictly religious spirit, to which any needless violence and cruelty were repugnant. As a result, at the siege of Belgrade several hundred Muslim soldiers successfully appealed to him personally, in order to avoid being massacred upon capture."[6] Actions such as this demonstrated the spirit of Jesus Christ even in the context of war.

Marco d'Aviano - Monument in front of the Church of the Capuchins in Vienna
Picture 2005 taken by Herwig Reidlinger.
Creative Commons

Marco d'Aviano also saw the threat to the Christian faith posed by Islam and worked fervently to get the shortsighted Christian churches, Catholic, Orthodox, and Protestant, to unite against the Muslim threat to the Kingdom of Jesus Christ. He was the spiritual confidant of Leopold I, Holy Roman Emperor, and had access and influence among the Christian nobility. Much credit goes to Marco d'Aviano for building the coalition of Christian forces required to defeat the stronghold of Islam both in the realm of the spirit and on the battlefield.

He spent most of the day of the battle, September 12th, in prayer in a small chapel, except for the time depicted in the statue to the left, when he stood with a Cross against the army of Islam before the great cavalry charge that won the battle. (This is depicted in the famous statue of him in Vienna,

290

Austria.)

Jan III Sobieski, the King of Poland, fought in the warrior role of Joshua. He put aside his political differences and ambitions to heed the call of the Pope to go to the aid of Vienna to save Western Christendom from Islam. He was well equipped for this decisive battle. He had served in Istanbul as an ambassador, was fluent in Turkish, and knew and respected the Ottomans. He had defeated them in other battles. What is more, he had developed the best cavalry of the time in the Winged Hussars. He was also a man of great faith and tactical skill.

After Sobieski's victory, he revealed the true nature of his faith and character when he paraphrased Julius Caesar's famous

quotation "Veni, vidi, vici," (I came, I saw, I conquered) by saying "Veni, vidi, Deus vicit" (I came, I saw, God conquered)[7]

King John III Sobieski sending Message of Victory to the Pope, after the Battle of Vienna - Public Domain

As a glimpse into the character of the stronghold of Islam embodied in the Ottoman Caliphate that sent this invasion force, we have this account: "The Muslim commander, at one point during the battle, Kara Mustafa panicked and ordered the execution of 30,000 Christian hostages—mostly women and children."[8]

Perhaps he panicked? But then again, perhaps not! In the face of certain defeat, he could just as well have panicked and shown mercy and released them. However, Islam is not a religion of mercy. The murder of the 30,000 defenseless captive Christians reveals the heart of Muhammad's religion and Satan's plans for genocide of

Jews and Christians through the strongholds built from the Quran and the Hadith. It is also consistent with Muslims' genocidal behavior for centuries as well as in the present.[9] The fate of Kara Mustafa was also consistent with that of one of the Sultan's slaves who disappointed his master. After escaping death at the battle, he was strangled to death on orders of the Sultan.

Jon III Sobieski went on to win other battles against the armies of Islam. The Pope named him "Defender of the Faith."[10] Marco d'Aviano, the Capuchin friar, continued as intercessor Moses. This service to the Church and the advancement of the Kingdom of God was acknowledged on April 27, 2003, when Pope John Paul II beatified him. "In order to honour his valiant defense of the Faith, the countless conversions and miracles he inspired in his own lifetime and the incredible graces that he gave to Austria and Vienna..."[11]

The Four Qualities Leaders Need to Defeat Radical Islam

From this summary of the Battle of Vienna, supplemented with a study of other similar battles, I have concluded the following that our Father worked to bring victory by raising up a team of military, political, cultural and spiritual leaders who converged to provide 17th century Moses and Joshua. A team of leaders today will need to have the following characteristics:

1. First, the leaders must be able to discern and name the deadly threat that Radical Islam poses not just to the Jewish and Christian faith, but also to Western culture and our institutions of individual liberty and diversity.

2. Second, the leaders must be able to draw together a coalition of governments and peoples of diverse faiths, cultures, and interests to fight Radical Islam.

3. Third, the leaders must be warriors who know the enemy and who can mobilize the strengths of the West to defeat the jihadist armies decisively.

4. Fourth, the leaders must understand the spiritual dimensions of the battle with Islam and can mobilize the spiritual resources that are available, which would include welcoming the work of intercessors.

Our role as intercessors will first be to pray for Father to raise up leaders with these characteristics. Secondly, we must support them in prayer as they wage war.

As we survey the cast of those in leadership at any moment in the flow of world events, there are many potential leaders whom God could use. But there needs to be the right convergence of people, as well as empowered positions, for this to take place.

Part of the difficulty in praying for and working for this convergence (such as voting politicians in or out of office) is that in the fog of the moment, we often do not know what is taking place in the counsels of government or in relationships between leaders. Often these convergences are seen only in retrospect, and when the fruit of their concerted actions have been proven over time. The battle named above at the gates of Vienna in 1683 is a prime example. We now know, by hindsight, that this was the first step in forcing the long slow retreat of Islam from Europe. We also know that this decisive victory required the convergence of several leaders coming together—the Pope, Marco d'Aviano, and the King of Poland, Jon III Sobieski with his Winged Hussars. But for those Christians called to pray for this desperate situation, very little was clear.

So how do we pray for leaders and the convergence of their talents and relationships when all is shrouded in the confusion of the moment?

- First, we must learn the facts and to analyze those facts. We must be students of history and stay attentive to unfolding human events.

- Second, we must ask the Lord about his big picture plans and whom he is calling to take part in his plans to defeat Islam. Take note these may not all be born again Christians, but they must be those who appreciate and will uphold our Judeo-Christian values and our Western democratic culture and ideals they have produced.

Our role is to pray for this convergence to take place before it is too late, before Satan has all the human means to unleash his plans for the full replacement of Jews and Christians through genocide and Islamic hegemony. For many of us having prayed for these leaders, the Holy Spirit may well keep us on duty to continue to pray for them.

Praying for the Soldiers on the Frontlines to Defeat Jihadist Armies

In addition to Joshua the commander, there is an entire army in the valley fighting in the field. What about them? In the biblical account, the focus is on the specific cohort of Moses, Aaron and Hur and the leader Joshua which also includes his army. This illustrates the principle that often an anointed cohort will be called to focus prayers on those at the top either of God's or Satan's chains of command. These are those with the most influence either in the Kingdom of God or in Satan's empire. The Holy Spirit, however, does not neglect the need for the same dynamic of intercessors praying for individuals on the frontlines. It is indeed the sum of their combined actions that enable the visions and battle plans of those in command to be fulfilled. In the case of the battle with Amalek, the powerful prayers of the cohort of Moses, Aaron and Hur, would have accomplished nothing had not Joshua been accompanied by an army in which each was doing his part in the fighting. In this vast drama of advancing the Kingdom of God over the empire of Satan, in which there are millions of actors, the Holy Spirit is managing the prayer work for the high-profile leaders as well as for the countless unnamed individuals. No other commander but Jesus can manage such a feat of support for all who are called to participate in his campaigns.

In the next chapter, I will illustrate the dynamics of Moses and Joshua and the four leadership characteristics I experienced as an intercessor for President George W. Bush in the War on Terror. I also address the important role of intercessors to pray for those on the frontlines of the battles against Satan's jihadist slave armies.

Interceding for President Bush and for Soldiers on the Frontlines

I seriously pondered leaving this chapter out of this book. I know that what follows may be a little much for many readers. It is one thing to deal with Islam's attacks against the West on September 11, 1683. It is risky to deal with Islam's attack against the West on September 11, 2001. It is especially hazardous to name President George W. Bush who led the counter-offensive against the demonic stronghold of Radical Islam in its al-Qaeda expression. Unlike the battle of Vienna, we do not look back over three centuries where we can fully appreciate the courageous decisions and heroic leadership by Marco d'Aviano and Jan III Sobieski. History has not yet rendered its verdict on the decisions and leadership provided during and after the terrorist attacks by the team of leaders gathered by President Bush. We are still in a war with Radical Islam in which the outcome is undecided.

In addition to the key leaders at the siege of Vienna in 1683, there were the thousands of individual soldiers whose courage and sacrifice enabled the leaders' strategy to be victorious. Their names are forgotten, but the fruit of their combined actions are vindicated by history. Not so with those warriors in our own day who fought in Iraq and Afghanistan. Even as I write in 2016 there are still many on the frontlines of this war with Radical Islam. Like those who lead them, the verdict is not yet in as to the long-term results of their actions.

I tell of these prayer engagements concerning President Bush and the soldiers on the frontlines, because these were the battlespaces where I learned to trust the Holy Spirit and to follow Jesus, our commander, into this battle with Radical Islam. I share these two stories to provide encouragement that our prayer engagements, whether for leaders or for the foot soldiers, really do make a difference. We all have a part in victory over evil.

The Call to Intercede for George W. Bush

In the second chapter of this book, I described my call first to pray for George W. Bush while the election was still undecided. I then was called into the gap to intercede for the President and the nation before, during and after the terrorist attacks of September 11, 2001. This call upon me did not lift until the end of his second term in January, 2009.

Over the years that followed, the Lord constantly gave me specific instructions of how to pray for the President and the prosecution of the war against Radical Islam. I was intensely aware that the Holy Spirit had called me to join a whole host of other Moses workers to provide the intercessory prayer support in the spiritual realm for a host of Joshua workers in the earthly realm also called into this battle. Chief among them was President Bush.

Most of the time during this prayer adventure I had no direct communication with President Bush or with any one in his administration. What kept me going and showed me that I was not delusional was in reading the *Wall Street Journal*, listening to Fox News, and after 2003, reading Robert Spencer's *Jihad Watch* web site. These reports confirmed that the prayer directions I was getting were connected to and facilitating the events in the human sphere.

The Spiritual Preparation for George W. Bush to Call Those into the Roles of Moses and Joshua

I believe that what prepared President George W. Bush for this assignment to lead the post 9/11 war against Islamic jihad were the same qualifications that equipped Marco d'Aviano, and Jon III Sobieski to take part in Jesus' victory over Islam at the gates of Vienna. It is his vital Christian faith that was biblical, Trinitarian, and centered in a personal relationship with Jesus Christ. [1]

In addition, all three of these leaders had the wisdom and humility to gather around themselves those who would provide talents and leadership to meet the challenges of their day. Moreover, whether by the direct guidance of the Holy Spirit, or the God given talent for leadership, they mobilized those characteristics needed to generally fit into God's way of advancing His Kingdom on earth, which is revealed in the motifs of Moses and Joshua.

President Bush in his memoir *Decision Points* reveals the careful process of finding the right people who could develop the strategies and implement the effective tactics to achieve the goals of winning the war over al-Qaeda. President Bush was also aware of the need for the role of the Moses workers.

Were we, this small group of PRMI intercessors, the only ones praying for the President? Of course not! I am sure that many thousands of Christians were praying for him. I also know from President Bush's own testimony that he had a personal relationship

Billy Graham. I live in the same community where Billy Graham lives and attend the same church that he and his wife Ruth attended. Often through prayer requests, we knew that Dr. Graham from time to time was in prayer with President Bush. There were other men and women of God in this Moses role who were no doubt part of this spiritual support network for President Bush. The President alludes to their role in his book by giving the example of the Camp David base chaplain.

> The chaplain in 2006, forty-eight-year-old Navy Lieutenant Commander Stan Fornea, was one of the best preachers I've ever heard. "Evil is real, biblical, and prevalent", he said in one sermon. "Some say ignore it, some say it doesn't exist. But evil must not be ignored, it must be restrained."[2]

A Surprise Invitation to the White House

I had a completely hidden Moses role of interceding for President Bush for years. Then in May of 2005 I received the astonishing invitation to visit President Bush at the White House. How this invitation came, to this day I do not know. It may have just been a small part of the Holy Spirit directing the Father's grand strategy of defeating evil and advancing the Kingdom of Jesus Christ. I arrived for the hour-and-a-half meeting with about twelve other church leaders. President Bush greeted each of us by name. When it came my turn I assured him that I had for a long time been interceding for him. He gave me a hug and said, "Yes, I know! Thank you! Please continue!" I was stunned!

Meeting President George W. Bush in 2005 at a small gathering at the White House

To put this strange meeting with key leaders of the evangelical and charismatic churches into perspective, we need to look back at the history. After the terrorist attacks of September 11th under President Bush's leadership, the war on terror was launched and had many successes. Then as the war wore on, 2005 and 2006 became low points for President Bush. Iraq was a disaster and *getting worse. Everything was* at the bottom. I realize now that the small group of us who were in various roles of spiritual leadership in the Church were invited to the White House at the nadir of the President's Freedom Agenda and the War on Terrorism. President Bush was reaching out to us as spiritual leaders in order to mobilize the work of prayer needed to reverse the tide of evil in Iraq and the world.

In our meeting, President Bush said as much! He shared his own personal testimony of coming to faith in Jesus Christ. He acknowledged that his decision to invade Iraq in the first place was no doubt problematic to some. He asked for prayer and said, "How can I ever tell the secular press how much I personally need prayer support, and how critically important prayer is in defeating these evils..." The meeting was concluded with laying hands on him and praying for him to have the wisdom and the anointing for Godly leadership. It was an altogether amazing experience, and I will tell you that I experienced the Holy Spirit powerfully present and Jesus Christ glorified in that meeting.

Although the Holy Spirit had already called me to be an

intercessor for President Bush and to be engaged in spiritual battles against Radical Islam, after that personal visit my intercessions increased. I suspect that it was the same for the others who attended that meeting. In 2007 President Bush, against all public opinion, launched the surge with the appointment of a gifted Joshua, General Petraeus, who gained the victory in Iraq. Dr. David Hanson named General Petraeus among the "Savior Generals" who won wars that were lost.[3]

General Petraeus was like a John III Sobieski, just the warrior needed to defeat this evil of an Islamic insurgency. He understood the enemy and came up with the right strategy and tactics. Of course, there were many Joshua workers involved with the coalition soldiers fighting on the frontlines. But it was President Bush who could see what was needed and gave him the command. All of this was being undergirded by a host of Moses workers who were not only praying for wisdom and guidance, but were being used by Jesus Christ to defeat the demonic powers in the heavenlies, clearing the way for victories on earth.

Another whole book could be written on the prayer engagements that took place during this period of the surge. What was learned has been distilled into the prayer tactics and strategies presented to you in this book. I felt it a great honor that the Holy Spirit called me into serving as an intercessor for President Bush during this tumultuous period in the war with Radical Islam. Frankly I find it all rather inexplicable that the Holy Spirit called me to have a part; but then, it is always that way for those of us called into this army of intercessors.

Now, looking at the present world situation with the strongholds of Radical Islam apparently in the ascendency, it is tempting either to blame the decisions of the Bush administration for the present disasters or to assume that nothing of value was achieved. But there were significant achievements and true victories over the strongholds of death and tyranny. President Bush summarizes the result of the surge as follows:

> Years from now, historians may look back and see the surge as a foregone conclusion, an inevitable bridge between the years of violence that followed liberation and the democracy that emerged. Nothing about the surge felt inevitable at the time. Public opinion ran strongly against it. Congress tried to block it. The enemy fought relentlessly to break our will.
>
> Yet thanks to the skill and courage of our troops, the new counter-insurgency strategy we adopted, the superb coordination between our civilian and military efforts, and the strong support we provided for Iraq's political leaders, a war widely written off as a failure has a chance to end in success. By the time I left office, the violence had declined dramatically. Economic and political activity had resumed. Al Qaeda had suffered a significant military and ideological defeat. In March 2010, Iraqis went to the polls again. In a headline unimaginable three years earlier, Newsweek ran a cover story titled "Victory at Last: Emergence of a Democratic Iraq."
>
> ....
>
> Every American who served in Iraq hoped to make our nation safer, gave twenty-five million people the chance to live in freedom, and changed the direction of the Middle East for generations to come. There are things we got wrong in Iraq, but that cause is eternally right."[4]

That this is not just President Bush trying to justify his decisions and claim his legacy is affirmed by Victor Davis Hanson and many others. That victory, however, was squandered by both the leaders of Iraq and by President Obama, who pulled all US forces out of Iraq against the advice of both military and government leaders, and against the lessons of history.[5] Those failures of vision, leadership and common sense do not detract from the astonishing achievement of brilliant leadership represented by President Bush, who was able to pull together a winning team that included capable Moses and Joshua workers that God has established as his means for defeating Satan's strongholds.

One other aspect of President Bush's leadership that is rarely acknowledged and certainly not appreciated, but which, in my perspective, confirms that he was God's chosen leader is this: he had the foresight and the courage to wage preemptive war against the demonic strongholds of death that were being built in al-Qaeda and the genocidal regime of Saddam Hussein. The problem with waging spiritual and earthly preemptive war is that the world sees only the inevitable disasters and foibles that always take place in any war, and for which the leader is always blamed. It is also easy to do what many are doing now, which is blaming the present rise of ISIS and Iran on President Bush's war on terror and the invasion of Iraq. The problem is that most people cannot imagine what the consequences of not waging preemptive war would have been.

Only the few with the gift of spiritual discernment see with clarity what would have happened if the course of appeasement would have been followed and the strongholds had been left to grow to full maturity. With the advent of nuclear weapons, where one bomb can wipe a whole nation off the map, we need leaders with the spiritual and political gifts demonstrated by President George W. Bush. Praying in such leaders will be the urgent task of the intercessors as the storm of Radical Islam continues to gather strength.

Praying for Those on the Frontlines of the Battlespace

In God's master strategy for victory some intercessors will be called to pray for those in positions of significant leadership. It is there that Father will often use our prayers to have national or global impact. Lord will also call intercessors to focus on those who are not in major leadership roles but on the frontlines of the battles.

During this period of the wars in Afghanistan and Iraq, many of us in Canada, the United Kingdom and the United States have friends or relatives in the military. Of course, we are called to pray for them. They are the Joshua workers on the front lines. We on the home front are called to do the Moses work of intercession for them.

These wars in far off places have been close to home for my family. My son-in-law has been deployed a number of times in the Middle East for extended periods in combat. I was often burdened for my daughter while her husband was deployed. We would arrange for her to come home for extended visits. My wife would also go visit her to help with the children, especially when there were special needs. I would call my daughter at least once a day to check in and support her, and she would often tell me specific prayer requests that had come in from her husband. He could give no details, but would say we have some challenges today. My daughter would pass those on to me.

An Engagement Praying for My Son-in-law

Most of the time, my prayers for her husband and for the other coalition solders were general prayers for protection and guidance. Then one morning I received urgent guidance to pray for his protection, as if he were under major attack and in grave danger, though whether physical or spiritual I did not know. A part of the guidance was, "Lord, speak clearly to my son-in-law and let him hear and obey instantly so as to avoid danger." I felt the Holy Spirit moving through me and then the anointing for this prayer lifted and I went on with the day. That evening my daughter called saying, "Daddy, were you called to pray today more than normal?" I told her what had happened. It turned out that her mother-in-law and the prayer group at her church, who had become an intercessory prayer cohort, had also been strongly impressed to pray.

"I thought so! Praise God!" My daughter shouted into the phone. Her husband had just come from the battlefield to say, "You must have been praying for me today. I nearly got killed." He told her that his unit had provided cover for a bomb squad to defuse the bomb in a van. They had disarmed the bomb. Then my son-in-law went up to the van to confirm it was ok before waving his troops forward. The bomb squad said all was ok, but just at that moment my son-in-law said, "I got this crazy nudge that I had to go back to my Humvee to check on some paper work. It was so strong and emphatic that I turned immediately and got into the Humvee. The moment I shut the door, there was an enormous explosion killing the two soldiers in the bomb squad, but my platoon was safe, and amazingly so was I! I felt God's protection."

God had just provided me with a startling example of the Moses-Joshua principle at work. As a remarkable coincidence, I was on an airplane several weeks later returning to England and sat beside an American military officer. In our conversation, I learned that he knew about this incident. I told him that a group of us had been led to pray. He said, "You know, while the loss of the two was tragic, we have many times felt the prayers and through them God's protection for many of our solders." I told him about the dynamic between the Moses intercessors on the mountain in prayer and the Joshua warriors in the valley fighting the enemies. His response was, "Yes! I see the dynamic at work often! Please encourage the intercessors. Let them know how much we need them if we are going to win this war."

Praying for the Military to Destroy the Demonic Stronghold of Radical Islam

We are called to pray for victory over the stronghold of Radical Islam that is both spiritual as well as military because strongholds are both human and demonic. The tragic reality is that Satan's stronghold through Radical Islam is not just spiritual in nature, but also political, cultural and military.

We must pray for those in political leadership who have a God-given responsibility to wage war against all who have declared war against the nations ISIS has named the "Nations of the Cross." This includes all nations that have been influenced by Christianity. For those in the demonic stronghold of Radical Islam, it matters not that we are divided into Roman Catholic, Orthodox or Protestant expressions. We are condemned to either subjugation or extermination regardless. We must unite to defeat this common foe as it morphs and twists itself into new forms. We must also pray for those who are fighting on the frontlines who the ones carrying out the battle plans of the leaders. We must pray for total and decisive victory over Satan's jihadist slave armies.

Does this mean total war against all Muslims?

Does this mean total war against all Muslims? Of course not. It does mean waging defensive and offensive war against Radical Islamists who have declared war on us. Radical Islam has also declared war on many fellow Muslims who do not measure up to the Islamist fanatical Wahhabi creed, or who refuse to submit to enslavement by Iranian clerics. Those Muslims are our allies in this battle. Indeed, they are on the frontlines of the war because this deadly cancer threatens to destroy them before us.

This is why we are called beyond purely defensive operations into the offensive of advancing the Kingdom of Jesus Christ. In the final part of this prayer strategy, we move to interceding according to the Father's strategy of sending waves of the Holy Spirit into Muslim lands. These waves, which we have learned to call "great awakenings," are moving history closer to fulfilling the Great Commission by sweeping large numbers of Muslims into the Kingdom of Jesus Christ.   These waves of the Holy Spirit are mobilizing, equipping and deploying Christ's armies of the Cross, bringing liberation to all humanity.

Part V
Closing the Ring

Four Waves of the Holy Spirit Converging on Jerusalem
Bringing the Gospel into the Muslim World

-

The Father's Strategy to Fulfill the Great Commission

Defeating the demonic strongholds of Radical Islam in the heavenlies and on earthly battlefields is the Father's secondary campaign. His primary campaign is the advancement of the Gospel of Jesus Christ into the Muslim world and the fulfillment of the Great Commission. The Father's will is that all those in bondage to Islam know his love and salvation through His Son Jesus. The Holy Spirit is calling us as his friends and coworkers to join the work of achieving this goal. For all who are weary of the struggles of intercession and unrelenting warfare, this next part is the reward for all our labors.

The Father's Master Strategy for Fulfilling the Great Commission

Having received all authority in heaven and on earth, Jesus gave the Church the commission to, "go and make disciples of all nations, baptizing them in the name of the Father and the Son and the Holy Spirit, teaching them to obey everything I have commanded you." (Matthew 28:18-20) This is a mission of God's grace that is based on all the points that are rejected by Satan through the deception of Islam.

> [46]Thus it stands written that the Christ would suffer and would rise from the dead on the third day, [47]and repentance for the forgiveness of sins would be proclaimed in his name to all nations, beginning from Jerusalem. [48]You are witnesses of these things. (Luke 24:46-48)

How are we to fulfill this humanly impossible mission? We have already addressed this question in Book I, contrasting God's methods with Satan's methods of genocide and subjugation to extend the creed of Islam. Heaven or hell, life or death, the plans of God or the plans of Satan all hinge on the means chosen. In much of this prayer strategy, as we have had engagements with demons, exposed human depravity, and had our hands uplifted like Moses in support of the Joshuas fighting on bloody battlefields, we have skirted dangerously close to Satan's evil means. It is imperative that we be anchored in the Father's means of fulfilling the evangelistic mission through the Lord Jesus.

The Father's master strategy for extending the Gospel to all nations and people on earth began with wave upon wave of the Holy Spirit to advance the Kingdom of God to all humanity starting in Jerusalem; and it will end with returning to Jerusalem. One of these waves of the Holy Spirit is restoring the kingdom to Israel through the Jewish people returning to the Land of Israel and to saving faith in Messiah Jesus. We see this master plan of world evangelism encapsulated in Acts 1:4-8.

[4]While he was with them, he declared, "Do not leave Jerusalem, but wait there for what my Father promised, which you heard about from me. [5]For John baptized with water, but you will be baptized with the Holy Spirit not many days from now." [6]So when they had gathered together, they began to ask him, "Lord, is this the time when you are restoring the kingdom to Israel?" [7]He told them, "You are not permitted to know the times or periods that the Father has set by his own authority. [8]But you will receive power when the Holy Spirit has come upon you, and you will be my witnesses in Jerusalem, and in all Judea and Samaria, and to the farthest parts of the earth."

We shall deal with the Father's strategy of restoring the Kingdom to Israel in the next chapter. Here we will focus on the Father's tactic of sending waves of the Holy Spirit.

Acts 1:8 Waves of the Holy Spirit

The important concept revealed to us in Acts 1:8, and in the whole book of Acts, is that beginning with Pentecost, the Holy Spirit has worked in successive waves or pulses to advance the Kingdom of God. This is crucial to understanding how our God is working in the first part of the 21st century to bring the Muslim world to faith in Jesus Christ.

The great Reformed theologian Jonathan Edwards discerned this dynamic of the Lord advancing the Kingdom through pulses or waves of the Holy Spirit:

Edwards conceived of the Christian movement as a kind of army of spiritual liberation moving out to free the world from an occupying force of demons that had already been defeated in principle at the Cross...

According to Edwards' postmillennial optimism, Christianity is destined to sweep outwards in a series of such pulsations until the whole earth is full of the knowledge and the glory of God, as the waters cover the sea.[1]

These pulsations of the Holy Spirit are actually the pattern of God's working in the book of Acts. Peter himself prophesied these waves in his second sermon, laying out God's strategy, in Acts 3:19-21. The strategy consisted of two parts:

- Times of refreshing from the presence of the Lord, during the present age of the Spirit; then
- The return of the King at the end of the present age, according to the prophets of old.

The first "time of refreshing from the presence of the Lord" happened in Jerusalem at Pentecost, which initiated the Father's campaign that "repentance for the forgiveness of sins would be proclaimed in his name to all nations, beginning from Jerusalem." (Luke 24:47) Other outpourings followed, each extending the Kingdom of God. The first one after Pentecost took place in Jerusalem after the disciples had come under persecution.

[29]"Now, Lord, consider their threats and enable your servants to speak your word with great boldness. [30]Stretch out your hand to heal and perform miraculous signs and wonders through the name of your holy servant Jesus." [31]After they prayed, the place where they were meeting was shaken. And they were all filled with the Holy Spirit and spoke the word of God boldly. (Acts 4:29-31)

It is significant that this outpouring with signs and wonders and empowered preaching took place so soon after the Pentecost outpouring. This establishes the reality that while the outpouring of the Holy Spirit at Pentecost was an initial event, it was not to be seen as a single unique event, but rather the beginning of a pattern extending until the return of Jesus Christ the King. This also clarifies this usage of "filled with the Holy Spirit" as having the same meaning as the "Holy Spirit falling upon people for power." These waves of the Holy Spirit include both the corporate expression of the Church and individuals who are filled with the Holy Spirit.

We see this same outpouring of the Holy Spirit taking place through Philip with the Samaritans in Acts 8, then Peter in the home of Cornelius in Acts 10, and later in Chapter 19 with Paul in Corinth. The rest of the book of Acts is a picture of these waves or moves of the Holy Spirit, each connected with anointed individuals who are part of the Church, the Body of Christ.

These waves or outpourings of the Holy Spirit have continued to take place throughout history. They advance the Kingdom of God by bringing people into the purposes of God, empowering and equipping them to fulfill these purposes. A review of Church history reveals this pattern of moves of the Holy Spirit and the advancement of the Kingdom of God.[2]

Our Call as Intercessors is Praying for and Participating in these Waves of the Holy Spirit

All through the history of the advancement of the Gospel of Jesus Christ, the role of intercessors will be to pray for these waves and be a part of them as the Holy Spirit calls us to engage in them. While these waves or pulses of the Holy Spirit come at God's initiative, we do have a role in Him sending these waves. He has decreed that we will cooperate with Him by means of prayer.

This is modeled for us in the book of Acts where each wave of the Holy Spirit was preceded by the work of earnest prayer. A good example is an amazing prayer meeting preparing for the outpouring at Pentecost. After Jesus ascended into heaven from the Mount of Olives,

> [13]When they had entered Jerusalem, they went to the upstairs room where they were staying. Peter and John, and James, and Andrew, Philip and Thomas, Bartholomew and Matthew, James son of Alphaeus and Simon the Zealot, and Judas son of James were there. [14]All these continued together in prayer with one mind, together with the women, along with Mary the mother of Jesus, and his brothers. (Acts 1:13-14)

This gathering together of the body—not just the apostles, but other men and women who were followers of Jesus—praying in one accord, is the model of our role in preparing for all future waves of the Holy Spirit.

In the case of the Holy Spirit's wave of the Gospel to the Gentiles, the Jewish believers did not appear to know the Gentiles were even to be included, and so apparently failed to have done the work of prayer in that direction. Instead, the Holy Spirit stirred a Roman centurion named Cornelius to earnest prayer, which then opened the door for the Father to send the same kind of Holy Spirit wave which came upon the Jewish believers at Pentecost. (Acts 10:1-4, Acts 11:15-16) The lesson is that prayer ordinarily precedes moves of the Holy Spirit. We have already quoted Jonathan Edwards in chapter two, the beginning of the book. Now at the end I must quote him again as he provides the biblical rationale for this entire prayer strategy:

It is God's will through His wonderful grace, that the prayers of His saints should be one of the great principal means of carrying on the designs of Christ's kingdom in the world.

When God has something very great to accomplish for His church, it is His will that there should precede it the extraordinary prayers of His people; as is manifest by Ezekiel 36:37.

And it is revealed that, when God is about to accomplish great things for His church, He will begin by remarkably pouring out the spirit of grace and supplication (see Zechariah 12:10).[3]

In our present era in the war against Radical Islam, the Father is relentlessly working out his purposes to advance the Gospel of Jesus Christ into the entire Muslim world. He is sending four great waves of the Holy Spirit that are in succession with the two thousand year westward blowing wind of the Holy Spirit that started in Jerusalem. The Father's intention is to flood as with a tsunami the Islamic world with a powerful transforming witness to the Gospel. (Acts 2)

These four waves are as follows:

1. The Holy Spirit is bringing Jewish people back to the Land of Israel and to faith in Jesus Christ as their Messiah.

2. A great outpouring of the Holy Spirit is occurring among those of Confucian culture, empowering them for witness to Muslim peoples worldwide—the *Back to Jerusalem* movement.

3. The third great wave is the outpouring of the Holy Spirit within the Church globally, renewing Trinitarian faith and

mobilizing the Body of Christ to contribute to the fulfillment of the Great Commission.[4]

4. The fourth great wave of the Holy Spirit is within the house of Islam itself. There are, by far, more Muslims coming to faith in Jesus Christ now than at any other time in history.

Here we gain a glimpse of the big picture—our Father is advancing the Kingdom by these waves of the Holy Spirit, each a westward blowing wind of the Holy Spirit originating from Jerusalem at Pentecost in Acts 2, and then over the centuries continuing in a predominantly westward movement to return and converge in Jerusalem.

In the Father's master plan for extending the Gospel of Jesus Christ to all nations and people on earth, each wave contributes significantly to "closing the ring" of the Kingdom of Jesus Christ on the Islamic world. I take this image "closing the ring" from Winston Churchill's work, *Closing the Ring*, the theme is "How Nazi Germany was Isolated and Assailed on All Sides."[5] The Father, Son and Holy Spirit are implementing a similar strategy to encircle and assault on all sides the fortress of Islam with the first three waves of the Holy Spirit. A fourth wave of the Holy Spirit moving within the House of Islam itself is closing the ring. This is comparable to a "fifth column" or an insurgency of faith in Jesus Christ within the fortress of Islam.

In our present epochal period, these waves are beginning the convergence in Jerusalem. The assault on the demonic deception of Islam is beginning its final phases. This is not just the defeat of the strongholds Satan has built out of Islam, but of the lie of Islam itself. The present phase of the Father's campaign, these waves of the Holy Spirit converging in Jerusalem, if not thwarted by Satan through our lack of faith and obedience, will soon deluge the Islamic world with the powerful transforming witness to the Gospel. Through the floodtide of the Holy Spirit moving in love, power, and signs and wonders, the "Prophet Isa," the Lord Jesus himself and not the Islamic impostor, will be knocking at the door of every Muslim heart offering freedom from the spiritual and political tyranny of Islam. Jesus will be extending the invitation to receive him by faith and thus receive the gift of forgiveness of sins and resurrection life.

Jews Returning to the Land of Israel and to Yeshua

The Father reveals his strategy for world evangelization in Acts 1:8, baptizing us, his disciples, with the Holy Spirit. The Holy Spirit, in turn, provides the empowerment and equipping to be witnesses to Jesus Christ to the ends of the Earth.

For the last 30 years of teaching on the Holy Spirit, I have jumped over what seemed to me to be a misguided question asked by Jesus' Jewish disciples, *"Lord, is this the time when you are restoring the kingdom to Israel?"* (Acts 1:6) I just dismissed this as an example of Jewish wrongheadedness. Embedded in the hearts of these fishermen were old prophecies about the role of the Jewish people, the Land of Israel, and the Jewish Messiah. Of course, with Jesus Christ standing before them in a resurrected, nail-scarred body, speaking of the promised Holy Spirit, they expected all the Old Testament prophesies to be fulfilled within months, if not days.

What I did not notice (until Messianic Jewish scholars pointed it out to me) is that Jesus does not tell them that the Kingdom would not be restored to Israel. Jesus is simply putting this restoration off to a later date, after a season of preaching the Gospel of the Kingdom around the world, to every *ethnos.* Messiah Jesus also gives them the method by which their deepest hopes for the restoration of Israel will be restored: by being "baptized with the Holy Spirit" (Acts 1:4) and by "the Holy Spirit falling upon them to be witnesses from Jerusalem to all the nations of the world." (Acts 1:8)

The great plan of the Father is sending wave upon wave of the Holy Spirit who advances the Kingdom of God to all humanity starting in Jerusalem and returning to Jerusalem. One of those waves of the Holy Spirit is bringing the Jewish people back to the Land of Israel and to saving faith in Jesus Christ today. We see this master plan of world evangelism encapsulated in Acts 1:4-8, with the Apostle Paul filling out the details of the restoration of the Jewish people and the Kingdom restored to Israel, in Romans 11.

The outpouring of Pentecost that launched the entire evangelistic endeavor started with Jewish believers in Yeshua as Messiah. While there has always been a faithful remnant of Israel following Yeshua as the Messiah, Jewish hearts have been hardened due to Satan's plans, the sin of the Church, and the mystery of God's providence. This river of the Holy Spirit has largely gone underground. However, for the last one hundred and fifty years, like a spring bubbling up to a stream and river, now like an ocean wave, the Holy Spirit is moving among Jewish people, bringing them to faith in Jesus as their long-awaited Messiah. Yet, they do remain Jewish! They are also being restored to the Land of Israel in fulfillment of the Old Testament prophecies. This is an unprecedented outpouring of the Holy Spirit, in which Jewish people are coming to faith in Jesus while retaining their Jewish identity. This same movement of the Holy Spirit is bringing the Church of Jesus Christ into unity with the redeemed remnant of Israel to gather in Jerusalem as an army of intercessors. This gathering is not just to defend Israel against Satan's assaults, but to become the launching pad of the Father's great offensive to bring the Muslim world to Jesus Christ, and ultimately to fulfill the Great Commission.

Satan can read the Bible prophecies and see the signs of the times, often better than we do. Every biblical revelation of the Father's heart given to His friends can be just as easily read by his enemies. That is why Jesus had to be careful about whom he revealed the secrets of the Kingdom to, especially at first. He knew his Kingdom was opposed. Today, Satan knows that this move of the Holy Spirit, restoring the Kingdom to Israel, is an existential threat to his plans for world domination. No wonder Satan is frantically driving his plans of genocide for Jews and Christians through the strongholds of Radical Islam. No wonder Islamists, seeking the weapons necessary to destroy Israel and America, are in overdrive. Satan sees the converging waves of the Holy Spirit in Jerusalem and is taking desperate measures to prevent the fulfillment of the Great Commission. No wonder fourteen hundred years ago the Prophet Muhammad had a special hatred of the "People of the Book" and called for our conversion, subjugation or death. No wonder Islamic fanatics the world over, chant death to America and death to Israel. Together America and Israel as the embodiments of our Judeo-Christian heritage are the world's leaders against Islamic jihad and the spiritual and earthy bulwark against Satan fulfilling his terrible plans.

Understanding What the Bible Says about Israel and the Jewish People

I understood none of this until (as I have already related in Chapter 15) I found that our authority to defeat the strongholds of Islam is incomplete unless we were joined by born again, Holy

Spirit-empowered Jewish followers of Jesus Christ. I realized that God was raising up an army of intercessors composed of the "one new humanity," that is Jew and Gentile men and women, born again through faith in Jesus Christ. It was then, in my meeting with Messianic Bible scholars who took me through Romans 11, that I started to see with Jewish and New Testament eyes.

Here are the verses that changed me completely and caused me to rewrite this entire prayer strategy to be consistent with plans for defeating strongholds and bringing the Muslim world—indeed the whole world—to hear the Gospel of Jesus Christ.

> [11]I ask then, they did not stumble into an irrevocable fall, did they? Absolutely not! But by their transgression salvation has come to the Gentiles, to make Israel jealous. [12]Now if their transgression means riches for the world and their defeat means riches for the Gentiles, how much more will their full restoration bring? (Romans 11:11-12)

> [15]For if their rejection is the reconciliation of the world, what will their acceptance be but life from the dead? [16]If the first portion of the dough offered is holy, then the whole batch is holy, and if the root is holy, so too are the branches. (Romans 11:15-16)

> [23]And even they—if they do not continue in their unbelief—will be grafted in, for God is able to graft them in again. [24]For if you were cut off from what is by nature a wild olive tree, and grafted, contrary to nature, into a cultivated olive tree, how much more will these natural branches be grafted back into their own olive tree? [25]For I do not want you to be ignorant of this mystery, brothers and sisters, so that you may not be conceited: A partial hardening has happened to Israel until the full number of

the Gentiles has come in. [26]And so all Israel will be saved, as it is written: "The Deliverer will come out of Zion; he will remove ungodliness from Jacob. [27]And this is my covenant with them, when I take away their sins." [28]In regard to the gospel they are enemies for your sake, but in regard to election they are dearly loved for the sake of the fathers. [29]For the gifts and the call of God are irrevocable. (Romans 11:23-29)

I have read and re-read these verses. I meditated on them in Chinese and in English versions. I will tell you honestly that I did not get it, however, until I went to Israel and saw firsthand the results of this wave of the Holy Spirit at work restoring the Kingdom of Israel by Jews trusting Yeshua as their Messiah.

The Vision of the Whole World
Turning Around the City of Jerusalem

As evidence that God is calling us to join Him to advance His Kingdom over Islam, I share with you what I experienced while I was in Israel during February, 2015. Doug and Carla McMurry and my wife Laura joined me on this trip.

While staying at the St. George Cathedral Pilgrim Guest House in Jerusalem, I received the following vision which I recorded in my journal:

Last night I had a strange dream that was more than a dream—a revelation and actually being there. In the dream/vision I was walking up steps that looked very much like the Cathedral complex we were staying in. I arrived at the top of a high stone turret overlooking the whole Old and New city of Jerusalem. Out on all sides was the Holy Land of Israel, a panorama dissolving into the distance of desert and mountains. In the dream, or awake, or in the Spirit, I do not know, I was overcome with emotion.

All my life, starting as a child in Sunday school, I had heard of this city. Now I was actually here seeing it with my own eyes, walking the narrow streets, standing inside the Garden Tomb, touching with my own hands the cold stone that had been seared with the light of Jesus' resurrection. I was also in the vision seeing Jerusalem with all its pasts. Level after level, sort of the way Charles Williams envisioned London with all past Londons going back to Roman times, all superimposed on each other.[1] That was what I was seeing in regards to Jerusalem: all the Jerusalems going back to Melchizedek, King David, King Herod, the Romans, Jesus, the Apostles, the crusader kingdoms, the restoration of Israel, to the present. Layer after layer, century after century, all superimposed upon each other.

Then suddenly, in the dream-vision, I could actually feel the whole earth, human history, and the cosmic battle for the salvation of humankind all turning around this one city as the fixed point in the universe, as if this was the axis on which the earth turned, not the North and South Poles. Even in the vision I asked the Lord, "What does this mean? Why does everything turn around this one city?" The Lord answered, "Wait and I will show you!"

The next morning, after a restless night, it was Shabbat, the Sabbath. We got a taxi to a shopping center with a fourteen-story building. Here in the Clal Building were located the offices of King of Kings Family of Ministries and the site of several Messianic congregations. Rabbi Asher Intrater and his wife Beth had invited us to this service. They said it would all be in Hebrew with no translation, but we were welcome to come early to join in prayer before the service.

The four of us arrived early and spent an hour and a half praying with the leadership team. I stepped into the prayer basement room and immediately the Holy Spirit fell upon me and I prayed in tongues the whole time. I noticed the same thing happening to Laura and the McMurrys. Then the service began. The worship was fantastic. All wonderfully led and filled with the Holy Spirit. The group was mostly Jewish, but there, mingled among these Jewish believers, were representatives from the nations of the world—from China, Taiwan, Korea, Brazil, America, Great Britain, various nations of Africa, Japan, and others I did not recognize, all with their hands lifted in praise to Yeshua.

Truly, the international Church was there joining the Messianic Jews in worshiping the Father in spirit and in truth. The one new humanity in which there is [11]"neither Greek nor Jew, circumcised or uncircumcised, barbarian, Scythian, slave or free, but Christ is all and in all." (Colossians 3:11) It was then that I started to gain at least a partial answer to the question in the vision. Here in the city of Jerusalem, Jesus was drawing together the nations of the world and gathering them around the saved remnant of the Jewish people. In this congregation, I saw the convergence of all the present moves of the Holy Spirit from Asia, Africa, Europe, North and South America, Eurasia, and Russia. I saw that they were already the army of the one new humanity gathered through one faith, one baptism and one Spirit in Yeshua, the Jewish Messiah who came to save the world.

I saw what Jesus spoke of to the woman at the well, happening:

[21]Jesus said to her, "Believe me, woman, a time is coming when you will worship the Father neither on this mountain nor in Jerusalem. [22]You people worship what you do not

know. We worship what we know, because salvation is from the Jews. [23]But a time is coming—and now is here—when the true worshipers will worship the Father in spirit and truth, for the Father seeks such people to be his worshipers. [24]God is spirit, and the people who worship him must worship in spirit and truth." (John 4:21-24)

This was worship in spirit and in truth! But God was showing me more. Later Doug McMurry and I went back to meet some of the leaders of the Messianic movement that is rapidly growing in Israel with many new fellowships and thousands of new Jewish believers. We had a good conversation and were impressed with all their ministries including connecting with the Palestinian and Arab Christians. Then the leader said, "There is just time before the service begins for us to go to the 14th floor and visit the Jerusalem Prayer Tower where 24-7 prayer takes place.

As Doug and I skirted the four corners of this bastion of prayer, I looked out over the old and new cities of Jerusalem and The Land of Israel like a Google Earth map, but seen with my own eyes, stretching off into a distant haze of desert and mountains. Suddenly I was back in my vision. This was the view I had seen, now with the added dimension of people praying as individuals and in groups. Some were Koreans. Others were praying with American or British accents. I heard German and Chinese. Then we turned a corner, and looked out over the vista of the Old City with the Dome of the Rock gleaming in the sun. Beyond was the Mount of Olives and to the left Mount Scopus. Right in the next room I heard Hebrew, a Messianic Jewish group praying fervently in the name of Yeshua. Representatives of the nations were gathered there once again, with the Jewish root all together as the "one new man" or, as the NRSV translates it, "one new humanity." The army of One doing the work of intercession in the power of the Holy Spirit in the name of Jesus Christ—Yeshua—to the Father.

We were seeing the actual fulfillment of St. Paul's promise of the working of Jesus Christ, bringing Jews and Gentiles together:

> [11]Therefore remember that formerly you, the Gentiles in the flesh—who are called "uncircumcision" by the so-called "circumcision" that is performed on the body by human hands—[2]that you were at that time without the Messiah, alienated from the citizenship of Israel and strangers to the covenants of promise, having no hope and without God in the world. [13]But now in Christ Jesus you who used to be far away have been brought near by the blood of Christ. [14]For he is our peace, the one who made both groups into one and who destroyed the middle wall of partition, the hostility, [15]when he nullified in his flesh the law of commandments in decrees. He did this to create in himself one new man out of two, thus making peace, [16]and to reconcile them both in one body to God through the cross, by which the hostility has been killed. [17]And he came and preached peace to you who were far off and peace to those who were near, [18]so that through him we both have access in one Spirit to the Father. (Ephesians 2:11-18)

I still did not understand. Why Jerusalem? What was so

strategic about this "one new humanity" gathered in fellowship, prayer and worship in Jerusalem? Why was it not gathered at any of the great historic Christian churches all over the world? What's so special about Jerusalem? There are many dynamic prayer centers in much safer locations in Korea or in America. Why this Jewish Messianic Prayer Tower overlooking the temple Mount and the Mount of Olives?

Then I understood. This "one new humanity" gathering in Jerusalem is the harbinger and concrete evidence of God's two great interdependent plans for redemption of all humanity: The first is the fulfillment of the Great Commission of the Gospel going to all the nations of the world (Matthew 28:18-20).[2] Secondly, in order for the full redemption of humanity and the culmination of history to come, the Jewish people are to be fully restored by the same means all are restored, which is by faith in Jesus Christ.[3] (See Romans 11: 12-15).

Jewish believer and apostolic leader Asher Intrater explains why the convergence of these great rivers of the Holy Spirit are taking place in the actual geographic location of the city of Jerusalem.

Everything begins in Jerusalem and ends in Jerusalem. In the biblical viewpoint, Jerusalem is the center of the world. At the end of the Bible, we find new heavens and a new earth. That paradise is pictured as the restoration of the Garden of Eden. This renewed Eden has the tree of life in it again, and the rivers of pure water (see Rev. 22:1-2). This paradise is seen not only as a renewal of Eden but also as a renewal of Jerusalem. Revelation 21:1-2 "I saw a new heaven and a new earth... I saw...the holy city, New Jerusalem, coming down out of heaven..."[4]

The preaching of the gospel and the restoration of the Promised Land are both part of bringing the Kingdom of

God to earth. As the Kingdom of God begins and ends in Jerusalem, so does the preaching of the Gospel begin and end in Jerusalem. As Abraham's commission to return to the Promised Land went westward, so does the general plan for the spread of the gospel move westward."[5]

If one follows this westward blowing wind of the Holy Spirit that starts in Jerusalem, wave upon wave, century after century, one ends up back at Jerusalem. This is actually happening in this city. We are witnessing the fulfillment of Old and New Testament prophecy at this time in history, not only in the realm of the Spirit and in the international Church of Jesus Christ, but in the actual geographical location of the city of Jerusalem, Israel, in which born-again Jews and Gentiles pray and worship as the "one new humanity."

This "One New Humanity" in Jerusalem is a Key to Jesus' Victory over Radical Islam

An important key to defeating Radical Islam and bringing Muslims together with the whole world to faith in Jesus Christ is in this international fellowship worshipping the Father in Spirit and in Truth. How fitting that it would be Jerusalem! How solid is Yahweh's promise to Abraham that the world would be blessed through his seed, the Lord Jesus, his plan for the salvation of humanity *"from the Jews"* (see John 4: 22). This is the vanguard of God's Army that He is raising up not only to defeat Satan's work in Radical Islam, but to bring the Gospel of Jesus Christ to the entire Muslim world.

The battle has been joined! The vanguard of the Kingdom of God has been formed at the epicenter of the battle, in the city of Jerusalem, the axis around which the world turns and the end-time gathering point of all the nations. Intercessors called into this army by the blood of Jesus are already connected to this fellowship. We worship "in the Spirit and in truth" (John 4:23) which brings a woven connection of all who have been born into the Kingdom God worldwide.

I have been on a steep learning curve about the biblical role of the Jewish people and Jerusalem in God's plans and purposes. I am still learning what this means in practice. Jesus has showed me that neither the Christian Church nor our Messianic friends will have the know-how or authority to defeat Radical Islam unless we do it together.

I am convinced that while there is no call for us all to move to Israel or to join Messianic fellowships, we must recognize that together we are part of the Body of Jesus Christ and together we are in this battle against Radical Islam. I am personally still working out how this unity in Christ and the army of the "one new humanity" is to be strategically and tactically deployed. I do, however, trust that as we get past the barriers that divide us—there are many on the Jewish as well as the Gentile side—that the Holy Spirit will guide us as to how we can support each other and work together in this battle. As we work out this unity in our own hearts and in the spiritual battlefield, Jesus Christ will use our unity to prevail over Satan's slaves who shout death to America and death to Israel. They will replace their curses of death with songs of praise and blessings of Jewish and gentile Christians who have faithfully prayed them into the river of life.

The "People Who Use Chopsticks" Taking the Gospel Back to Jerusalem

Over the last 150 years there has been a great move of the Holy Spirit among peoples influenced by Confucian culture—China, Korea and Japan—bringing them to faith in Jesus Christ. The Father is pouring out the Holy Spirit to equip these Asian believers to take their place in fulfilling the Great Commission. Astonishingly, in the last 80 years they have been bearing witness to Muslims in what has been named the "Back to Jerusalem Movement." (傳回耶路撒冷運動)

I have served in theological education and equipping of Church leaders in Korea, Japan, Taiwan, and China for many years. All this is very close to my heart, but, more importantly, close to

Jesus' heart. I believe this movement is the Father's master plan for fulfilling the Great Commission. This was confirmed not just in the trip to Israel in February, 2015, but in a trip to South Korea in March. Rev. Dr. John Chang, Dr. Ji Dong Shan, and I (the Chinese speaking team) were in Korea to join our Korean brothers and sisters in establishing the PRMI Dunamis Fellowship Korea.[1]

One of the Korean leaders told us the story of how a Korean pastor during a conference received a vision of "of a large hand holding a pair of chopsticks." He shared the image to the group saying: "I do not know what this means." Another pastor jumped up and said, "God is saying that it is the people who use chopsticks who will be used to take part in bringing to conclusion the Great Commission." When Dr. John Chang and I heard this, the Holy Spirit fell upon both of us. We suddenly saw that pair of hands holding chopsticks becoming millions of hands holding chopsticks. With this vision the Lord spoke, "I am pouring out my Holy Spirit upon the people of China, Korea, Taiwan and Japan, bringing healing from past hurt and divisions so that in a unity of faith in Jesus Christ the next great wave of the Holy Spirit may advance the Gospel not only to Muslims but into the whole world."

A vast movement of the Holy Spirit that first started in Korea, Taiwan, Hong Kong, and Singapore, is now beginning to gain momentum in Japan. It has now become a great torrent in China. There are millions upon millions of people being caught up into this move of the Lord, with potential for millions more. As people with a common Chinese/Confucian culture, these are the "people of the chopsticks." Each subcultural group brings special gifts to the work of advancing the Kingdom of God. However, for this unity of the army in Christ to be built and these tremendous cultural and national character assets to be mobilized, we must pray for reconciliation among Christians from mainland China, Korea, Japan, and Taiwan. There are deep scars from war, subjugation and national arrogance, mutual animosities, and conflicting ideologies that Satan has utilized to build strongholds to destroy the unity of the army Christ is building among the people of the chopsticks.

Why Send Christians from Confucian Cultures?

While the West still has a vital role to play in this movement, those most suitable for witnessing to Muslims are no longer Western Christians, but Asian Christians. Confucian cultures have much less conflict with Islamic culture than do cultures based on a Judeo-Christian worldview. It is easier for Asian Christians to bridge the hostility gap with Muslims and to present to them the Gospel, than it is for Western Christians.

This is confirmed by Samuel Huntington's book *The Clash of Civilizations.*[2] Below, I present his chart of the clash of civilizations, which helps explains the Father's plans for sending waves of Asians into Muslim lands. In one glimpse this gives us the Father's rationale for why He sent the Holy Spirit in a Westward, rather than an Eastward, direction.[3]

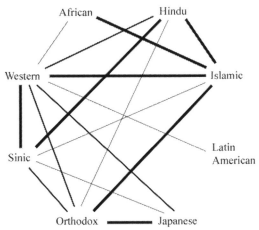

"Emerging alignments" of civilizations, per Samuel Huntinton's theory in *The Clash of Civilizations* (1996).

Greater line thickness represents more conflict in the civilizational relationship.

Notice from the chart that the least level of conflict is between

"Sinic" cultures (or cultures which are influenced by Confucianism) and Islamic culture; while the maximum conflict for Islamic cultures is with all other major cultures. Historically the greatest level of conflict has been with those cultures influenced by Biblical faith. The implication is that there are fewer obstacles to Muslims hearing the Gospel through Asian Christians than through Western Christians. This accounts for the Father's remarkable long term plans of world evangelization. Knowing Satan's battle plan of developing a false religion in Arabia to replace Christianity and its Jewish roots, the Father sent the Holy Spirit in wave upon wave in a Western direction. Onward to Europe the Gospel spread, where— through the Spanish, French, and British maritime empires—the waves of the Holy Spirit moved to Africa to North and South America, and to outposts in Asia.

During the present wave of the Holy Spirit in Korea, Taiwan and China, many leaders have received a vision of taking the Gospel back along the "silk road" to the Muslim world and to the geographical starting place of God's covenant of salvation: Jerusalem. This "Back to Jerusalem Movement" [4] vision has its origins in the 1920s in the "Jesus Family." [5]

How the Christian Faith Crossed Over the
Hostility Gap into Sinic Cultures

In Huntington's chart, there is a high level of conflict between Chinese cultures and Western culture. So how did the Christian Faith coming from the West initially move across that hostility gap (a feat rarely accomplished in the Muslim world)? First, it was through the efforts of many missionaries—both Catholic and Protestant—who put aside their Western dress and culture and crossed over into Chinese culture. For instance, Hudson Taylor, the missionary founder of the China Inland Mission, adopted Chinese

James Hudson Taylor (1832-1905)
https://omf.org/us/about/our-story/james-hudson-taylor/

culture in his personal lifestyle. One needs to see him in his Chinese clothes to understand this. Not all western missionaries were able to make this shift. Many did not. But through Taylor, the seeds of the Gospel were planted by the Holy Spirit in the hearts of Chinese believers without Western packaging. This process of indigenization was accelerated in 1949 with the Communist takeover. They expelled the foreign missionaries and through vicious persecution striped away the cultural chaff leaving the fertile seeds of biblical Christianity. The Church could and would now explode with growth in its own Chinese form.

Another part of the "Sinic" Confucian world where the Gospel crossed over from the West was into Korea. This was a remarkable development and strategic to God's westward moving wind of the Holy Spirit.

The Role of the Korean Church

The Gospel crossed over into Korean culture from Western Culture over a period of decades. In 1784 Korean diplomats brought the Christian faith to Korea and established a lay Catholic Christian community. However, persecution in which most believers were martyred nearly extinguished this first planting. [6] The next sowing wave came from Presbyterian Missionaries from the United States with Horace Newton Allen in 1884.

There are many aspects of Presbyterianism that fit well in the Confucian culture of Korea. For instance, the role of the pastor as scholar and teacher fit well the Confucian system which honors a sage as the leader. There is also a similarity in the disciplined focus on building social systems that provide order and prosperity for humanity. In the great outpouring of the Holy Spirit starting in 1903-07[7] in Pyongyang, the work of prayer and the experiential aspects of the Christian faith entered Korea. These elements set well with the shamanistic and mystical Buddhist aspects of Korean culture.

A real leap forward came during the Japanese occupation of Korea in which Christians, especially Presbyterians and Methodists, stood up to the Japanese attempt to destroy Korean culture and identity. The Japanese plan was to make Koreans the obedient subjects of their empire as pawns in their invasion of China. However, Presbyterian and Methodist missionaries and Korean believers refused to bow to the Japanese Emperor. Their schools were closed, clergy imprisoned or killed, and churches destroyed, but their courageous opposition and martyrdom led to the Christian faith taking root in the Korean heart. It was no longer a foreign import, but indigenous Korean faith. This process of refinement through suffering continued through the Korean War. After the war, when many missionaries returned (many of them from China after being driven out by the Communists), they contributed to the rebuilding of the shattered nation.

After the war, during continuing moves of the Holy Spirit, the Christian faith shed still more of its western baggage, yet with a grateful openness especially to English, Scottish, Canadian and American Christianity.[8] The Korean Church, famous for its focus on prayer and evangelism, sends more missionaries out worldwide than any other nation except the United States.

The key to the extraordinary dynamics of faith and passion for missions comes from the work of prayer. Prayer is the furnace that impassions Asians to advance the Gospel into the Muslim world.

Throughout Korea there are prayer centers focused on doing the work of prayer. For years, I have personally been involved with one of them: Jesus Abbey, an Anglican charismatic prayer community on the east coast of Korea. Starting in 1966, this community has been in focused intercessory prayer for the outpouring of the Holy Spirit in Korea and for the Gospel to go forth to China. Many Koreans have a deep burden to pray for their *older brother*, the Chinese, whom they passionately pray will come to know Jesus Christ. This has been a theme of prayer at Jesus Abbey for years: praying for China—and praying for Jerusalem. What's more, the Korean Church is sending many missionaries into China.

This is a major contribution to the advance of the Gospel and to the moves of the Holy Spirit into the Muslim world. The Korean Church is the vanguard of this whole prayer movement that is undergirding the worldwide advance of the Gospel. They have been on the frontlines of the Father's missionary strategy for over fifty years and are moving to an even larger role in this battle with Radical Islam.

While there is great excitement and focus on what God is doing in China, we must never forget that it is the Korean Christians who have been providing the work of extraordinary prayer that Jonathan Edwards said in 1740 was the essential beginning place for God to do something great through the Church. We see this dynamic now moving from Korea through China into the countries of the Muslim world.[9]

Is the *Back to Jerusalem* Movement Real?

There is quite a bit of controversy about this movement. Some even question whether it is happening at all. I have been involved in equipping Korean and Chinese Church leaders for many years. I have witnessed firsthand the move of the Holy Spirit taking place both in Korea and in China. Some have shared with me their vision of taking the Gospel to the Muslim world. I knew that Koreans were praying for the Gospel to go to the Muslim world, but were they really there in the frontlines? I admit my own concern. I had no hard evidence that the Holy Spirit was sending Chinese Christians to the Muslim world.

But during our trip to Israel in 2015, Laura and I visited the Ahavat Yeshua congregation in Jerusalem. Though many were Messianic Jews, people from all over the world gathered there. There was a large contingent of Koreans and Chinese present. In fact, there are prayer places all over the Holy City in which Koreans are in intercession. There were so many Koreans at the Messianic service that they even had their own translator with earphones.

Most astonishing to me was meeting the Chinese who were there. In the time of passing the peace, I went up to greet several of the groups of Chinese, but did not have time to ask why they were there. Later, in the service my back was hurting so much that I had to get up to walk around. I went outside into the large open courtyard, just praying in the Spirit. Thinking no one was about; I began to pray in a loud voice in tongues. After a moment, the Holy Spirit nudged me to shift from my prayer language into Mandarin Chinese. I turned a corner and there was a lovely young Chinese woman about my daughter's age holding a baby. Startled, I stopped shouting prayers in Chinese. Then, I awkwardly said something like, "Well, hello! You have a cute baby!" She was stunned that I was speaking Chinese. That started a brief exchange. She asked how I could speak her language. I told her that I had been a missionary for nine years in Taiwan and had been many times to China. I asked where she was from. She named a city in mainland China. Then I asked why she was in Israel. Her answer blew me away. She said that she and her husband were part of a church in China. One

Sunday the Holy Spirit had fallen upon the fellowship and told them clearly to send two young couples to Jerusalem as missionaries. I said, "That is amazing! Who are you working with here in Israel, the Jews?" "Oh no," she said, "We are here with our Messianic Jewish brothers and sisters for fellowship and spiritual support. Our mission is to the Muslims, the Arabs!" I asked, "How do they receive you and receive the Gospel of Jesus Christ?" Her answer stunned me. "Oh, they are open to receive from us as Chinese and are eager to know about how to believe in Jesus." She saw my amazement and asked, "Have you ever heard of the Back to Jerusalem Movement? Well, it is really happening. That is why we are here!" She abruptly turned and walked way. I suspect she feared she had revealed too much to me, a complete stranger. I stood there caught up in praise and worship.

This was the first confirmation for me personally that the Lord was undeniably sending this great wave of the people who use chopsticks, surging along the Silk Road back to Jerusalem with the Gospel of Jesus Christ. That builds a highway for the Lord right through the center of Islamic cultures, setting them free to become disciples of Jesus Christ.

How to Pray for the People Who Use Chopsticks

What about those of us who do not use chopsticks, how do we fit into this picture? Our job is to do the "Moses" work of intercession for those Asian brothers and sisters who are risking their lives in Muslim countries along the "Silk Road." First, let us pray that the Holy Spirit will continue to be poured out on Asians, that they may become powerful witnesses to Jesus Christ within their own cultures.

Second, let us pray that there will be deep healing and reconciliation among the Christians in these nations. Because deep wounding has taken place over centuries of their joint history, reconciliation must precede effective work to advance the Kingdom westward. This will necessitate the removal of demonic spirits that have taken root both at the personal and corporate levels.

Third, let us pray that those of us in the West who are called to cross over into these Chinese/Confucian cultures will be spiritually and financially equipped to train and support the Asian believers.

Finally, let us pray that in addition to the challenges of evangelizing their own people, they will not lose the missionary vision of taking the Gospel to the Muslim world. The specific challenge is to pray that these movements will stay focused on Jesus Christ as the only way of salvation, will be grounded in the Bible as the Word of God, and will be open to the power of the Holy Spirit to advance the Kingdom of God.

Closing the Ring on Fortress Islam

In this prayer strategy, we have focused on the first two great waves of the Holy Spirit: Jews returning to Israel and to faith in Messiah Jesus, and people of the chopsticks bearing witness to Jesus back to Jerusalem. To see the strategic significance of these two movements in the Father's plans, imagine a mechanical vise for woodworking. There are two jaws; the moving jaw presses the wood firmly against the fixed jaw. In the Father's strategy, the Jewish People in the Land of Israel are the fixed jaw—the axis around which salvation history has turned and the beginning and destination points of the waves of the Holy Spirit. The moving jaw represents the waves of the Holy Spirit circling the globe to advance the Kingdom of God to every tribe and tongue. At this time in history, the moving jaw—the people who use chopsticks—is closing in on the fixed jaw, providing Satan with a very uncomfortable squeeze. He knows, now more than ever, that his time is near.

"Closing the Ring"
The Third Great Wave

Now let's add the image used by Winston Churchill— "Closing the Ring." This is the name he used to describe the phase in World War II when Nazi Germany was "isolated and assailed on all sides" by allied armies.[1] Reaching this point of being able to close the ring on Hitler's Germany was the result of the master strategy devised by Churchill and Roosevelt for the overall conduct of the war. Today, our Father is deploying a similar strategy of closing the ring on Satan's empire of Islam.

Islam is now being encircled and pressed on all sides. Jesus Christ is accomplishing this by adding to the first two waves in the Chinese world and Jewish world, a third great wave of the Holy Spirit in the Western and Eastern expressions of the Body of Jesus Christ. A full description of this wave is beyond the scope of this prayer strategy. But it has been moving for at least 150 years in the preaching of R.A. Torrey and D.L. Moody, the Welsh Revival and the Azusa Street revival. In the 1950s, Billy Graham's evangelistic crusades spanned a half-century, followed by the Charismatic movement and Third Waves of the Holy Spirit. The impact of these movements is still gaining momentum worldwide.

These moves of the Holy Spirit are renewing Biblical faith in churches in the West from North America to the British Isles and to Europe. The result is the re-evangelization into biblical faith of many in Westernized cultures where the Church of Jesus Christ had grown feeble. There is a new vibrancy of faith and a massive prayer movement manifesting worldwide. Africa, Brazil and the Spanish speaking world are experiencing revival fire. The Holy Spirit is coming upon the younger generation with an explosive passion of faith and love for God. Wherever these Christians have been filled with the Holy Spirit, an evangelistic zeal has taken hold, both in outreach to Muslim neighborhoods in Western cities, and to world centers of Islamic culture.

The Western Church Empowered to Reach out to Muslims in their Midst

With the threat of radical Islamic terrorism growing in North America, the United Kingdom, Western Europe and Africa, Satan is working hard to stir up hatred and distrust of Muslims. It serves his purposes well if Muslims living in Islamic enclaves are so dehumanized that they are viewed as cancers that must be destroyed. Satan's strategy is being thwarted wherever the Holy Spirit is welcomed to work within Christian fellowships. He is opening spiritual eyes to see such enclaves not as threats, but opportunities for reaching out in love and friendship with the gospel of Jesus Christ. This goes beyond concepts of equality, justice, inclusiveness and multiculturalism, to the Kingdom of God that is entered through faith in the Lord Jesus, and extended under the anointing of the Holy Spirit.

I share here one inspiring example of the Holy Spirit on the move. At the edge of a large Muslim enclave in the United Kingdom, a Christian congregation has been growing in the anointing of the Holy Spirit and prayer. The Holy Spirit led them into persistent prayer that Muslims would come to know Jesus as Savior and Lord. The work of prayer was led by several members who had lived in the Muslim world, were fluent in Arabic, and had a deep love for these people in bondage to Islam.

During the Christmas season, they experienced the Lord speaking to them in their prayer meeting saying, "This year when you do your annual Christmas caroling, do not walk through your normal safe neighborhoods where people always welcome you with hot drinks. Instead, go as I will guide you into Muslim neighborhoods." The little group of fifteen were rather concerned about this guidance, but those who knew Muslims personally and spoke Arabic encouraged them forward. So, after earnest prayers for guidance and protection, with pleas for the Holy Spirit to use them to sow seeds of faith, they started out. The first direction was to divide into two smaller groups with three people left behind at the church to provide prayer cover. The fear was that they could appear to be a mob if there were too many of them together. They recognized, too, that some were not called to go out but were being directed to stay back at the church as intercessors.

Here is my summary of what the Arabic-speaking leader of one of the groups shared with me. As they went out into the cold, snow-covered streets singing traditional Christmas carols, heavily curtained windows remained closed at first. But as they persisted their caroling down the street, the curtains started to open. People looked out in wonderment.

Then many started to come out onto their porches. Some were waving and smiling. Many were taking pictures with their iPhones of these singing Christians—a sight they had never seen before. Then, in English and in Arabic, the group wished them peace and the blessings of Christmas. The people responded with words of "peace!"—the older people in Arabic and the younger ones in English.

As they were getting ready to move to the next block, the Arabic-speaking leader received a sudden nudge of the Holy Spirit. He called out, "Do you have any prayer requests that we may pray to God for you?" At this everyone looked awkward. Finally, one of the younger women said, "Yes! I have my exams coming up. I am very worried about failing and need prayer!" That broke the spiritual ice; other prayer requests followed. The Christians prayed in the name of Jesus Christ in English and in Arabic for the people. This ended with warm thanks from the Muslims and appreciative good-byes and "Please come again," over and over. The leader was getting very excited; he could feel the Holy Spirit at work.

As the group headed down the street, suddenly a young man approached them, and said, "Please come this way, the people can't hear you. Please follow me!" He turned down a narrow alley. A moment of fear came over some members of the group. Was this an ambush? The Arabic-speaker said, "Let us follow him. It is the Lord leading us." So down the alley they went, and found themselves in a courtyard of an apartment complex. People on their porches around them welcomed them. The caroling group sang several Christian hymns about the coming of Jesus Christ and concluded with *Joy to the World*. This was followed by a momentary reverent silence. Then some of the older folks stepped forward and excitedly invited the carolers to come in out of the cold, into the large living room filled with people of all ages, with food and hot drinks. They stayed for a long time. Warm fellowship and food were shared by all. The Christians shared Jesus with their hosts naturally and without hesitation, explaining the songs they were singing.

Only the Holy Spirit knows fully what came from that wondrous evening of Muslims and Christians spending time together. Whether the Muslim hosts welcomed Jesus into their lives as well I cannot say. The carolers simply testified to the Holy Spirit's presence and power to break down barriers. New friendships developed. Relationships of trust and caring were established. How the Lord will use this remains to be seen.

The one who shared this story with me marveled at how gracious the Holy Spirit was to lead their group in this unexpected way. This is the great dance of the Holy Spirit in which he invites us to join him in reaching out to those who don't yet know the love and forgiveness of the Father in Jesus. Yes, it is likely to move us into risky relationships and to stretch us out of our comfort zones. Let us accept the Father's invitation to dance!

Equipping and Sending Missionaries

Another aspect of this great wave of the Holy Spirit is the equipping and sending of missionaries. The Holy Spirit is calling and equipping Western Christians to go out with the love of Jesus. Of course, I will not reveal here the exact details, names and locations. They are giving their lives in accordance with the Father's strategic plan to close the ring by equipping and deploying wave upon wave of Holy Spirit-anointed missionaries to Muslim lands.

There is a vast mobilization underway, directed by the Holy Spirit to enable Christians in the First World to provide the education, equipping, organization, and finances for Holy Spirit-anointed Christians from Africa, Latin America, and East Asia to re-evangelize Western Europe and to launch a frontal spiritual assault against the Empire of Islam in the power of the Holy Spirit. From my knowledge and experience, much of this world missionary movement is driven by Korean Christians in Korea and in countless outposts worldwide serving as intercessors. They are the prayer dynamo for these present-day waves of the Holy Spirit converging on Jerusalem.

The Fifth Column

It is indeed happening! The ring is closing, but not without ferocious resistance from Satan in his battle engines of Radical Islamic jihad. Islam and Islamic culture is a vast empire of oppression. It is under assault both from Western culture and the Kingdom of God, but at its heart it is impregnable from outside forces because the strongholds themselves are within the hearts of Muslims.

The military operations of Radical Islam may be destroyed, Islamic warriors killed, terrorist plots exposed and thwarted. Still the fact persists that Satan's lies in the Quran and the Hadith are embedded in the hearts of Muslims. These lies remain a bulwark against completely closing the ring. No one can change hearts but the Lord alone, sometimes working through his servants, and sometimes independently in answer to the prayers of his royal priesthood.

The Father is the master strategist. He has taken all this into account, and has provided another tactic in the campaign to close the ring and bring the Muslim world to faith in Christ. It is a "fifth column," a move of the Holy Spirit within the House of Islam itself, getting past all the defenses of Islam, and reaching directly into Muslim hearts. Already the Holy Spirit, largely invisible, akin to an underground stream, is leading Muslims to Jesus whose truth is undermining the edifice formed from the lies of Satan. As the ring continues to be closed, the structure of deception of Islam will crumble from within.

An Imam in Training Meets Jesus

I had, of course, heard rumors and reports of this great move of the Holy Spirit from within Islam whereby signs and wonders, dreams and visions make Jesus real to Muslims. I did not appreciate the full significance until I met a man from Africa, a Muslim, who had begun to follow the Lord Jesus and was now a pastor. Here is a summary of the story he told me. Stories like this are being told all over the Islamic world.

Originally from Muslim North Africa, this brother came from a family of high-ranking powerful imams. He was himself an extremely devout Muslim. He was in training to follow in his father's and grandfather's footsteps by becoming an imam. The training was rigorous. One day he was alone in his room sitting up on the bed reciting the Quran in Arabic. He assured me that he was not asleep nor dozing off, but wide awake. He said, "I was looking up from the book, when there materialized before me in my room without opening the door, Jesus wearing a brilliant white robe." He stood there gazing at me with great love. Then, he made himself at home in my room by sitting down in my chair. Still looking at me with such love like I had never experienced before, he said in an audible voice in my native language, "You will not find me in that book, but go read in my book, John 14:6." With that, he vanished.

After this visionary experience, this man dared not tell anyone what had happened to him for fear that he would be ostracized by his family. He also questioned his own sanity, and wondered if it had not just been a hallucination. But there was birthed in him a deep yearning to know Jesus. Surreptitiously he began to look for a Bible. Finally, after three years of seeking, while also doubting the entire experience, he found a New Testament in his native language. He opened it to John 14:6 and read the words of Jesus, *"I am the way, and the truth, and the life. No one comes to the Father except through me."*

That was the breakthrough! Later he sought out some Christians and heard the Gospel. Then he set about to read the whole Bible. He received Jesus as his Lord and Savior and experienced new birth in Christ. This born-again Muslim had to flee his native country where he would have been murdered as an apostate. He is now the pastor of several flourishing congregations with many members having come out of spiritual bondage to Islam into the freedom and life of Jesus Christ.

The Holy Spirit is moving among Muslims in this great wave in an unprecedented way over the 1400 years of Islam. There are now more Muslims coming to faith in Jesus than at any other time in history. Don't take my word for it. Turn to David Garrison's *A Wind in the House of Islam: How God is drawing Muslims around the world to faith in Jesus Christ.* [2] Our God loves the people in Islamic captivity, and therefore He is sending a new wave of the Holy Spirit.

Garrison's opening declaration is stunning:

> A wind is blowing through the House of Islam. The House
> of Islam, Dar al-Islam in Arabic, is the name Muslims give
> to an invisible religious empire that stretches from West
> Africa to the Indonesian archipelago, encompassing 49
> nations and 1.6 billion Muslims. Dwarfing the size of any
> previous earthly kingdom, Islam directs the spiritual
> affairs of nearly a quarter of the world's population. But
> something is happening today that is challenging the hold
> that Islam exercises over its adherents. Muslim
> movements to Jesus Christ are taking place in numbers
> we've never before seen.[3]
>
> It is this long history of frustration, a history that has seen
> tens of millions of Christians absorbed into the Muslim
> world that makes the current events all the more striking.
> In only the first 12 years of the 21st century, an additional
> 69 movements to Christ of at least 1,000 baptized Muslim-
> background believers or 100 new worshiping fellowships
> have appeared. These 21st Century movements are not
> isolated to one or two corners of the world. They are taking
> place throughout the House of Islam: in sub-Saharan
> Africa, in the Persian world, in the Arab world, in
> Turkestan, in South Asia and in Southeast Asia. Something
> is happening—something historic, something
> unprecedented. A wind is blowing through the House of
> Islam. [4]

Our role in this Fifth Column move of the Holy Spirit within the
heart of Islam is to pray for the Holy Spirit to continue to manifest
in this way. As we see from Acts 5, we can ask the Lord to move in
signs and wonders to advance the Gospel. So we are praying into
reality the words of Jesus Christ.

No one can come to me unless the Father who sent me draws him, and I will raise him up at the last day. It is written in the prophets, 'And they will all be taught by God.' Everyone who hears and learns from the Father comes to me. (John 6:44-45)

Concluding Vision and Our Call to Pray into the Father's Strategy

Let us draw together these four great moves of the Holy Spirit, all part of the Father's plans for world evangelization. Ours is the work of earnest prayer in unity, in the name of Jesus Christ. Where Jesus is present and we are led by the Holy Spirit, we actually pray Jesus' prayers which the Father always hears and answers. The following prayer experience that took place in Korea provides a glimpse into the work that is so crucial if the demonic strongholds are to be defeated and the victory of Jesus Christ secured.

One such occasion took place in 2014 at a location at the Jesus Abbey annex—the high ridge mountain cow pastures of the Fourth River Project in South Korea. A stone altar was placed there with a large flat stone on top. In the stone is engraved a map of Korea marking that point as the watershed of three rivers. One river runs to the west coast of Korea and faces China. Another river runs east across the ocean to Japan and further to North America. There is a river streaming south to the end of the Korean Peninsula across the oceans to South Asia and to the largest Muslim majority nation in the world, Indonesia. Not etched in the stone map, but living in the hearts of many Koreans and the founder of the Fourth River Project, Ben Torrey, is a fourth river flowing north into North Korea and Manchuria. This represents the River of Life in Jesus Christ. Groups of intercessors have gathered there by the hundreds to pray for the waves of the Holy Spirit represented by those four rivers.

On this occasion, Ben Torrey and I were joined by a team from America, Taiwan, Korea and China, with one of the American women present having spent her early childhood in Japan. We gathered around the stone map and were caught up praying in the Spirit. Suddenly, in the same way that I was caught up into the heavenlies at the Community of the Cross and given terrifying visions of an Islamic jihadist apocalypse resulting in the genocide of billions, I was caught up again. I saw physical rivers representing rivers of living water flowing from the Father's throne, all welcomed and conducted by our prayers, faith and obedience. That afternoon our prayers were joining the chorus of prayers of a vast host of Koreans, all part of the Holy Spirit's global symphony of intercession. In the vision I heard Jesus say, "Now, face west, pray for my river of life surging into China. As we all faced toward China with the Chinese-speakers praying in Mandarin, I saw millions upon millions of Chinese coming to faith in Jesus. They were being equipped through our teaching on the Holy Spirit, filled with the Holy Spirit, and then surging on toward the Muslim world. We were caught up in praying for healing between the Chinese, the Koreans, and the Japanese.

Then Jesus said, "Now turn east, and pray for the outpouring of the Holy Spirit upon those who identify with my chosen people that they may join the mission." We were also called to pray in English for the entire Western World that there would be mighty rivers of revival.

Then Jesus led Ben Torrey to call us all to lift our hands. He began to pray in Korean for the river of life into North Korea. Finally, we faced south and prayed for the river to go to South Asia. Then in the vision I was having, suddenly I begin to see rivers and rivers of Asian faces. As the faces were coming into higher definition, I realized with a shock of joy that I recognized many of the faces. They were from Indonesia, Taiwan, Korea, Japan, China, North and South

America, and the United Kingdom and Africa—the very people with whom our team had gathered around the stone map.

Then the Lord said, "These rivers have already begun. Now pray for the next phase to close the ring on the Muslim world, that they may also be swept up into the river of life." After these last prayers, the Holy Spirit lifted from us and we went back down the mountain rejoicing.

In retrospect, as I was reviewing this remarkable experience, I kept being drawn back to the fourth river of life that was flowing north to North Korea. Suddenly I grasped that this is not a call to prayer for North Korea alone, but a prayer for the Holy Spirit to move directly through visions, dreams, signs and wonders within the hearts of those who are enslaved in any oppressive totalitarian government or system. This is prayer for the fifth column, the Wind of the Holy Spirit within the House of Islam.

We have been given this vision and this command, "These rivers of my Holy Spirit have already begun to flow. Now, pray for the next phase to advance my Kingdom. Pray that these waves will converge together, closing the ring on the Muslim world, that they may also be swept up into the river of life." We must pray together, "Come, Lord Jesus, come! Father, draw to yourself all your children, including from the House of Islam."

The result will be the fulfillment of the vision given in Philippians 2:8-11:

> [8]And being found in appearance as a man, he humbled himself by becoming obedient to death—even death on a cross! [9]Therefore God exalted him to the highest place and gave him the name that is above every name, [10]that at the name of Jesus every knee should bow, in heaven and on earth and under the earth, [11]and every tongue acknowledge that Jesus Christ is Lord, to the glory of God

the Father.

The Holy Spirit Mobilizing, Equipping and Deploying Jesus' Army of Intercessors

I believe the Holy Spirit is speaking prophetic words from Jesus Christ that implement the Father's master plans in this present "kairos moment" to counter the works of Satan in this "hour of the power of darkness" and to advance the Gospel into the entire Muslim world. These prophetic words are intended to mobilize, equip and deploy an army of intercessors to support the four great waves of the Holy Spirit converging on Jerusalem through the Father's 21st century campaigns:

Jesus is calling for a 21st century campaign of love for all those in bondage to Islam. Because He says, "For this is the way God loved the world: He gave his one and only Son, so that everyone who believes in him will not perish but have eternal life." (John 3:16)

Jesus Christ is calling for a campaign to defeat the demonic strongholds of Radical Islam and advance the Kingdom of God into the entire Muslim world. The Lord says:

[18]..."I saw Satan fall like lightning from heaven. [19]Look, I have given you authority to tread on snakes and scorpions and on the full force of the enemy, and nothing will hurt you. [20]Nevertheless, do not rejoice that the spirits submit to you, but rejoice that your names stand written in heaven." (Luke 10:18-20)

The Lord Jesus is calling for a campaign of intercessory prayer, that we would bid the Father, "Thy Kingdom come" according to Jesus' command. This will by necessity include praying for those in governmental authority entrusted by God with, "a sword to be drawn against all murderers"[1] to destroy the works of the Devil through the war machine of Radical Islam.

Jesus Christ is calling for a campaign of prayer and evangelistic outreach for the liberation of Muslims from the bondage of death by overcoming the deception of Islam. Jesus says, "I am the way, and the truth, and the life. No one comes to the Father except through me." (John 14:6)

Jesus Christ is calling for a campaign of the Cross to overcome the power of death embodied in the Crescent with his power of resurrection life. Jesus Christ who died on the cross, says:

[25]"I am the resurrection and the life. The one who believes in me will live even if he dies, [26]and the one who lives and believes in me will never die. Do you believe this?" (John 11:25-26)

A Waking Vision of the Menorah, the Olive Trees, Jesus' Cross, and the Descending Dove

As I was rewriting this chapter and praying for guidance about the nature of the Father's campaigns to advance the Kingdom of Jesus Christ, I took a break for a nap. As I lay in bed praying in tongues, I drifted off and had a dream/vision, which continued after I woke up.

In the Spirit, I saw a flaming golden menorah. On either side of the menorah growing in wild profusion were two olive trees laden with fruit. Then, between the olive trees, but growing out of the center of the menorah, was the empty cross of Jesus Christ. Then a flaming dove descended and remained on the menorah, the olive trees and the cross. Each symbol was distinct, but organically connected by the intermingled fire of the dove and the menorah. I then saw the hand of God pushing this flaming structure against a sinister black fortress that I knew to be Islam. The walls of fortress Islam were crumbling and being swept away by rivers of living water flowing in the wake of the flaming structure.

In this waking dream/vision, I felt the Holy Spirit impressing upon me the message that the 21st century campaign of love, prayer and evangelism will fulfill the Father's purposes only if born again Jews and Gentiles are moving in unity with one another as God's covenant people. This unity is the basis of the spiritual authority to divide and scatter Satan's kingdom of Islam. Jesus' campaigns must also be conducted according to God's means which is by the authority of Jesus Christ and the empowering of the Holy Spirit.

I had been meditating on the vision of the menorah of pure gold and the two olive trees in Zechariah 4:1-5. That must be where the images came from. However, the flaming dove representing the Holy Spirit is not in Zechariah's vision. It is given in God's interpretation of the vision. *Therefore he told me, "These signify the word of the LORD to Zerubbabel: 'Not by strength and not by power, but by my Spirit,' says the LORD who rules over all."* (Zechariah 4:6) This is clear guidance to me that these campaigns which must be launched into this present kairos moment to defeat Satan's plans can only be accomplished by the means Jesus has given us in Acts 1:4-8, which is, *"by my Spirit."*

> [5]For John baptized with water, but you will be baptized with the Holy Spirit not many days from now."

> [6]So when they had gathered together, they began to ask him, "Lord, is this the time when you are restoring the kingdom to Israel?" [7]He told them, "You are not permitted to know the times or periods that the Father has set by his own authority.

> [8]But you will receive power when the Holy Spirit has come upon you, and you will be my witnesses in Jerusalem, and in all Judea and Samaria, and to the farthest parts of the earth."

The commission Jesus has given his disciples in Acts 1:4-8 is a New Covenant updating of the vision given in Zechariah 4:1-6. In Jesus' campaign, my vision of the flaming menorah, the two olive trees, the cross and the descending dove reveal its character and the means we are to use to achieve this victory. The only way that individual Christians and the Church of Jesus Christ can take part in this campaign of love, prayer and evangelism is in the power of the Holy Spirit.

The baptism with the Holy Spirit given in Acts 1:5 is the gateway into the dynamic of receiving the power and gifts of the Holy Spirit for participating in Jesus' campaign to defeat demonic strongholds, to set the captives free, and to advance the Kingdom of

Jesus into the Muslim world. Through this vision and prophetic word calling us to participate in these campaigns, we are being given a kairos moment of opportunity as the Holy Spirit is calling us to cooperate with Jesus in fulfilling the Great Commission.

Resurrection Life of Jesus Christ Embodied in the Cross Overcoming the Power of Death in the Crescent

In another age the term *crusade* would have been used instead of *campaign*. But *crusade* carries too much negative baggage. The positive meaning of the term *crusade* is that all who are called into this war by Jesus must take up their cross and follow Him. This term points to the core of the clash between Christianity and Islam. The armies of Christ in a crusade of life warring against the slave armies of Satan in a Jihad of death.

From the beginning of Islam through the false prophet Muhammad, Satan has waged a war against the cross of Jesus Christ.[2] The cross is the heart of the Christian message, but Satan rejects and replaces that message through the deception of Islam. As already confirmed, Islam rejects the historical fact that Jesus died on the cross, rejects the New Testament witness that that he rose from the dead, rejects that he ascended into heaven, and fundamentally rejects the biblical revelation that Jesus Christ is the Son of God, the second person of the One True God. In rejecting the cross, Islam rejects God's way of salvation that is based on the covenants with Israel fulfilled by Jesus' life, death and resurrection.

These intentions of Satan in Islam are explicitly and publicly stated by Satan's agents who identify themselves as following the example of Muhammad and obeying the commands of Allah in the Quran. The leaders of the Islamic State have declared a war based on their Islamic faith against the "Nations of the Cross." And the Iranian Mullahs require Allah's slaves in all their Mosques each

Friday to chant, "Death to America and death to Israel."[3] This means murdering the members of those cultures that have their roots in Judeo-Christian (the Menorah and the Cross) values. This is Islam's war of extermination of Jews and Christians and against Western culture.

Additionally, the Islamic jihadists clearly state that their war is not just against the people and our culture, but also against our spiritual root which is our biblical faith.

BREAK THE CROSS

http://www.clarionproject.org/factsheets-files/islamic-state-magazine-dabiq-fifteen-breaking-the-cross.pdf

The 15th issue of *Dabiq*, their propaganda magazine, is titled "Break the Cross." This is an eighty-page declaration of war against Christians and Christianity—a satanically inspired curse based on the deceptions of Islam, spoken against the cross of Jesus Christ, the basis of our faith. The cover of the Dabiq magazine exposes the war plans of Radical Islam: The Cross of Jesus Christ is being replaced by the Black Flag of ISIS which displays in white the creed of Islam. "There is no God but Allah and Muhammad is his Messenger." This word from ISIS "Break the Cross" is being spoken into the "hour of the power of darkness" where Satan is already carrying out his four deadly plans through Radical Islam. The first plan is the replacement of God's way of salvation with the deception of Islam. This curse has been released publicly for demons everywhere to use to mobilize anyone who has been deceived by Islam to join Satan's cause of destroying God's way of salvation by dismantling crosses, destroying churches, and murdering or subjugating Christians.

The word the Holy Spirit is giving in order to counter and

defeat Satan's movement embodied in the name "Breaking the Cross," is a "Campaign of the Cross of Jesus Christ overcoming the power of death embodied in the Crescent with the power of resurrection life." It is at this point that *crusade* is the actual word that I believe Jesus is speaking this word into the kairos moment to mobilize and direct our warfare to defeat the strongholds of Radical Islam and to overcome the deception of Islam with the truth of Jesus Christ. Jesus died on the cross; therefore, he declares to all humanity, [25]*"I am the resurrection and the life. The one who believes in me will live even if he dies,* [26]*and the one who lives and believes in me will never die..."* (John 11:25-26) All who are called to serve in Jesus' campaigns and sent into combat in any one or all of the three battlespaces must do so according to Jesus' command, [34]*"Whosoever will come after me, let him deny himself, and take up his cross, and follow me."* (Mark_8:34)

The 21st Century Campaign of Intercession

Encountering Jesus Christ in a mystical vision prompted me to develop the Prayer Strategy for Jesus' Victory over Radical Islam. This happened while I was in prayer on March 20, 2010. First, the Lord gave me visions of the unleashing of Satan's schemes through Radical Islam. The Holy Spirit overwhelmed me with vivid pictures of worldwide jihad, a second holocaust of Jews and Christians of not millions, but billions, murdered, and the replacement of God's way of life with Satan's way of death. The Lord said, "I have given you a glimpse of Satan's plans for the world; these are not my plans." Then came another word of command that reverberated through my whole being, "I am calling and anointing you with the Holy Spirit to cooperate with Jesus Christ in mobilizing, equipping and deploying an army of intercessors to defeat Satan's plans in Radical Islam and to advance the Kingdom of Jesus to the ends of the Earth."

In obedience to this calling, I have written these books,

prepared teaching materials, and have been working with a growing international team to provide the contexts for the Holy Spirit to equip and deploy intercessors.

As I demonstrated throughout both book I and II, our enemy is not the human structures of the demonic strongholds created from the core deceptions of Muhammad, but the demonic powers behind Muhammad, the religious political system of Islam and the strongholds constructed by Satan. (Ephesians 6:12)

In this struggle, our primary weapons are spiritual. Foremost are intercession and tactics of spiritual warfare. This campaign of intercession is rooted in the prayer that Jesus Christ taught his first disciples to pray. [9] *"So pray this way: Our Father in heaven, may your name be honored,* [10]*may your kingdom come, may your will be done on earth as it is in heaven."* (Matthew 6:9-10) When intercessors pray, "Father, your Kingdom come" we are asking him in the name of Jesus Christ to pour out his Holy Spirit in waves to advance the Gospel. We will also be praying for those in governmental authority entrusted by God with "a sword to be drawn against all murderers"[4] to destroy the war machine of Radical Islam that has chosen tyranny to enslave their own and the murder of all who do not submit. Our role as intercessors is to be in the position of Moses, Aaron and Hur in support of Joshua and the army fighting against the enemies of God.

The Father has ordained that prayer is the basis and wellspring of advancing his Kingdom in the world. Therefore, the intercessors are the vanguard in Jesus' 21st century campaigns.

The Recapture of Dabiq Confirming this Strategy

Above I referred to the ISIS propaganda magazine Dabiq making the the declaration of the curse against the Christian faith, "Breaking the Cross." Just as this book was about to go to press in

December 2016 one of our intercessors noted that the magazine Dabiq is no longer being published![5]

To understand the significance of this event the title of this propaganda publication is the name of a small desert town in Northern Syria that had been held by ISIS. The town had very little military significance. However this. Islamic jihadist believed an ancient prophecy that Dabiq would be the location where their "Messiah" known as the "Mahdi" would bring the final victory over all the infidels. The name Dabiq thus became a battle cry for ISIS and the "victory" that this Mahdi would bring.

However, in the October 18, 2016 edition of Breaking Israeli News had this headline: *Islamic Messianic Dreams Shattered as ISIS Defeated in Dabiq* [6]

Turkish Foreign Minister Mevlut Cavusoglu announced on Sunday that Dabiq was fully under control of Turkish-backed Syrian rebels. The Islamic State(ISIS) reinforced the small city with over 1,200 fighters, carpeting the surrounding area with mines and Improvised Explosive Devices (IED). Approximately 2,000 rebel fighters, supported by Turkish tanks and infantry, and US-led coalition air-support, faced off against the terrorists.

This defeat of ISIS at the keystone of their apocalyptic vison confirms that the Holy Spirit is implementing this prayer strategy which includes all three battlespaces and the interface between the roles of Moses the intercessor and Joshua the warrior. Glory to God! This battlefield victory over ISIS also confirms the constantly morphing nature of Satan's strongholds and tactics based on Islam. Even as you are reading this book, the names of the leaders and the nature of the threat will be changing. Just as the stronghold of ISIS gained the power to implement Satan's agenda suddenly burst onto the in 2014 they could just as quickly be replaced by another expression of the same deadly stronghold based on Islam. Intercessors as well as our political and military leaders must remain constantly alert and prepared.

Jesus calls us as his friends and coworkers to persist with him, in this campaign of intercession until Satan's lies sown in the hearts of Muslims are replaced by the indwelling of the Holy Spirit bringing God's truth. This takes us to the next campaign.

The 21st Century Campaign of Evangelism in the Power of the Holy Spirit

The Father, through the sending of Jesus Christ and the outpouring of the Holy Spirit has already launched this campaign of evangelism. These campaigns are a necessary adaptation of the means of fulfilling the Great Commission due to the deadly challenges posed by Radical Islam designed for replacing God's way of salvation and exterminating Jews and Christians.[7]

In the 21st century campaigns, unlike the 11th century Crusades, there is a clear separation between the role of the Church of Jesus Christ and the role of government responsible for the military aspects in the defensive and offensive war against the Islamic jihad. The Church is called to the spiritual aspects of this war—intercession and witnessing to Muslims about Jesus Christ as the way of life. This is already happening and is intensifying in the four great waves of the Holy Spirit as I already discussed. These campaigns are in continuity with the Father's plans for redemption of all humanity through Jesus Christ, the only name given under heaven by which humanity may be saved. (Acts 4:12)

The victory of Jesus Christ over Radical Islam consists not only in setting the captives free from Islamic tyranny which will require military victories over Jihadist armies but also in offering the opportunity to enter into the Kingdom of God through faith in Jesus

Christ. This is accomplished not in human power and might, but only in the power of the Holy Spirit and the Father's love.

Is the Holy Spirit Calling you to join Jesus' 21st Century Campaign?

Let me summarize the call. Listen to the Holy Spirit speaking through many prophetic voices. The call is being given to join Jesus' campaign to defeat Satan's plans and to advance the Kingdom of God.

In this epoch, Satan is mustering the forces to destroy both the Church of Jesus Christ and Western culture through the demonic strongholds of Radical Islam, strongholds wielding demonic, cultural and military power. Counteracting Satan's plans, the two millenniums westward blowing wind of the Holy Spirit which started in Jerusalem is now converging on Jerusalem. Jesus is mobilizing, equipping and deploying a global army of intercessors who are the vanguard of these 21st century campaigns of love, prayer and evangelism. God has so arranged it that he will not accomplish the victory goals for this campaign unless we say, "Yes, I am in."

The challenge before us as individuals, as a culture and above all as the Church of Jesus Christ is to say, "Yes, we are in." The future depends on our faith and obedience. In all the various roles in the army of intercessors, Jesus is calling us to take up our crosses, and in the power and guidance of the Holy Spirit, follow him.

The storm clouds are gathering! Is God calling you into the war which Satan has declared against the Kingdom of God and all humanity? This war transcends the clash of civilizations and becomes the clash of the Kingdom of God on earth against the evil empire of Satan. Neither secularists nor Muslims have any idea where history is headed. Only those with a biblical worldview can know the true choice before each of us and the means and goals of

Jesus' 21st century campaign.

The choice is simple: Satan's kingdom or the Kingdom of God? Jesus alone has paid the price for the redemption of creation and to him alone is given authority and judgment over the nations. (Rev. 5:12) Jesus alone is the One from above; He alone sees clearly. (John 8:23) All others, including Muhammad, are "from below." Those who are in Christ are treated as friends of God. (John 15:15) God reveals to us his secrets and shows us where history is leading us all, including Muslims. It is we, not Muslims, nor governments, who wield the iron scepter of prayer over the nations. (Rev. 2:26-27) There can be no other conclusion than the one clearly described in the Bible—the complete defeat of Satan's host and the triumph of God's appointed Messiah. (Rev. 19, 20)

Jesus is Victor!

Notes

Chapter 1
Facing the Dire Threat of Radical Islam

1. Patrick Goodenough, "4 Sunni Muslim Groups Responsible for 66% of All 17,958 Terror Killings in 2013," Nov. 19, 2014, CNS News, http://www.cnsnews.com/news/article/patrick-goodenough/4-sunni-muslim-groups-responsible-66-all-17958-terror-killings-2013.

2. Jonathan Edwards, *Thoughts on the Revival in New England* – 1740 Part V 7 Sec III. New-York : American Tract Society, [1844 or 1845], http://www.worldcat.org/title/thoughts-on-the-revival-of-religion-in-new-england-1740-to-which-is-prefixed-a-narrative-of-the-surprising-work-of-god-in-northampton-mass-1735/oclc/002085705

3. "Iran Supporting More than 100 Shiite Terror Groups," Jun. 17 2015, The Clarion Project, http://www.clarionproject.org/news/iran-supporting-more-100-shiite-terror-groups-report.

4. "Muslim Terrorist Attack at Orlando Gay Club, At Least 50 Dead, More than 53 Wounded," Jun. 12 2016, Bare Naked Islam, http://www.barenaked islam.com/2016/06/12/muslim-terrorist-attack-at-orlando-gay-club-at-least-50-dead-more-than-53-wounded/.

Chapter 2
Who Serve in the Army of Intercessors?

1. Samantha Levine, "Hanging Chads: As the Florida Recount Implodes, the Supreme Court Decides Bush v. Gore," Jan. 17 2008, U.S. News, http://www.usnews.com/news/articles/2008/01/17/the-legacy-of-hanging-chads

2. Kenneth Leach, *True Prayer* (Harper, San Francisco, 1980), 25.

Chapter 3
Cohorts of Intercessors for Defeating Strongholds

1. Don Hooser, "9/11 and the Apparent Miracles on that Day," Sep. 9 2011, Beyond Today, https://www.ucg.org/beyond-today/blogs/911-and-the-apparent-miracles-on-that-day.

2. "Moravian Revival," Jul. 6 2005, Evan Wiggs, http://www.evanwiggs.com/revival/history/moravian.html.

3. Jesus Abbey's website, http://www.jabbey.org/bbs/main.php. "Jesus Abbey's Three Seas Center," Jesus Abbey, http://www.the fourthriver.org/PDF%20Documents/Main%20Brochure%20English.pdf.

4. The International House of Prayer (IHOP) was started on May 7, 1999 by Mike Bickle. http://www.ihopkc.org/ihopu/.

5. Jerusalem Prayer Tower, http://www.jerusalemprayertower.org/.

6. "Islamic Terror on Christians," The Religion of Peace, http://www.the religionofpeace.com/attacks/christian-attacks.aspx.

7. This process of receiving vision is given in detail in the book I (Brad Long) wrote with Doug McMurry: *Prayer That Shapes the Future: Praying with Power and Authority* (Zondervan, Grand Rapids, MI, 1999).

8. Major Brian R. Reinwald, US Army, "Tactical Intuition," Military Review, September-October 2000, https://www.questia.com/library/p5876/military-review.

9. "Back in the 1990s, the British anthropologist Robin Dunbar noticed a remarkable correlation between primate brain size and the social groups they formed. This correlation was simple: the bigger their brains, the larger their social groups. And the explanation seemed reasonable: animals with bigger brains can remember, and therefore interact meaningfully with, more of their peers. That led Dunbar to a famous prediction. By plotting the correlation and extrapolating the curve to the size of the human brain, he predicted that humans could have no more than about 150 people in their social sphere. Humans really do seem to have a natural limit to the number of meaningful relationships they can have. And this number is about 150." Emerging Technology from the arXiv, "Your Brain Limits You to Just Five BFFs," Apr. 29 2016, MIT Technology Review, https://www.technology.review.com/s/601369/your-brain-limits-you-to-just-five-bffs/.

Notes

Chapter 4
Opposing War Aims of the Lord and of Satan

1. Carl Von Clausewitz, *On War*, Edited and Translated by Michael Howard and Peter Paret (Princeton University Press, 1976), 128.
2. Ibid..
3. Ibid., 87.
4. Declaration of Independence, Preamble (U.S. 1776), The National Archives, http://www.archives.gov/exhibits/charters/declaration transcript.html.
5. Dr. Sebastian Gorka, *Defeating Jihad: The Winnable War* (Regnery Publishing, Washington DC., 2016), 105.
6. Ibid., 106.
7. Ibid.
8. The concept of a cluster of leaders is articulated in Peggy Noonan's article in the Wall Street Journal. She called such a gathering a "genius cluster." Peggy Noonan, "A World in Crisis, and No Geniuses in Sight: An Old Order is Being Swept Away, and Political Leaders Everywhere Seem Lost," Jul. 1 2016, The Wall Street Journal, http://www.wsj.com/articles/a-world-in-crisis-and-no-genius-in-sight-1467328674.

Chapter 5
Into the Gap: Engagements with the Enemy

1. Clausewitz, *On War*, 128.
2. Ibid., 182.
3. Evan Perez, "Cleric Issues Call to Kill Americans," Nov. 8 2010, The Wall Street Journal, http://www.wsj.com/articles/SB10001424052748703 51490457560292412695l244?alg=y.
4. "Anwar al-Awlaki killed in Yemen: Officials confirm death in al-Jawf of dual Yemeni-American citizen accused by US of spreading al-Qaeda's message," Sep. 30 2011, Aljazeera Middle East News, http://www.aljazeera.com/ news/middleeast/2011/09/201193083340115111.html.

Chapter 6
The Holy Spirit's Strategy and Tactics

1. Clausewitz, *On War*, 177.

Chapter 7
Intelligence Preparation of the Battlespace

1. Fundamentals of Intelligence, Preparation of the Battlefield/Battlespace, pg. 1, http://armypubs.army.mil/doctrine/DR_pubs/dra/pdf/atp201x3.pdf.

2. David Garrison, *A Wind in the House of Islam: How God is Drawing Muslims around the World to Faith in Jesus Christ*, (Monument, CO: WIGTake Resources LLC, 2014).

3. United States, Office of the Press Secretary, George W. Bush, "Address to a Joint Session of Congress and the American People," Sep. 20 2001, https://georgewbush-whitehouse.archives.gov/news/releases/2001/09/print/20010920-8.html.

4. Joel Richardson, *Will Islam be Our Future?* Chapter 6, "The Muslim Jesus" Answering Islam, http://www.answeringislam.org/Authors/JR/Future/ch06_the_muslim_jesus.htm.

5. I have been profoundly helped in understanding this complex process of the formation of strongholds that are intermingled spiritual and human realities by the two following sources: *A Study of History*, by Arnold J. Toynbee, and *The Social Construction of Reality: A Treatise in the Sociology of Knowledge*, by Peter L. Berger and Thomas Luckmann.
    Toynbee explains the role of the mystic with a vision of reality. A "creative minority" forms around the mystic, and it is through them that the vision actualized in human society.
    Section II of Berger and Luckmann's book elucidates the principles of how a social structure such as the Islamic State, with its own social and spiritual reality, may be formed.
    Arnold J. Toynbee, *A Study of History*, Abridgement of Volumes I-VI by D.C. Somervell (Oxford University Press, New York, 1947), 214-217.
    Peter L. Berger & Thomas Luckmann, *The Social Construction of Reality: A Treatise in the Sociology of Knowledge* (Garden City, NY, Doubleday & Company, 1966).

6. The Lord Jesus points to what we may call demonic kairos moments or a demonic moment of opportunity while he is being arrested. "Day after day when I was with you in the temple courts, you did not arrest me. But this is your hour, and that of the power of darkness!" (Luke 22:53 NET) "Hour" here

Notes

is for "hour" or "season" and not "kairos," but it is clearly the opportunity when the conditions were right for the Devil to work within human history.

7. The "routinization of charisma" is Max Weber's term for how charismatic, prophetic leadership becomes structured, organized, and made transferable to others.
   "Charismatic Authority," Mar. 11 2016, Wikipedia, The Free Encyclopedia, https://en.wikipedia.org/wiki/Charismatic_authority.
8. "Sun Tzu>Quotes>Quotable Quote," Apr. 20 2016, Quotable Quotes, *Good Reads*, http://www.goodreads.com/quotes/17976-if-you-know-the-enemy-and-know-yourself-you-need.
9. "Out of intense complexities, intense simplicities emerge," Winston Churchill Quotes, winstonchurchill.com, http://aboutwinston churchill.com/127/2013/09/out-of-intense-complexities-intense-simplicities-emerge-winston-churchill-2/.
10. Jonathan Sandys and Wallace Henley, *God & Churchill: How Great Leader's Sense of Divine Destiny Changed His Troubled World and Offers Hope for Ours* (Tyndale Momentum, 2015, http://tyndalemomentum.com/books/god-and-churchill/), 117.
11. Winston Churchill, "Minister Winston Churchill's Broadcast on the Soviet-German War," Jun. 22 1941, The BBC, Radio, http://www.ibiblio.org/pha/policy/1941/410622d.html.
12. This statement is based on my experience of working with non-Christians in China, Taiwan, Korea, and Africa who—while involved in non-Christian religions including Islam—were neither possessed nor, in many cases, occupied by demons. They were people whom the Bible would call "God fearers" and were like Cornelius in Acts 10. They were also those whom Paul talks about in Romans 2:13-16. I must also affirm that in many more cases when those outside of the Christian faith—including Muslims—came to faith in Jesus Christ, their conversions were accompanied by the casting out of demons who had gotten attached to them through both their unconfessed sins of violating the Ten Commandments and/or participating in non-Christian beliefs and practices.

Chapter 8
Tactics for Piercing the Demonic Cloaking

1. This is the purpose of the Presbyterian Reformed Ministries International's Dunamis Project, which provides a safe place through the love of Jesus Christ, prayer, worship, community discernment and biblical teaching. Here one may experience the Holy Spirit working. www.prmi.org. Other ministries offer similar such opportunities to experience the real presence of Jesus Christ.

2. This is a composite of several experiences with high level demons that I had while being mentored by Archer Torrey. On another occasion, after a time of praying for the advancement of the Gospel of Jesus Christ, another archon manifested. Its name was given as Dagon. That was another major prayer battle that took most of the night.

3. Spoken to me in a personal conversation. For more of this story, see his excellent book telling of his own experience of Islam, *Lost Boy No More: A True Story of Survival and Salvation* (by Abraham Nhial and DiAnn Mill, B&H Publishing Group, Nashville, 2004). Also see the report on CBS Sixty Minutes featuring the Lost Boys: Scott Pelley, "The Lost Boys," Jan. 19 2014, 60 Minutes, cbsnews.com, http://www.cbsnews.com/news/60-minutes-presents-tales-of-survival/.

4. Another person who is a credible witness is Robert Spencer. He is a brilliant writer and speaker. He maintains a web site called Jihad Watch (https://www.jihadwatch.org/). There are many others.

5. Matthew Dalton, William Horobin, Inti Landauro, and Thomas Valera, "Seven Militants Led Deadly Paris Attacks," Nov. 14, 2015, The Wall Street Journal, http://www.wsj.com/articles/paris-attacks-were-an-act-of-war-by-islamic-state-french-president-francois-hollande-says-1447498080.

6. Arwa Damon, Jethro Mullen, Catherine E. Sholchet, "Russian Plane Crash in Sinai: Questions Swirl as 224 Aboard are Mourned," Nov. 2 2015, CNN, http://www.cnn.com/2015/11/01/middleeast/egypt-sinai-russian-plane-crash/.

7. Steve Almasy, Jason Hanna, and Ed Payne, "Deadly Mali Hotel Attack: 'They were shooting at anything that moved'," CNN, http://www.cnn.com/2015/11/20/africa/mali-shooting/.

8. I go into much more detail and give the biblical bases for the nature of "Kairos

Moments" when the Holy Spirit is at work and the "Hour of the Power of Darkness" when Satan is at work in Chapter 23.

9. "For Want of a Nail," Nov. 1 2016, Wikipedia, The Free Encyclopedia, https://en.wikipedia.org/wiki/For_Want_of_a_Nail.

10. "Belgian Authorities Arrest 16 in Anti-Terror Raids," Nov. 22 2015, FoxNews.com, http://www.foxnews.com/world/2015/11/22/belgian-authorities-arrest-six-in-anti-terror-raids/?intcmp=hpbt3.

11. Jay Akbar, Jennifer Newton, and Julian Robinson, "Dramatic Moment World's Most Wanted Terrorist Dragged Away: ISIS Fugitive Behind Paris Massacre is Caught Trying to Flee His Brussels Hideout Run Past Armed Police," DailyMail.com, http://www.dailymail.co.uk/news/article-3498786/Prime-suspect-Paris-attacks-escaped-police-Brussels-shoot-Salah-Abdeslam-s-fingerprints-raided-flat.html.

12. "19 Yazidi Girls Burned Alive for Refusing to Have Sex with Their ISIS Captors," Jun. 6 2016, FoxNews.com, http://www.foxnews.com/world/2016/06/06/19-yazidi-girls-burned-alive-for-refusing-to-have-sex-with-their-isis-captors.html.

Chapter 9
Are Intercessors Authorized to Engage the Archons?

1. Job 1:6-7. Now the day came when the sons of God came to present themselves before the LORD—and Satan also arrived among them. (7) The LORD said to Satan, "Where have you come from?" And Satan answered the LORD, "From roving about on the earth, and from walking back and forth across it."

2. 2 Corinthians 12:2-4. (2) I know a man in Christ who fourteen years ago (whether in the body or out of the body I do not know, God knows) was caught up to the third heaven. (3) And I know that this man (whether in the body or apart from the body I do not know, God knows) (4) was caught up into paradise and heard things too sacred to be put into words, things that a person is not permitted to speak.

3. Revelation 4:5. From the throne came out flashes of lightning and roaring and crashes of thunder. Seven flaming torches, which are the seven spirits of God, were burning in front of the throne. Revelation 5:6. Then I saw standing in the middle of the throne and of the four living creatures, and in the middle of the elders, a Lamb that appeared to have been killed. He had seven horns and

seven eyes, which are the seven spirits of God sent out into all the earth.
4. Mark 6:7 . Jesus called the twelve and began to send them out two by two. He gave them authority over the unclean spirits.
5. Associated Press, "Al-Qaida in Iraq's al-Zarqawi 'Terminated'," Jun. 8 2006, NBC News, http://www.nbcnews.com/id/13195017/ns/world_news-mideast_n_africa/t/al-qaida-iraqs-al-zarqawi-terminated/#.VrDx5PkrIU0.

Chapter 10
The Intercessor Standing Between Heaven and Earth

1. Athansius, *Life of St. Anthony*, revised and edited for New Advent by Kevin Knight, New Advent, http://www.newadvent.org/fathers/2811.htm.
2. "Saints Who Fought the Devil: The Temptation of St. Anthony," Oct. 23 2015, Adapted from the Portuguese by Elizabeth Lavigne, Aleteia, http://aleteia.org/2015/10/23/saints-who-fought-the-devil-the-temptation-of-st-anthony/.
3. Ibid..
4. From a personal interview with The Rev. Archer Torrey at Jesus Abbey, South Korea. Brad Long and Cindy Strickler, *The Dunamis Course #3 The Power of Prayer* (PRMI, Black Mountain, NC, 2011, http://dunamisinstitute.org/courses/pluginfile.php/823/mod_resource/content/0/06 Lesson 8 Work of Intercession.pdf), 148.
5. This is a composite of a number of prayer battles that I experienced with Archer Torrey while at Jesus Abbey – the Prayer Community in the Mountains of South Korea.
6. Norman Grubb, *Rees Howells: Intercessor* (CLC Publications, Fort Washington, PA, 1983), 254.
7. This is a written account of the complete vision:
Zeb Bradford Long, http://prmi.org/files/jesuscalltomissions.pdf.
This is a video of the whole mystical experience when I was caught up in heaven and had an astonishing encounter with the Father, Son and Holy Spirit:
Zeb Bradford Long, "010 Jan Video of 1996 Caught up into Heaven and Encountering Jesus Christ and being Called into Missions," Jan. 16 2010, Online video clip, Vimeo, https://vimeo.com/8777809.
8 *The Hymnbook*, Published by Presbyterian Church in the United States,

Notes

Presbyterian Church in the United States of America, United Presbyterian Church of North America, Reformed Church in America , Richmond, Philadelphia, Pittsburgh, New York MCMLV. p. 135, Hymn # 148 Let All Mortal Flesh Keep Silence.

9. The United Presbyterian Church in the U.S.A. and the The Reformed Church in the United States, *Hymnbook Published by the Presbyterian Church in the United States*, Hymn 91 (Richmond, Philadelphia, New York, 1955), 87.

Chapter 11
Binding the Demons at Work in the Leaders

1. I am adopting this term from President George W. Bush's 2002 State of the Union Address. He named the nations involved—Iran, Iraq, and North Korea. KellyWurx, "President Bush Axis of Evil Speech," Apr. 2 2013. YouTube, https://www.youtube.com/watch?v=btkJhAM7hZw.
2. "Remilitarization of the Rhineland," Sep. 8 2016, Wikipedia, the Free Encyclopedia, https://en.wikipedia.org/wiki/Remilitarization of the Rhineland.
3. Grubb, *Rees Howells: Intercessor*, 246.
4. Ibid., 222.
5. Ibid., 223-224.
6. Ibid., 225.
7. Ibid., 222.
8. Ibid., 223.
9. Ibid., 232.
10. Ibid., 223.
11. Dutch Sheets, *Authority in Prayer,* (Bethany House Publishers, Bloomington, MN. 2006), 20.
12. Joel Richardson, *Will Islam be Our Future: A Study of Biblical and Islamic Eschatology*, Chapter 5: "Comparing the Biblical Antichrist and the Mahdi," Answering Islam, http://www.answering-islam.org/Authors/JR/Future/ ch05 comparing the biblical antichrist.htm.
13. "Iranian President Prepares for 12th Imams Reappearance," 2006, CBN.com, http://www1.cbn.com/onlinediscipleship/iranian-president-prepares-for-12th-imam%27s-reappearance.
14. Bernard Lewis, "August 22," Aug. 8 2006, The Wall Street Journal,

http://www.wsj.com/articles/SB115500154638829470.
15. "Mutual assured destruction, " Nov. 22 2016, Wikipedia, the Free Encyclopedia, https://en.wikipedia.org/wiki/Mutual_assured_destruction.
16. Bernard Lewis, "August 22," Aug. 8 2006, The Wall Street Journal, http://www.wsj.com/articles/SB115500154638829470.
17. "Alliance of Builders of Islamic Iran," Nov. 7 2016, Wikipedia, the Free Encyclopedia, https://en.wikipedia.org/wiki/Alliance_of_Builders_of_Islamic_Iran.
18. "Mahmoud Ahmadinejad," Nov. 18 2016, Wikipedia, the Free Encyclopedia, https://en.wikipedia.org/wiki/Mahmoud_Ahmadinejad.
19. "Ex-Hostages: Iran's President was Captor," Jul. 1 2005, Fox News, http://www.foxnews.com/story/2005/07/01/ex-hostages-iran-president-was-captor.html.
20. Stoyan Zaimov, "Iranian President Ahmadinejad Tells UN Jesus Christ and 'Ultimate Savior' are Coming," The Christian Reporter, http://www.christianpost.com/news/iranian-president-ahmadinejad-tells-un-jesus-christ-and-ultimate-savior-are-coming-82336/.
It is about 30 minutes into the speech that he makes this prophetic announcement.
wesawthat1, "iran's president mahmoud ahmadinejad address to the 67th un general assembly 2012," Sep. 27 2012, YouTube, https://www.youtube.com/watch?v=BHyvkQpqQTE.
21. "Isa (Jesus) in the Hadith - 'Isa the destroyer of Christianity. The prophet 'Isa will have an important role in the end times, establishing Islam and making war until he destroys all religions save Islam. He shall kill the Evil One (Dajjal), an apocalyptic anti-Christ figure. In one tradition of Muhammad we read that no further prophets will come to earth until Isa returns as 'a man of medium height, or reddish complexion, wearing two light garments, looking as if drops were falling down from his head although it will not be wet. He will fight for the cause of Islam. He will break the cross, kill pigs, and abolish the poll-tax. Allah will destroy all religions except Islam. He ('Isa) will destroy the Evil One and will live on the earth for forty years and then he will die'. (Sunan Abu Dawud, 37:4310) The Sahih Muslim has a variant of this tradition: 'The son of Mary ... will soon descend among you as a just judge. He will ... abolish the poll-tax, and the wealth will pour forth to such an extent that no one will accept charitable gifts.' (Sahih Muslim 287) What do these

Notes

sayings mean? The cross is a symbol of Christianity. Breaking crosses means abolishing Christianity. Pigs are associated with Christians. Killing them is another way of speaking of the destruction of Christianity. Under Islamic law the poll-tax buys the protection of the lives and property of conquered 'people of the Book'. (At-Taubah 9:29) The abolition of the poll-tax means jihad is restarted against Christians (and Jews) living under Islam, who should convert to Islam, or else be killed or enslaved. The abundance of wealth refers to booty flowing to the Muslims from this conquest. This is what the Muslim 'Isa will do when he returns in the last days. Muslim jurists confirm these interpretations: Consider, for example, the ruling of Ahmad bin Naqib al-Misri (d. 1368). '... the time and the place for [the poll tax] is before the final descent of Jesus (upon whom be peace). After his final coming, nothing but Islam will be accepted from them, for taking the poll tax is only effective until Jesus' descent (upon him and our Prophet be peace) ... (The Reliance of the Traveller. Trans. Nuh Ha Mim Keller, p. 603). Ibn Naqib goes on to state that when Jesus returns, he will rule 'as a follower' of Muhammad." Dr. Mark Durie, "'Isa, the Muslim Jesus," Answering Islam, http://www.answering-islam.org/authors/durie/islamic_jesus.html.

22. Hitler's words and William Shirer's reflections: "'If the international Jewish financiers... should again succeed in plunging the nations into a world war the result will be... the annihilation of the Jewish race throughout Europe.' This was a prophecy, he said, and he repeated it five times, verbatim, in subsequent public utterances."
William L. Shire, *The Rise and Fall of the Third Reich*, (Simon and Schuster, New York, 1960), 964.

23. "Mahmoud Ahmadinejad," Nov. 18 2016, Wikipedia, the Free Encyclopedia, https://en.wikipedia.org/wiki/Mahmoud_Ahmadinejad.

24. "WARNING GRAPHIC PHOTOS (RAW) - ISIS begins killing Christians in Mosul, CHILDREN BEHEADED," Aug. 8 2014, Catholic Online, http://www.catholic.org/news/international/middle_east/story.php?id=56481.

25 Allegedly from a mid-sixteenth-century statement by John Bradford (1510–1555) an English Reformer "There but for the grace of God, goes John Bradford", in reference to a group of prisoners being led to execution. A paraphrase from the Bible, 1 Corinthians 15:8-10, which states, "Last of all, as to one born abnormally, he appeared to me. For I am the least of the apostles, not fit to be called an apostle, because I persecuted the church of

God. But by the grace of God I am what I am..."
https://en.wiktionary.org/wiki/there_but_for_the_grace_of_God_g
o_I

26. As this experience of hatred for the Devil and his works washed over me, I think I experienced what C.S. Lewis described in the book *Perelandra* about perfect hatred. This is from Chapter 12 when Ransom had to kill Weston with his own bare hands to keep the Devil from tempting the Green Lady (Eve) into disobeying Maleldil (God the Father, Son, and Holy Spirit).

26. Mark 3:27 (NET). But no one is able to enter a strong man's house and steal his property unless he first ties up the strong man. Then he can thoroughly plunder his house.

27. Used with permission.

Chapter 12
Breaking Satan's Curses

1. PRMI offers teaching on this dynamic in our Dunamis Project Unit #2, *In the Spirit's Power*, and in the books *Prayer that Shapes the Future* and *Growing the Church in the Power of the Holy Spirit.* See www.prmi.org or https://dunamisinstitute.org/.

2. "Fatwa," Nov. 17 2016, Wikipedia, the Free Encyclopedia, https://en.wikipedia.org/wiki/Fatwa.

3. Reza Kahlili, "Ayatollah: Kill All Jews, Annihilate Israel," Feb. 5 2012, World Net Daily, http://www.wnd.com/2012/02/ayatollah-kill-all-jews-annihilate-israel/.

4. Ibid.

5. Reza Kahlili, *A Time to Betray*, (Threshold Editions, 2010), http://superstore.wnd.com/A-Time-to-Betray-Hardcover.

6. Reza Kahlili, "Iran Warns World of Coming Great Event," Feb. 2 2012, World Net Daily, http://www.wnd.com/2012/02/iran-warns-world-of-coming-great-event/#qwM7TXttluhle5eg.99.

7. I do believe that--while perhaps not in the specifics of exterminating all the Jews in the world--the Holy Spirit did reveal Hitler's intentions to destroy the Jewish people.
This knowledge was based on astute observation and divine guidance. It did guide the actions and prayers of these two great leaders. For the historical

Notes

evidence concerning Winston Churchill, see:
Martin Gilbert, "Churchill and the Holocaust: The Possible and the Impossible," Nov. 8 1993, The International Churchill Society, http://www.winstonchurchill.org/support?catid=0&id=596.
For Rees Howells, see:
Norman Grubb, *Rees Howells: Intercessor* (CLC Publications, Fort Washington, PA, 1983).

8. "ISIS: We will raise our flag in the White House," Aug. 4 2014 , The Week, http://theweek.com/speedreads/448499/isis-raise-flag-white-house.

9. Walid Shoebat, "ISIS Sends Out This Message To All Christians: 'You Will Soon See An Ocean Of Blood For All The Nation Of The Cross'," Feb. 15 2015, Shoebat Foundation, http://shoebat.com/2015/02/15/isis-sends-message-christians-will-soon-see-ocean-blood-nation-cross/.

10. I got this summary from the following source:
dgitrader, "Are These Verses Really in the Quran?" May 8 2013, Nairaland Forum, http://www.nairaland.com/1283381/these-verses-really-quran.

11. Dale Hurd, "Brave German Woman Rebukes Islam's Lie," Sep. 7 2014, CBN News, http://www.cbn.com/cbnnews/world/2014/February/German-Woman-Publicly-Rebuking-Islam-Goes-Viral-/.

12. Boorstein, Michelle, "In a first, Washington National Cathedral to host Friday Muslim prayer service," Nov. 10 2014, The Washington Post, https://www.washingtonpost.com/local/in-a-first-washington-national-cathedral-to-host-regular-friday-muslim-prayer/2014/11/10/53d3425e-6916-11e4-9fb4-a622dae742a2_story.html.

13. Dale Hurd, "Brave German Woman Rebukes Islam's Lie," Sep. 7 2014, CBN News, http://www.cbn.com/cbnnews/world/2014/February/German-Woman-Publicly-Rebuking-Islam-Goes-Viral-/.

14. Winston Churchill, "Blood, Toil. Tears and Sweat," May 13 1940, The House of Commons, The International Churchill Society, http://www.winston churchill.org/resources/speeches/1940-the-finest-hour/blood-toil-tears-and-sweat.

15. Ibid.

16 Grubb, *Rees Howells: Intercessor*, 248.

17. Ibid., 253.

Chapter 13
Dividing Satan's Kingdom

1. In this long study entitled *THE PUNISHMENT FOR APOSTASY FROM ISLAM* by Silas, the author concludes: "We have examined the theological foundation of Islam and found that Islam's established ruling is that apostates are to be killed wherever they are. The Quran implies this while the Hadith, Sira, and works of jurisprudence state it clearly. When the breadth and depth of Islam are examined, this is the only conclusion that can be drawn."
Silas, *The Punishment for Apostasy from Islam*, Jan. 24 2007, Introduction, Answering Islam, http://www.answering-islam.org/Silas/apostasy.htm.

2. In this book, Asher offers profound biblical prophetic insights into the nature of the war we are in. Meeting him in Israel in 2015 and hearing him teach had a profound impact on me, changing my understanding of the battle that we are in and the role of the Jewish people in God's redemptive plans.
Asher Intrater, *From Iraq to Armageddon: The Final Showdown Approaches* (Destiny Image Publishers, Inc., Shippensburg, PA, 2003), 150-152.

3. This is a direct quote. Asher has refused to give Satan the credit or honor of capitalizing its name, even if this is against grammatical conventions.

4. Ibid., 150-152.

5. Christianity is the religion of the second chance. With Islam, it's often one strike and you're out. Jesus tells the woman caught in adultery, after He has shamed those who might have condemned her publicly, "Go and sin no more." One hadith (verse) tells about a woman pregnant by adultery coming to Muhammad: He has her treated decently until she gives birth, and then has her stoned to death. Islam teaches that Allah loves the righteous, but Christianity teaches, "While we were yet sinners, Christ died for us."
Marvin Olasky, "Brutality and dictatorship: How Islam affects society", Oct 27, 2001, *World.*

Chapter 14
Unity in Biblical, Trinitarian Faith

1. Luke 11:17, "But Jesus, realizing their thoughts, said to them, 'Every kingdom divided against itself is destroyed, and a divided household falls'."

2. John 17:21,"That they will all be one, just as you, Father, are in me and I am in you. I pray that they will be in us, so that the world will believe that you

sent me."

3. From a personal e-mail to me from Asher Intrater.

4. Once again we have an important topic that we do not have room to explore fully in this prayer strategy. I am speaking here of the divide between the liberal and evangelical sides of the Church. Liberal Christians have often focused on social transformation, issues of justice, and recently on climate change to the neglect of the spiritual message of the Gospel of salvation and eternal life. Evangelicals have often focused on the spiritual dimensions of the gospel as well as the ethical and moral imperatives of the Bible, and neglected the social justice issues. A Biblical understanding of the Kingdom of God has no such divide.

5. Father Ben Torrey, a Priest in the Church of the East is one of those called to serve as a link between the Eastern and Western Church.

6. (A disclaimer before defining these various terms.) I basically did a quick search on Google just to give a summary definition of these various heresies. They are not meant to be definitive of the often elaborate and complex theological debates that went into the formation of the creeds defining Biblical Trinitarian Faith. For some of that history I recommend the book *Early Christian Creeds* by J.N.D. Kelly (David McKay Company, New York, 1972).

    "*Arianism* is a nontrinitarian belief that asserts that Jesus Christ is the Son of God, created by God the Father, distinct from the Father and therefore subordinate to the Father. *Arian* teachings were first attributed to *Arius* (c. AD 250–336), a Christian presbyter in Alexandria, Egypt."

    "Arianism," Nov. 20 2016, Wikipedia, the Free Encyclopedia, https://en.wikipedia.org/wiki/Arianism.

7. "**Nestorianism** is a form of dyophysitism, and can be seen as the antithesis to monophysitism, which emerged in reaction to Nestorianism. Where Nestorianism holds that Christ had two loosely united natures, divine and human, monophysitism holds that he had but a single nature, his human nature being absorbed into his divinity. A brief definition of Nestorian Christology can be given as: 'Jesus Christ, who is not identical with the Son but personally united with the Son, who lives in him, is one hypostasis and one nature: human.'[1] Both Nestorianism and monophysitism were condemned as heretical at the Council of Chalcedon. Monophysitism survived and developed into the Miaphysitism of the modern Oriental

Orthodox churches."

"Nestorianism," Nov. 19 2016, Wikipedia, the Free Encyclopedia, https://en.wikipedia.org/wiki/Nestorianism.

8. **Monophysitism** (/məˈnɒfɨsaɪtɨzəm/ or /məˈnɒfɨsɪtɨzəm/; Greek: μονοφυσιτισμός from μόνος monos, 'only, single' and φύσις physis, 'nature'), is the Christological position that, after the union of the divine and the human in the historical Incarnation, Jesus Christ, as the incarnation of the eternal Son or Word (Logos) of God, had only a single 'nature' which was either divine or a synthesis of divine and human. Monophysitism is contrasted to dyophysitism (or dia-, dio-, or duophysitism) which maintains that Christ maintained two natures, one divine and one human, after the Incarnation. Historically, Monophysitism (usually capitalized in this sense) refers primarily to the position of those (especially in Egypt and to a lesser extent Syria) who rejected the Council of Chalcedon in 451 (the Fourth Ecumenical Council). The moderate members of this group, however, maintained a 'Miaphysite' theology that became that of the Oriental Orthodox churches. Many Oriental Orthodox reject the label 'Monophysite' even as a generic term, but it is extensively used in the historical literature."

"Monophysitism," Nov. 17 2016, Wikipedia, the Free Encyclopedia, https://en.wikipedia.org/wiki/Monophysitism.

9. "**Ebionites** (Greek: Ἐβιωναῖοι Ebionaioi, derived from Hebrew אביונים ebyonim, ebionim, meaning "the poor" or "poor ones"), is a patristic term referring to a Jewish Christian movement that existed during the early centuries of the Christian Era.[1] They regarded Jesus of Nazareth as the Messiah while rejecting his divinity[2] and insisted on the necessity of following Jewish law and rites.[3] The Ebionites used only one of the Jewish Gospels, revered James the Just, and rejected Paul the Apostle as an apostate from the Law.[4] Their name suggests that they placed a special value on voluntary poverty. Ebionim was one of the terms used by the sect at Qumran that sought to separate themselves from the corruption of the Temple, whom many believe were Essenes.[5]"

"Ebionites," Nov. 20 2016, Wikipedia, the Free Encyclopedia, https://en.wikipedia.org/wiki/Ebionites.

10. "The Nazarenes, then, recognized Jesus, though it appears from occasional references to them that they considered the Mosaic law binding only for those born within Judaism, while the Ebionites considered this law binding

Notes

for all men (Hippolytus, 'Comm. in Jes.' i. 12). The Nazarenes therefore rejected Paul, the apostle to the Gentiles. Some accordingly declared even that the Nazarenes were Jews, as, for instance, Theodoret ('Hær. Fab.' ii. 2: οἱ δὲ Ναζωραῖοι Ἰουδαῖοί εἰσι); that they exalted Jesus as a just man, and that they read the Gospel of Peter; fragments of this Gospel of Peter have been preserved (Preuschen, l.c. p. 13). Aside from these references, Theodoret, however, makes the mistake of confounding the Nazarenes and Ebionites; he is the last one of the Church Fathers to refer to the Nazarenes, who probably were absorbed in the course of the fifth century partly by Judaism and partly by Christianity."
Samuel Krauss, "Nazarenes," *The Jewish Encyclopedia*, 1906, http://www.jewishencyclopedia.com/articles/11393-nazarenes
For an excellent review of these early movements by Messianic Scholar Dan Juster, see chapter 5 of his book, *Jewish Roots: Understanding Your Jewish Faith*, Destiny Image Publishers, Inc. Shippensburg, PA, 2013.

11. Geert Wilders, *Marked for Death: Islam's War against the West and Me*, (Regnery Publishing, Washington, D.C., 2012), 40–41.

12. This schism in understanding the biblical vision of the Kingdom of God has in the past and even today played into Satan's plans for replacement of Christianity with Islam. For instance, after Constantine accepted Christianity as the official religion of the empire and the Jews were excluded from the fellowship of Christians by the Edict of Milan in 313 AD, the church was severed from the doctrinal roots of the Kingdom of God in the Torah and the Hebrew scriptures (The Old Testament). The Torah describes human beings created in equality as male and female, and given joint dominion over the earth shared with Yahweh. With the fall, Satan destroyed this unity and equality between male and female and introduced male domination. Using this foundational division at the core of humanity, Satan was able to develop systems of domination and inequality affecting every dimension of humanity. One of these was the shifting of all human beings created in the image of God having dominion over the earth to just the few land owners having control. This, in a practical way, resulted in domination over other human beings who now had no access to the land except as surfs or slaves. The Old Testament vision of the Year of Jubilee was intended to reverse these tendencies of control over the land by the few and restore access to all people. (Leviticus 25) When Islam came with the message that Allah, not the land owners,

owned the land, there was a ready acceptance of this doctrine by those living in oppression. (These insights are based on conversations with the Rev. Archer Torrey who wrote and taught extensively on the Biblical understanding of the Land and Economics.) See:

Archer Torrey, *Biblical Economics* (Henry George Institute, 1985), condensed and hosted by Land Reform, http://www.landreform. org/be1.htm.

Archer Torrey, "The Land and Biblical Economics," *Land and Liberty*, Jul.-Aug. 1979, reprinted by The School of Cooperative Individualism, http://www.cooperative-individualism.org/torrey-archer land-and-biblical-economics-1979.htm.

R. Archer Torrey, *Biblical Economics* (Jesus Abbey, 1999), https://www.amazon.com/Biblical-Economics-Archer-Torrey/dp/1401022804/ref=sr_1_1?ie=UTF8&qid=1479849487&sr=8-1&keywords=Archer+Torrey+Biblical+Economics#reader_B0052EM76E.

13. Father Ben Torrey notes that the Christological issues were dominated by the economic and political issues. This has been recognized in recent years by rapprochements among Roman, Greek Orthodox, Miaphysite and Diaphysite traditions. They have come to see that much of the differences in expression of the doctrine of the Trinity were cultural and linguistic issues and that it was political jockeying that forced the issues. To be accurate and truthful in the detail, you need to review a lot more history and the theology of the 3rd to 6th Centuries—the era of the Great Councils. (From a personal review of the book.)

14. Just view the recent history of one great denomination after another, such as the Presbyterian Church in the USA or the Episcopal Church in the USA, both of which for the sake of organizational unity have rejected the authority of the Word of God, quenched the Spirit of God, or, worst of all, rejected the "singular saving Lordship of Jesus Christ." In 2000 the GAC of the PC(USA) co-sponsored the "Peace Making Conference" in which a Presbyterian Pastor spoke on "What is the big deal about Jesus?" He seems to have rejected that Jesus Christ is the only way of salvation. His statements and the PC(USA)'s support of this conference was so offensive to Bible believing Christians that thousands of congregations called for an official rejection of the unorthodox doctrines proposed by this peacemaking confirmation conference and called for a reaffirmation of our basic doctrine that Jesus Christ is the only way of

Notes

salvation. The Rev. Garret Dawson of the Presbytery of Western North Carolina with the full backing of the Presbyterian Lay Committee and PRMI brought an overture to the 2001, GA which asked the GA to affirm "The Singular Saving Lordship of Jesus Christ." The General Assembly, after hours of debate, could not affirm the "Singular Saving Lordship of Jesus Christ," but sent it to a study committee. This was the decisive battle in the war for the soul of the PC(USA). While the study committee may have confirmed the Saving Lordship of Jesus Christ, it was too late, the doors were opened and Satan completed his work of building the stronghold of Liberal Progressivism at the leadership levels of the denomination. From this a number of actions followed to reject both the authority of the Word of God and the Lordship of Jesus Christ. The result has been that the denomination has continued to descend into apostasy and to move from holding people and congregations in its fold through inspiration and faithfulness to Christ, to now holding them with coercion. (This denomination rejected the renewing Christ centered movement of the Holy Spirit represented by PRMI and others in the 1990's.)

15. The PRMI Dunamis Fellowship International. See http://prmi.org/dunamis-fellowship-international.

Chapter 15
The Authority of Born Again Jews and Gentiles in Unity

1. Daniel Juster, *Jewish Roots: Understanding Your Jewish Faith*, Revised Edition (Destiny Image, Shippensburg, PA, 2013), 110-111.
2. David Rudolph and Joel Willitts, *Introduction to Messianic Judaism: Its Ecclesial Context and Biblical Foundations* (Zondervan, Grand Rapids, MI, 2013), 23.
3. Romans 11:11-24.
4. Rodney Aist, "The Edict of Milan," Feb. 4 2013, Medieval Milanetc, https://medievalmilanetc.wordpress.com/2013/02/04/the-edit-of-milan/.
5. David Rudolph and Joel Willitts, *Introduction to Messianic Judaism: Its Ecclesial Context and Biblical Foundations* (Zondervan, Grand Rapids, MI, 2013), 25.
6. "What Does Islam Teach About...Violence," 2016, The Religion of Peace,

http://www.thereligionofpeace.com/quran/023-violence.htm.

7   In Hebrew, "tikkun" means restoration. The purpose of the ministry is "Partnering for the Full Restoration of Israel and the Church." http://www.tikkunministries.org/.

8.   "One new man out of two": The note in the (NET) Bible helps clarify this term. (Ephesians 2:15, Note 30). In this context the author is not referring to a new individual, but instead to a new corporate entity united in Christ (cf. BDAG 497 s.v. καινός 3.b: "All the Christians together appear as κ. ἄνθρωπος Eph 2:15. ") This is clear from the comparison made between the Gentiles and Israel in the immediately preceding verses and the assertion in v. 14 that Christ "made both groups into one." This is a different metaphor than the "new man" of Eph 4:24. In that passage the "new man" refers to the new life a believer has through a relationship to Christ. (This is from the online version http://NETbible.com/ The New English Translation)

9.   For the Biblical basis and theology behind these statements I urge you to read the books by Daniel Juster and Asher Intrater or view any of their excellent video teaching. Just google their names. I recommend the following books: Daniel Juster, *Jewish Roots: Understanding Your Jewish Faith* (Destiny Image, Shippensburg, PA, 2013).
Asher (Keith) Intrater and Daniel Juster, *Israel the Church and the Last Days: Understanding the Last Days, the Hope of the World, The Kingdom of God* (Destiny Image, Shippensburg, PA, 2003).

10.   John 17:20-21. (20) I am not praying only on their behalf, but also on behalf of those who believe in me through their testimony, (21) that they will all be one, just as you, Father, are in me and I am in you. I pray that they will be in us, so that the world will believe that you sent me.

11.   Shire, *The Rise and Fall of the Third Reich*, 240.

Chapter 16
God Removes the Leaders through Conversion to Christ

1.   Dr. Sebastian Gorka, *Defeating Jihad: The Winnable War* (Regnery Publishing, Washington, D.C., 2016) 18.

2.   Geert Wilders, *Marked for Death: Islam's War against the West and Me*, (Regnery Publishing, Washington, D.C., 2012), 32.

Notes

lkl3. Sam Harris, *The End of Faith: Religion, Terror, and the Future of Reason* (Norton & Company, New York and London, 2004) 109.
4. Daniel Greenfield, a Shillman Journalism Fellow at the David Horowitz Freedom Center, is a New York writer focusing on radical Islam.
   Daniel Greenfield, "De-Islamization is the Only Way to Fight ISIS," May 18, 2015, Frontpage Magazine, http://www.frontpagemag.com/fpm/257157/de-islamization-only-way-fight-isis-daniel-greenfield.

5. W. Cleon Skousen, *The Five Thousand Year Leap: 28 Great Ideas That Changed the World*, Revised 30 Year Anniversary Edition (PowerThink Publishing, LLC, 2009).
6. J. Lee Grady, "How to Pray When Terrorists are Beheading Christians," Feb. 18 2015, Charisma Magazine, http://www.charismamag.com/blogs/fire-in-my-bones/22581-how-to-pray-when-terrorists-are-beheading-christians.
7. Ibid.
8. Nicola Menzie, "Report: ISIS Fighter who 'Enjoyed' Killing Christians Wants to Follow Jesus After Dreaming of Man in White who Told Him 'You are Killing my People'," Jun. 3 2015, The Christian Post, http://www.christianpost.com/news/report-isis-fighter-who-enjoyed-killing-christians-wants-to-follow-jesus-after-dreaming-of-man-in-white-who-told-him-you-are-killing-my-people-139880/#xjBs4xU9ypvrGzve.99.http://www.christianpost.com/news/report-isis-fighter-who-enjoyed-killing-christians-wants-to-follow-jesus-after-dreaming-of-man-in-white-who-told-him-you-are-killing-my-people-139880/#xjBs4xU9ypvrGzve.99..
   Watch this incredible video telling how god is reaching Muslims through dreams and visions of Jesus Christ: https://www.youtube.com/watch?v=6E076Nia7bM
9. Nicola Menzie, "Report: ISIS Fighter who 'Enjoyed' Killing Christians Wants to Follow Jesus After Dreaming of Man in White who Told Him 'You are Killing my People'," Jun. 3 2015, The Christian Post, http://www.christianpost.com/news/report-isis-fighter-who-enjoyed-killing-christians-wants-to-follow-jesus-after-dreaming-of-man-in-white-who-told-him-you-are-killing-my-people-139880/#xjBs4xU9ypvrGzve.99.

10. "Christian Martyrs," Nov. 22 2016, Wikipedia, the Free Encyclopedia, http://en.wikipedia.org/wiki/Christian_martyrs.

Chapter 17
God Removes the Leaders of Radical Islam by Death

1. Reuben Archer Torrey, *How to Pray* (Fleming H. Revell Company, 1900), 34-37.

Chapter 18
Military Force Destroying Jihadists Armies

1. C. N. Trueman, "Robert Ley," Aug. 16 2016, The History Learning Site, http://www.historylearningsite.co.uk/Rhineland_1936.htm.
2. Clausewitz, *On War*, 184-185.
3. *The Heidelberg Catechism* (The Christian Reformed Church Synod, 1975), The Christian Reformed Church, 2016, http://www.crcna.org/welcome/beliefs/confessions/heidelberg-catechism.

    The Scripture references are as follows:

    1) Ps. 119:5, 105; 143:10; Matt. 6:33
    2) Ps. 122:6-9; Matt. 16:18; Acts 2:42-47
    3) Rom. 16:20; 1 John 3:8
    4) Rom. 8:22-23; 1 Cor. 15:28; Rev. 22:17, 20

4. Robert Spencer, "Separation of religion and state is not an option for Muslims because it requires us to abandon Allah's decree for that of a man," Sep. 4 2010, Jihad Watch, http://www.jihadwatch.org/2010/09/separation-of-religion-and-state-is-not-an-option-for-muslims-because-is-requires-us-to-abandon-alla.

5. Barak Obama, "Remarks by the President at the University of Cairo 6-04-09," Jun. 4 2009, The University of Cairo, Office of the Press Secretary, https://www.whitehouse.gov/the-press-office/remarks-president-cairo-university-6-04-09.

    Or watch it on YouTube here:
    C-Span, "President Obama Speech to Muslim World in Cairo," Jun. 4 2009, YouTube, https://www.youtube.com/watch?v=B_889oBKkNU.

Notes

6. I read the original and Wilders. In this book Adams provides a lucid, biblically sound commentary on the differences in the doctrines and the fruit of Christianity and Islam. Adams brings what is rare in our generation of leaders: a Biblical Christian worldview to his analysis of the threat posed by the religion of Islam as embodied in the false prophet Muhammad.
Geert Wilders, *Marked for Death: Islam's War against the West and Me* (Regnery Publishing, Washington, D.C., 2012), 17.
For the comments by Adams, go to "John Quincy Adams" in Joseph Blunt, *The American Annual Register; the Years 1827-8-9* (E. & G. W. Blunt, 1830), http://www.archive.org/stream/p1americanannual29blunuoft.

7. Geert Wilders, *Marked for Death: Islam's War against the West and Me,* (Regnery Publishing, Washington, D.C., 2012) 41.

8. Refers to the October 10, 732 Battle of Tours: "With perhaps 1,500 soldiers, Charles Martel halted a Muslim force of around 40,000 to 60,000 cavalry under Abd el-Rahman Al Ghafiqi from moving farther into Europe. Many regard this battle as being decisive in saving Europe from Muslim control. Gibbon wrote: "A victorious line of march had been prolonged above a thousand miles from the rock of Gibraltar to the banks of the Loire; the repetition of an equal space would have carried the Saracens to the confines of Poland and the Highlands of Scotland; the Rhine is not more impassable than the Nile or Euphrates, and the Arabian fleet might have sailed without a naval combat into the mouth of the Thames. Perhaps the interpretation of the Koran would now be taught in the schools of Oxford, and her pulpits might demonstrate to a circumcised people the sanctity and truth of the revelation of Muhammad."
"Islam and Europe Timeline (355-1291 A.D.)," The Latin Library, http://www.thelatinlibrary.com/imperialism/notes/islamchron.html.
Victor Davis Hanson, *Carnage and Culture*, (Anchor Books, Random House, Inc., New York, 2001.) 135-169.

9. Actually it was not Sobieki's sword but the Winged Hussars that defeated the army of 300,000 besieging the city of Vienna in 1683.
Anthony Pagden, "Turning the Ottoman Tide – John III Sobieski at Vienna 1683," Jul. 28 2008, History Net, http://www.history(NET).com/turning-the-ottoman-tide-john-iii-sobieski-at-vienna-1683.htm.
Stanislaus Tarnowski, "John Sobieski," *The Catholic Encyclopedia*, Vol. 14.

(Robert Appleton Company, 1912), New Advent, http://www.newadvent.
org/cathen/14061c.htm.

Chapter 19
The Responsibility of Government to Wage War

1. John Calvin, *Institutes of the Christian Religion*, Volume XXI, The Library of
    Christian Classics, Ed. John T. McNeill, Trans. Ford Lewis Battles (The
    Westminster Press, Philadelphia, 1960).
2. Ibid.
3. Wallace Henley and Jonathan Sandys, *God & Churchill: How the Great
    Leader's Sense of Divine Destiny Changed His Troubled World and Offers Hope
    for Ours*, (Tyndale House, 2015). 115-130, 236-237.

4. Sir Winston Spencer Churchill, *The River War*, first edition, Vol. II,
    (Longmans, Green & Co., London, 1899), 248-250.

5. Mark Steyn, *America Alone: The End of the World as We Know it*, (Regnery
    Publishing, Washington, D.C., 2006).
6. "America Alone," Oct. 18 2016, Wikipedia, the Free Encyclopedia,
    https://en.wikipedia.org/wiki/America_Alone.

Chapter 20
Joshua the Warrior Joins the Cohort

1. For references confirming how many people were murdered by Communist
    governments--the estimates range from 90 – 140 million people--see:
    Lawrence Person, "How Many People Did Communism Kill," May 7 2010,
    Lawrence Person's Battleswarm Blog,
    http://www.battleswarmblog.com/?p=1191.
    As for Nazi mass murder, once again there are estimates of from 11 million
    to 20 million people killed in nonmilitary operations.
    Matthew Day, "'Shocking' Holocaust Study Claims Nazis Killed Up To 20
    Million People," Mar. 4 2013, Business Insider, http://www.businessinsider
    .com/shocking-new-holocaust-study-claims-nazis-killed-up-to-20-million-
    people-2013-3.
2. "The Battle of Tours (often called the Battle of Poitiers, but not to be confused

Notes

with the Battle of Poitiers, 1356) was fought on October 10, 732 between forces under the Frankish leader Charles Martel and a massive invading Islamic army led by Emir Abdul Rahman Al Ghafiqi Abd al Rahman, near the city of Tours, France."
"The Battle of Tours," Nov. 18 2016, Wikipedia, the Free Encyclopedia, https://en.wikipedia.org/wiki/Battle of Tours.

3. "Battle of Lepanto,(October 7, 1571), naval engagement in the waters off southwestern Greece between the allied Christian forces of the Holy League and the Ottoman Turks during an Ottoman campaign to acquire the Venetian island of Cyprus. The battle marked the first significant victory for a Christian naval force over a Turkish fleet and the climax of the age of galley warfare in the Mediterranean.
The Editors of Encyclopedia Brittanica, "Battle of Lepanto," Mar. 12 2015, *Encyclopedia Brittanica*, http://www.britannica.com/event/Battle-of-Lepanto.
For the spiritual dimensions of this battle see: Christopher Check, "The Battle that Saved the Christian West," Mar. 2007, Catholic Answers Magazine, http://www.catholic.com/magazine/articles/the-battle-that-saved-the-christian-west.

4. Dr. Hanson does at times point to the spiritual and religious dimension of these battles. He does give the facts that show that both Christians as well as Muslims did indeed see their conflict as the clash of two faiths. The Christians saw their victories as God given and to the Glory of Jesus Christ. Dr. Hanson, in describing the battle of Lepanto October 7, 1571 where Christian navy forces halted centuries of Muslim advance, does note this after naming all the factors in the Christian victory that resulted from Western culture: "Or perhaps the edge was spiritual? Lepanto was fought on a Sunday morning, and the crew were given mass by priests on deck even as they prepared to kill" (p. 253).Dr. Hanson also provides another glimpse into the spiritual realities produced by two entirely different faiths. The Islamic Ottoman Caliphate was a slave state, whereas the Holy League consisted of free men. "While there were servile crews on both sides at Lepanto, the oarsmen of the Holy League still included free rowers, and the coalition was more likely to free those slaves it did employ. In contrast, Christian slaves on Turkish galleys were threatened with death before the battle should they raise their heads, and there is some indication that at least on a few ships they mutinied

in the midst of the battle."

In effect, there was not a single free fighter in the Turkish fleet--not the shackled oarsmen, not the Janissaries, not those peasants mustered under feudal service, not the renegade admirals and seamen, and not even Ali Pasha himself. Across the water, the Christian admirals at the battle were free aristocrats...None of these proud and often headstrong individuals could be arbitrarily executed by the pope, the doge at Venice, or King Philip II for simple failure to win at Lepanto. In contrast, Ali Pash and his commanders knew that an embarrassing defeat required a sufficient number of heads for the sultan" (p. 249).

In short, Satan has created bondage and slavery through Islamic culture, whereas Jesus Christ sets humanity free and creates free societies. Christianity, at heart, produces freedom; Islam produces slavery.

Victor Davis Hanson, *Carnage and Culture* (Anchor Books, Random House, Inc., New York, 2001).

5. Movie Clips Film Festivals and Indie Films, "Day of the Siege Official Trailer (2014) - F. Murray Abraham Epic Movie HD," Jun. 11 2014, YouTube, https://www.youtube.com/watch?v=HolSYyDsRJc.
    espadaX100, "charge of the polish winged hussar," Aug. 9 2014, YouTube, https://www.youtube.com/watch?v=cjdvf01pJXg.
    Resource777, "Siege of Vienna 1683 (Documentary)," Sep. 5 2014, YouTube, https://www.youtube.com/watch?v=pc-RWtovrqg.
6. "Marco D'Aviano," Sep. 17 2016, Wikipedia, the Free Encyclopedia, https://en.wikipedia.org/wiki/Marco_d%27Aviano.
7. "Battle of Vienna," Nov. 19 2016, Wikipedia, the Free Encyclopedia, https://en.wikipedia.org/wiki/Battle_of_Vienna.
8. Frank W. Thackeray and John E. Findling, *Events That Formed the Modern World: From the European Renaissance through the War on Terror* (ABC-CLIO, 2012), 267, http://www.abc-clio.com/ABC-CLIOCorporate/product.aspx?pc=A3543C.
9. Raymond Ibrahim, "The Islamic Genocide of Christians, Past and Present," Apr. 27 2015, Frontpage Magazine, http://www.frontpagemag.com/fpm/255940/islamic-genocide-christians-past-and-present-raymond-ibrahim.
    Also see Raymond Ibrahim's book for the documentation, history, and present practice of Satan's plans for genocide against Christians through employing the teaching and example of Mohammed in the building of

Notes

strongholds.

Raymond Ibrahim, *Crucified Again: Exposing Islam's New War on Christians* (Regnery Publishing, Inc., Washington, D.C., 2013).

10. "Battle of Vienna," Nov. 19 2016, Wikipedia, the Free Encyclopedia, https://en.wikipedia.org/wiki/Battle_of_Vienna.

11. Harriet Murphy, "Blessed Marco d'Aviano," Jan. 2004, Christian Order, http://www.christianorder.com/features/features_2004/features_jan04.html.

Chapter 21
Interceding for President Bush
and Soldiers on the Frontlines

1. George W. Bush, *Decision Points* (Crown Publishers, New York, 2010), 30-34.

2. Ibid., 368.

3. Victor Davis Hanson, *The Savior Generals: How Five Great Commanders Saved Wars That Were Lost - From Ancient Greece to Iraq* (Bloomsbury Press, 2013), https://www.amazon.com/Savior-Generals-Commanders-Ancient-Greece/dp/160819342X.

4. George W. Bush, *Decision Points*, 392-394.

5. "President Obama claims he inherited a mess in the Middle East. Not so....In Iraq, U.S. strategy hinged on forcing the fledgling democracy to create loose alliances between Kurds, Shiites, and Sunnis, with the understanding that they would all resist both al-Qaeda and Iranian-sponsored Shiite affiliates. And from 2009 to 2011, consensual government in Iraq seemed to be working, albeit mostly through the implied threats that nearby U.S. troops would intervene if it did not. The country was more quiet than not. Indeed, the U.S. military there was losing more personnel each month to accidents than to combat. In December 2009, three Americans were killed in Iraq — the lowest figure for any month since the war began. In December 2011, no Americans were lost. Obama, who had opposed the Iraq war, termed the country "secure" and "stable." Vice President Joe Biden, who as senator had voted for the war, bragged that it might become the Obama administration's "greatest achievement." American proconsuls kept the pressure on Iranophile Prime Minister Nouri al-Maliki to treat Sunni tribes more

equitably, and to keep Iraqi territory free of the Iranian military. Al-Qaeda in Iraq was comatose. Most Sunni Islamists had no desire for a replay of the Anbar Awakening and the Surge. Then, for the sake of a 2012 reelection campaign point, Obama pulled out all U.S. constabulary troops at the end of 2011. The result was a void that drew in the dregs of the Middle East, as ISIS and the Iranian-backed militias fought over the corpse of what used to be Syria and Iraq."

Victor Davis Hanson, "Five Middle East Blunders," Feb. 17 2015, National Review, http://www.nationalreview.com/article/398698/five-middle-east-blunders-victor-davis-hanson.

Chapter 22
The Father's Strategy to Fulfill the Great Commission

1. Richard Lovelace, *The Occult Revival in Historical Perspective*, *Demon Possession*, ed. Warwick Montgomery (Bethany Fellowship Inc., Minneapolis, MN, 1976), 87.
2. For a brilliant study of these waves of the Holy Spirit advancing the Kingdom of God, see Doug McMurry's video series entitled *Glory Through Time*. http://www.theclearing.us/video-teachings/glory-through-time/.
3. Jonathan Edwards, *Thoughts on the Revival in New England*, 1740, Part V Sec III.
4. This includes--but is more inclusive than--what Peter Wagner named the "Third Wave of the Holy Spirit" which was embodied by John Wimber and the Vineyard movement, which was preceded by the Pentecostal and Charismatic movements.
   Got Questions Ministries, "What is the Third Wave Movement," 2016, GotQuestions.org, http://www.gotquestions.org/Third-Wave-movement.html.
5. Winston Churchill, *The Second World War: Closing the Ring*, Preface (Houghton Mifflin Co., Boston, The Riverside Press, Cambridge, 1951).

Chapter 23
Jews Returning to the Land of Israel and to Yeshua

1. Charles Williams, *Descent into Hell*. New York : Pellegrini & Cudahy [1949]

Notes

2. Matthew 28:18-20 (NET). (18) Then Jesus came up and said to them, "All authority in heaven and on earth has been given to me. (19) Therefore go and make disciples of all nations, baptizing them in the name of the Father and the Son and the Holy Spirit, (20) teaching them to obey everything I have commanded you. And remember, I am with you always, to the end of the age."
3. Romans 11:12-15. (12) Now if their transgression means riches for the world and their defeat means riches for the Gentiles, how much more will their full restoration bring? (13) Now I am speaking to you Gentiles. Seeing that I am an apostle to the Gentiles, I magnify my ministry, (14) if somehow I could provoke my people to jealousy and save some of them. (15) For if their rejection is the reconciliation of the world, what will their acceptance be but life from the dead?
4. Asher (Keith) Intrater, *From Iraq to Armageddon: The Final Showdown Approaches* (Destiny Image Pub., Shippensburg, PA, 2003), 69.
5. Ibid., 72.

Chapter 24
The "People Who Use chopsticks"
Taking the Gospel Back to Jerusalem

1. The Rev. Dr. John Chang from Taiwan is the Pastor of Grace Community Churches in Staten Island and Flushing Queens, New York, and is the Director of PRMI's Asian Ministries. For more on the Presbyterian-Reformed Ministries International's global apostolic network, the Dunamis Fellowship, see http://prmi.org/about/dunamis-fellowship.
2. Samuel P. Huntington, *The Clash of Civilizations and the Remaking of World Order* (Simon and Schuster, New York, 1996), 245.
3. This turning point seems to have taken place after having planted churches in Asia when Paul was called to turn toward Rome instead of continuing to advance in Asia. (Acts 16:6)
4. From my own research as well as firsthand experience of equipping Chinese church leaders, I am convinced that this may well be the largest missional movement in history that is in large part being directed spontaneously by the Holy Spirit without the agency of mission boards. As an introduction to this movement see:
   "A Captivating Vision: Why Chinese house churches may just end up

fulfilling the Great Commission. An interview with Paul Hattaway," Apr. 1 2004, Christianity Today, http://www.christianitytoday.com/ct/2004/april/5.84.html.
Or the web site by that name: https://backtojerusalem.com/home/.

5. "Definition: The Jesus Family (Chinese: 耶穌家庭) was a Chinese Pentecostal communitarian church established in 1927 by Jing Dianying. It began in the rural village of Mazhuang, Taian County, Shandong Province. The church was primarily located in rural and semirural areas, where members had everything in common, inspired by the life of the apostles in the book of Acts. In 1949 there were over a hundred of these communities, numbering thousands of people.[1] The church emphasized a simple lifestyle, spiritual experiences like prophecy as well as the second coming of Christ. After the communist takeover in 1952, the Jesus Family was dismantled and its leader, Jing Dianying, was put into prison and died there."
"The Jesus Family," Nov. 2 2016, Wikipedia, the Free Encyclopedia, https://en.wikipedia.org/wiki/Jesus_Family.
I was first introduced to this amazing work of the Holy Spirit by Archer Torrey, founder of Jesus Abbey in Korea. He gave me the book The "Jesus Family" in Communist China: A Modern Miracle of New Testament Christianity by Delwyn Vaughan Rees (Import, 1970, Chinese Artist: Illustrator). The "Jesus Family" was part of God's preparation of the Church of Jesus Christ to survive the onslaught of Communism in China.

6. "A Church Established by Lay Initiative," Catholicism in Korea, http://popekorea.catholic.or.kr/en/korea/kcc_02.asp.

7. An amazing aspect of this move of the Holy Spirit included Koreans as well as Japanese who in 1905 had taken over Korea. From Jonathan Goforth's report: "Such extraordinary happenings could not but move the multitude, and the churches became crowded. Many came to mock, but in fear began to pray. The leader of a robber band, who came out of idle curiosity, was convicted and converted, and went straight to the magistrate and gave himself up. The astonished official said, 'You have no accuser; you accuse yourself; we have no law in Korea to meet your case'; and so dismissed him."
A Japanese officer at the time of the revival was quartered in Ping Yang. He had imbibed the agnostic ideas of the West, therefore to him spiritual things were beneath contempt. Still, the strange transformations which were taking

place, not only among great numbers of Koreans, but even among some Japanese, who could not possibly understand the language, so puzzled him that he attended the meetings to investigate. The final result was that all his unbelief was swept away and he became a follower of the Lord Jesus. Jonathan Goforth, *When the Spirit's Fire Swept Korea* (The Gospel Truth, 2012), http://www.gospeltruth.net/koreafire.htm.

8. This grateful openness comes not just from the history of missionaries coming to Korea from these nations but also because these were primarily those nations whose soldiers fought and died to rescue Korea from complete communist domination during the Korean War.

9. Beyond the scope of this book is the work of the Holy Spirit taking place among Japanese Christians.

Chapter 25
Closing the Ring on the Fortress Islam

1. Moral of the work: "In War: Resolution, In Defeat: Defiance, In Victory: Magnanimity, In Peace: Good Will". Theme of the volume: "How Nazi Germany was Isolated and Assailed on All Sides".
Winston S. Churchill, *"The Second World War, Closing the Ring,"* Preface, (Hougton Mifflin Company, Boston, 1951).

2. David Garrison, *A Wind in the House of Islam: How God is Drawing Muslims around the World to Faith in Jesus Christ* (WIGTake Resources, Monument, CO, 2014).
For reports on how this is happening please see the videos on the website, "A Wind in the House of Islam".
Part 1 https://www.youtube.com/watch?v=GP18dklJS3w.
Part 2 https://www.youtube.com/watch?v=KIG6T10ILKE.
Part 3 https://www.youtube.com/watch?v=1Rtzf1Uu3IA.
Watch these videos and you will see why our battle is not hopeless. Our God is at work! Pray for those outpourings of the Holy Spirit to continue and deepen.

3. Garrison, A Wind in the House of Islam, 5.

4. Ibid., 4.

Chapter 26
Prophetic Words for Mobilizing, Equipping and Deploying Jesus' Army of Intercessors

1. Calvin, *Institutes of the Christian Religion*, Book IV, Ch. XX, Sec. 10.
2. Raymond Ibrahim, "Islamic Hate for the Christian Cross," Jun. 20 2015, Raymond Ibrahim, http://www.raymondibrahim.com/2015/06/20/islamic-hate-for-the-christian-cross/.
3. For the confirmation of Iran's declared war against Jews and Christians and the obligation to chant Death to America and Death to Israel see the excellent video presentation: JihadWatchVideo, "Robert Spencer on the Islamic Republic of Iran's war against the US," Aug. 27 2016, YouTube, https://youtu.be/YY4tOIXOQ_E.
4. Calvin, *Institutes of the Christian Religion*, Book IV, Ch. XX, Sec. 10.
5. November 7, 2016 a publication out of Iraq showed that their propaganda arm of videos and printed page has been destroyed and that Dabiq magazine will no longer be published. http://www.iraqinews.com/iraq-war/isis-moviemaker-killed-group-ceases-mosuls-paper-propaganda/
6. *Islamic Messianic Dreams Shattered as ISIS Defeated in Dabiq* By Adam Eliyahu Berkowitz October 18, 2016 , 1:01 pm. https://www.breakingisraelnews.com/77246/islamic-messianic-dreams-shattered-isis-defeated-dabiq/#0hrhPOBXyziE3m1I.99
7. These adaptations to fulfilling the Great Commission when it comes to taking the Gospel to those enslaved in the strongholds of Radical Islam are required by the fact that they have chosen the means of death and subjugation in their system of deception to prevent the Gospel form reaching their hearts. I believe much well intended evangelism of Muslims over the ages has born so little fruit because these facts have not been considered. These adaptations consist of having to focus on the high-level demons who are behind the entire system. It also means that one must take up the sword in self-defense to prevent Islamic bondage from being imposed upon us by the sword of Muhammad. That is their choice not ours!

Presbyterian-Reformed Ministries International

PRMI was founded in 1966 to pray and work for the spiritual renewal of Presbyterian and Reformed churches. Over the past 50 years, we have grown to include parts of the Body of Christ in many nations, and continue to have a distinctive role in the world wide movement of the Holy Spirit advancing the Gospel of Jesus Christ for the fulfillment of the Great Commission. www.prmi.org

Dunamis Institute
Equipping the Church for the Advancement
of the Kingdom of Jesus Christ Worldwide

The Dunamis Institute is the teaching ministry of PRMI. It equips Christians to cooperate with the Holy Spirit in ministry, missions and evangelism, growing the Church and advancing the Kingdom of God. Free online video courses available, www.DunamisInstitute.org

Other books available by this author related to mobilizing prayer

Prayer that Shapes the Future: How to Pray with Power and Authority	*Receiving the Power:* Preparing the Way for the Holy Spirit	*Growing the Church in the Power of the Holy Spirit:* The Two Foundations and Seven Dynamics	*Discerning the Times:* Exposing Satan's Plans in Radical Islam

Order books online at www.prmi.org/resources

"But you will receive power when the Holy Spirit has come upon you, and you will be my witnesses in Jerusalem, and in all Judea and Samaria, and to the farthest parts of the earth." Acts 1:8

Learn how to cooperate with the Holy Spirit to be an effective witness to Jesus Christ by effectively engaging in ministries of prayer, healing, spiritual warfare, and evangelism for growing the Church and advancing the Kingdom of God.

Dunamis can help you deepen your walk with the Lord and prepare you for effective ministry wherever the Lord has called you. "Dunamis" is the Greek term for "power."

With the Dunamis teaching, you'll discover

- Solid biblical theology about the person and work of the Holy Spirit in the life of the believer.
- Teaching forged from the Scriptures, proven in ministry, and informed by 200 years of renewal and revival movements.
- Your spiritual gifts and how to use them effectively in the Kingdom of God.
- How to recognize God's guidance for ministry in a given moment through the experience based lab times and review debriefings.

The Dunamis Project consists of six units each taught over five days six months apart in the same location. Each event consists of intensive biblical teaching and practical application in the context of prayer and worship. These events are designed to enable every believer to grow in their faith, personal relationship with God and participation in the ministry of the Holy Spirit.

For more information, go to www.dunamisinstitute.org/dp

Equipping Projects are offered in English, Spanish, Korean, Japanese, Chinese, and other languages in the United States, Central and South America, Canada, the United Kingdom, South Korea, and other locations

Printed in Great Britain
by Amazon